No Bartók Before Breakfast

No Bartók Before Breakfast
A Musician's Memoir

John Manduell

with an Appreciation by
Anthony Gilbert

2016

Published by Arc Publications
Nanholme Mill, Shaw Wood Road
Todmorden OL14 6DA, UK
www.arcpublications.co.uk

Copyright © John Manduell, 2016
Copyright in the present edition © Arc Publications, 2016

978 1910345 58 0 (pbk)
978 1910345 59 7 (hbk)
978 1910345 60 3 (ebk)

Cover design by Tony Ward

Cover phtograph: © Hanya Chlala / ArenaPAL

John Manduell has asserted his right under the Copyright, Designs and Patents Act 1988, to be identified as the author of this Work. Subject to statutory exception and to provision of relevant collective licensing agreements, no reproduction of any part of this book may take place without the written permission of Arc Publications.

The publishers are grateful to the Ida Carroll Trust
for its financial support.

**Arc Music
Series Editor: Angela Jarman**

Author's Acknowledgements

This book owes its origin to the enthusiasm with which my wife, Renna, initially urged me to write it and to the insistence with which she eventually overcame my hesitation about doing so. It is, therefore, dedicated to her, gratefully recognising our long shared journey and recalling that sage old African saying: "When you want to go fast, go alone. When you want to go far, go together."

Many people have freely and generously given of their goodwill and knowledge in encouraging me to write it. They include: Christopher Audland, Kenneth Baird, Elaine Bevis, Bryan Fox, my sister Gillian and her husband John Hall, Gavin Henderson, Joyce Kennedy, the late Philip Ledger, Timothy and Hilary Reynish, John Turner, Anna Wright and the late Christopher Yates.

While this book might not have been written but for Renna's insistence, it would certainly never have been completed but for the dedication and determination of my collaborator and colleague, Jane Thompson, to whom so many features in the book are attributable and without whose professionalism it would long ago have stuttered to a halt.

John Manduell

Contents

Foreword / 11
Early Days / 12
Cloister Foibles / 21
Student Days
    Haileybury / 25
    Strasbourg / 28
    Cambridge / 36
    Durban / 39
    London / 43
A Few Domestic Byways
    Some Elderly Allsops / 53
    Trams / 55
    Cricketing / 56
The BBC
    Music Producer (1956-9) / 61
    BBC Symphony Orchestra (1959-61) / 78
    Midland Region (1961-4) / 88
    The Music Programme (1964-8) / 97
Prague Spring / 105
Lancaster University / 113
Some Music Competitions
    Segovia / 129
    BBC Young Musician of the Year / 132
    Transcontinental in Canada / 134
    Munich / 136
    Bucharest / 139
    And… / 142
[Plates 1-37]
Royal Northern College of Music
    A New Prospect / 143
    Preparing the Way / 147
    Assembling the Team / 157
    Making a Start / 167
    Out and About / 176
    Bombed Out / 191

[Plates 38-47]
Here and There
    Chetham's / 193
    El Sistema – an early glimpse / 196
    The British Council / 198
    The Arts Council / 203
    European Music Year / 206
    Northern Ballet / 212
    European Opera Centre / 215
    Cheltenham / 221
    Covent Garden / 222
    Codetta / 224

Appendix 1
    Manduell the Composer: an Appreciation
        by Anthony Gilbert / 229
Appendix 2
    Discography / 241
Appendix 3
    Cheltenham Firsts / 243

Index / 264

List of Illustrations

PLATE 1 Matthewman Donald Manduell, John's father, on the steps of Oribi. (Photo: Author's archive)

PLATE 2 Early formative influences: Kathleen & Hector McCurrach with Ida Carroll at an ISM conference. (Photo: Author's archive)

PLATE 3 A view of Knoersheim, Alsace, painted by John's sister, Anne, in 1960. (Painting: Author's archive)

PLATE 4 Michael and Lennox Berkeley in the garden at their home in Little Venice, 1984. (© George Newson / Lebrecht Music & Arts)

PLATE 5 Leonard Isaacs, Head of BBC Home Service Music.

PLATE 6 Peter Crossley-Holland, BBC Third Programme Music Organiser.

PLATE 7 Clifton Helliwell, veteran BBC Accompanist and subsequently the RNCM's first Head of Keyboard Studies, in his garden at Lower Peover. (Photo: RNCM archive)

PLATE 8 Sir William Glock, BBC Controller Music. (Photo: Charles Davis, DISS Archive)

PLATE 9 Frank Gillard, BBC Managing Director Radio. (Photo: Polygoon Hollands Nieuws)

PLATE 10 Rudolf Schwarz, BBC Symphony Orchestra Chief Conductor. (Photo: © hansgal.org 2014)

PLATE 11 The Manduell family at home in Yorkshire: Helen, Julius, Jonathan, Renna, David, John. (Photo: Author's archive)

PLATE 12 Petr Eben, leading Czech composer, shares a toast with John. (Photo: RNCM archive)

PLATE 13 Sir Charles Carter, Vice-Chancellor of Lancaster University.

PLATE 14 Sir Charles Groves, Music Director of the Royal Liverpool Philharmonic Orchestra and first Chairman of the RNCM Council. (Photo: Clive Barda. RNCM archive)

PLATE 15 John receives a Royal College of Music Fellowship from Her Majesty The Queen Mother. (Photo: Author's archive)

PLATE 16 The laying of the RNCM Foundation Stone on 1 April 1971. From L to R: John Bickerdike, architect, Frederic Cox CBE, Principal of the Royal Manchester College of Music, Ida Carroll OBE, Principal of the Northern School of Music and Dr. Kathleen Ollerenshaw. (Photo: RNCM archive)

PLATE 17 Bryan Fox, Administrator, RNCM Development 1971-73, subsequently appointed the College's first Accommodation Officer.

(© Lawrence The Photographers. RNCM archive).
PLATE 18 The RNCM under construction. (© Arthur Taylor. RNCM archive)
PLATE 19 John, an inveterate left-hander. (Photo: Author's archive)
PLATE 20 Terence Greaves, first Dean of Development. (Photo: RNCM archive)
PLATE 21 Ida Carroll OBE, former Principal of the Northern School of Music and RNCM's first Dean of Management. (Photo: RNCM archive)
PLATE 22 Dr. John Wray, the RNCM's first Dean of Studies. (Photo: RNCM archive)
PLATE 23 John Cameron (left) and Patrick McGuigan (right), School of Vocal Studies Senior Tutors, with John Wilson, Senior Staff Accompanist. (© Margaret Robinson Photography. RNCM archive)
PLATE 24 Cecil Aronowitz, international violist and the RNCM's first Head of School of Strings. (Photo: RNCM archive)
PLATE 25 Anthony Gilbert, the RNCM's first Senior Tutor in Composition. (Photo: Hanya Chlala. RNCM archive)
PLATE 26 Simon Holt, an early RNCM student and widely admired composer. (Photo: Richard Kalina. RNCM archive)
PLATE 27 Philip Jones, RNCM's first Head of School of Wind & Percussion. (RNCM archive)
Pate 28 Alexander (Basil) Young, RNCM's first Head of School of Vocal Studies. (Photo: Author's archive)
PLATE 29 Air Commodore, Mansel Vaughan, CBE, first Secretary, RNCM, 1972-1982. (© Elsam, Mann & Cooper. RNCM archive)
PLATE 30 Anthony Hodges, the RNCM's first Senior Librarian. (Photo: RNCM archive)
PLATE 31 John Bower, the RNCM's first Recording Manager. (Photo: RNCM archive)
PLATE 32 Colonel Robert and Dame Kathleen Ollerenshaw open the RNCM Roof Garden which they commissioned in memory of their daughter, Florence. (Photo: RNCM archive)
PLATE 33 The Ollerenshaw Roof Garden. (Photo: RNCM Archive)
PLATE 34 A view of the RNCM, as it appeared at the formal opening in June 1973. (Photo: RNCM Archive)
PLATE 35 HRH The Duchess of Kent, President of the RNCM, with

Michael and Joyce Kennedy and John. (© Lawrence The Photographers. RNCM archive)

PLATE 36 Staff v. students cricket match at Hartley Hall. (Photo: RNCM archive)

PLATE 37 Welcome line-up for Degree Congregation Day: Dame Kathleen Ollerenshaw (Chairman of the RNCM Court & Lord Mayor of Manchester), HRH The Duchess of Kent (RNCM President), John and Renna. (Photo: Author's archive)

PLATE 38 John at Buckingham Palace, with Renna and sons Julius and David (Lieut. RN), to receive his knighthood in 1989. (Photo: Author's archive)

PLATE 39 John Ogdon and conductor, Sir Charles Groves, at the conclusion of an early concert by the RNCM Symphony Orchestra. (© Lawrence the Photographers. RNCM archive)

PLATE 40 Joseph Ward, Director of Opera and Assistant Head of School of Vocal Studies. (© Kenneth Jarvis. RNCM archive)

PLATE 41 Glenville Hargreaves and Peter Bodenham in Gordon Crosse's opera *Purgatory*, recorded by Decca and subsequently toured by RNCM to London & Copenhagen. (Photo: RNCM archive)

PLATES 42 & 43 Juanita Waterson's costume designs for Oberon & Puck in Joseph Ward's 1973 production of Britten's *A Midsummer Night's Dream*. (Paintings: Author's archive)

PLATE 44 John, first recipient of Royal Philharmonic Society / Performing Right Society Leslie Boosey Award ("honouring champions of contemporary music") in 1980, admires the award in the form of Dame Elizabeth Frink's bronze sculpture 'Eagle'. (Photo: Author's archive)

PLATE 45 November 1986 in Red Square, Moscow, for the Conference of European Conservatoires hosted by the Tchaikovsky Conservatoire – John and Renna with Michael Gough Matthews, Director of the Royal College of Music, and their 'minder'. (Photo: Author's archive)

PLATE 46 Three Musical Knights: Sir John Manduell with Sir Michael Tippett and Sir Peter Maxwell Davies at the Cheltenham Festival 1994. (Photo: Martin Davis. Author's archive)

PLATE 47 John receives the Freedom of Cheltenham in 1994. (Photo: Author's archive)

Foreword

If twentieth-century musical life in Britain could be characterised as a stately vehicle capable of surprising bursts of exuberant acceleration, then a pivotal cog in its gearbox might well be called The Manduell. Because this vital component, which consists of a myriad parts – composer, BBC Producer, Festival Director, Principal of the Royal Northern College of Music and... cricketer – these all go to make up The Manduell.

John has enabled, eased and cajoled so much that is of value in our musical life with the kind of determination that marks out people who are really going to make things happen. Whether his early life in South Africa informed his ability to aim high as a musical big game hunter I do not know, but what I have personally born witness to is John's extraordinary sense of commitment and loyalty to those he believes in (including countless composers and students) and those he counts as his friends.

When I took over direction of the Cheltenham Festival from John in 1995 I found a devoted band of followers and sponsors, all charmed and frequently amused by his sense of mission and twinkling humour, qualities that radiate throughout his entertaining autobiography.

A gifted composer – the String Quartet is a particular favourite of mine – John has rarely pushed his own music though often in a position to do so.

The pages that follow are not only evidence of a wonderful and entertaining life but also paint a valuable portrait of a period of British music that is not well documented but is an important part of our cultural heritage.

Michael Berkeley CBE[1]

---

[1] Michael Berkeley (b. 1948), composer and broadcaster, ennobled as Baron Berkeley of Knighton, 2013.

Early Days

My ever-indulgent parents introduced me to the world at Oribi on 2 March 1928. Oribi was the designated house at Jeppe High School, Johannesburg's oldest boys' public school, which my father occupied as headmaster. One distinctive feature about Jeppe was that each of the houses bore the name of a South African buck: tsessebe, impala, duiker, eland, kudu and so on.

My father, Matthewman Donald [Plate 1], was born in 1877 to a long-established farming family near Wigton, in Cumberland. After six years at St. Bees School, which he represented at both cricket and rugby, captaining the First XV, he won a scholarship to Jesus College, Cambridge, specialising in Tacitus whose record as a preeminent Roman historian was to become a lifelong preoccupation for my father. After emerging from Jesus with a double first in Classics, he taught briefly at Dartford Grammar School but very soon found himself sailing for South Africa, having been recruited to form part of a team charged with establishing an initial school education structure for the Transvaal. This was a pioneering initiative made all the more challenging for being undertaken during an unsettled period in the wake of the gold rush on the Rand, and soon after the conclusion of the Boer War. Once that task was completed, my father reverted to being a schoolmaster, joining the staff at Jeppe as Head of Classics.

When Kitchener's call to arms reached South Africa, my father boarded a ship for England and volunteered for service in the Royal Field Artillery. In due course he rose to the rank of major and was decorated with both the Military Cross and the French Croix de Guerre. He was destined to survive the war without serious injury and to walk away, technically intact, from the blood-soaked fields of Flanders and France. But some scars became evident when he shunned any family contact for many months after the Armistice. The skin on his back remained badly scarred for the rest of his life – the result of being caught under a cloud of mustard gas. My mother also told me that, in later life, he would withdraw into solitary isolation on 1 July each year symbolically to join, albeit at a distance of some 6,000 miles, with those veterans attending, in Thiepval, the annual commemoration of the Battle of the Somme. I venerated the man for what he accomplished – as scholar, schoolmaster and soldier – just as I loved him for the kind and gentle counsellor he was, who never raised his voice to me nor, as I have been widely assured, to anyone else.

A Londoner by birth, and a globe-trotter by disposition, my mother, Theodora, an inveterate lacrosse enthusiast who essentially saw life as one long unfolding adventure, would seize almost greedily on every fresh opportunity while deflecting any difficulty with an insouciance which never really left her. It was, therefore, not altogether surprising that soon after qualifying as a physiotherapist she set sail for South Africa and in so doing unwittingly followed my father's earlier example of youthful wanderlust. She delighted in every aspect of life at the Cape where she developed a successful practice in the Wynberg district of Cape Town. There she met my father holidaying from Johannesburg. They married back in London on 30 April 1927 and honeymooned in a cottage on the shores of Lake Bala in North Wales. Had they been subscribers to any belief in serendipitous surprises, they might have found it curious, at the very least, to learn that thirteen years later their son would find himself living on the edge of another Welsh lake at nearby Vyrnwy.

That they only married in 1927 indicates that my father was already 50 before he allowed himself to take a marital plunge, perpetuating what seems to have been something of a family tradition. His own father, Jonathan, similarly retained the freedom of bachelor life until he had turned 50. A quick calculation suggests – facetiously, if you like, and only by a whisker – the improbable but technically accurate fact that my grandfather had briefly been a contemporary of both Beethoven and Schubert. Not surprisingly there is no suggestion that grandfather Jonathan, busily farming in Cumberland, ever visited Vienna.

Were my parents musical? My father would contend that his musical career was abruptly terminated while auditioning for his school choir at St. Bees. Asked to join in singing 'Three Blind Mice' in canon, his contribution was tersely cut short with a curt command: "Stop talking Manduell!" I never heard my mother sing or play but this was perhaps in deference to her mother, a formidable lady who looked like Queen Mary, and indeed dressed like her, and who was wont to deliver Victorian ballads in a stentorian contralto voice while accompanying herself, rather too enthusiastically, on the piano.

My own first memories are of discovering an upright piano in a corner of the Oribi dining hall. There I would spend many happy moments in breaks between school meals when the hall was deserted, experimenting to my heart's content. Ultimately this persuaded my parents to engage the services of a local piano teacher, Dorothy Boxall, who would come to give me lessons on that Oribi piano. The very first piece of music she gave me to learn happened to be 'The Jolly Farmer' from *Scenes at a Farm* by Walter Carroll. In so doing, the good Miss Boxall unintentionally looked ahead some forty years to when Carroll's daughter, Ida[2], would be one of my first senior appointments when we prepared to open the Royal Northern College of Music in Manchester.

My early boyhood was wonderfully happy. Whenever my sweet tooth craved a treat, I could implore Mrs. Harcourt, the Oribi cook, to let me have some tasty indulgence. Out of doors I could spend hours with our dog, a brown and white pointer called Puck, by then too portly to be really puckish. He and I would romp up to the memorial at the top of Oribi Koppie[3], from which vantage point we could look down on the school grounds and the surrounding Kensington district of Johannesburg.

For reasons best known to himself, Father did not favour my attending Jeppe's own prep school. Instead I was sent to Parktown Preparatory, the junior department of another leading school in Johannesburg and one frequently engaged in friendly sporting rivalry with Jeppe. Jeppe itself had a prominent and eminently successful sporting tradition, especially in rugby and cricket. My father was particularly proud of the fact that Jeppe could boast that it had provided at least one member of every South African cricket team touring in England from the 1900s onwards. This tradition continued after the Second World War, and only ceased when tours by all-white teams were suspended in the face of anti-apartheid protests.

My father and mother celebrated his retirement after seventeen years as Head at Jeppe by devising for themselves and their two children[4] a wonderful tour of the Dutch East Indies, as Indonesia

---

[2] Ida Carroll, OBE, former Principal of the Northern School of Music in Manchester, and subsequently Dean of Management at the RNCM.
[3] A hillock in Afrikaans.
[4] My sister, Anne, had been born in 1935. Gillian, my second sister, followed soon after our tour to Indonesia and Australasia.

was then styled, and Australasia. Until we reached New Zealand, our spirit of adventure was lent colourful variety through our leisurely journey being undertaken on an old Dutch tramp ship, the *Swartenhond*, inching its way at will in and out of successive ports in Sumatra, Java, Bali, and Papua New Guinea.

For me, a young lad then approaching ten, this whole tour richly provided a kaleidoscope of new sights, sounds and colourful experiences – none more so than when we made an excursion to the Borobudur Temple in central Java. This involved a half day's journey over rough roads from our hotel in Batavia, as Jakarta was then called. Originating in the ninth century during the Sailendra Dynasty, this magnificent terraced Buddhist temple left a particularly indelible romantic impression on me. The fact that when we arrived overgrown jungle was still being cleared away, while a multitude of chattering monkeys raced about us, encouraged my vivid boyish imagination to believe that we were engaged on a wonderful journey of discovery and exploration. This, in effect, we were.

When we reached Papua New Guinea, that country was still largely unexplored and the inhabitants we encountered still remained virtually unspoilt. As the *Swartenhond* nosed its way into Rabaul harbour, the flooded crater of an old volcano, I had been regaled by members of the crew with colourful stories about Papuan cannibals. When we docked my parents would not allow me to accompany them ashore, a restriction I naturally resented. Determined not to remain confined to the ship once they had gone, I slipped ashore and out through a large warehouse until I found myself on an open road leading away from the dockside. Suddenly, a group of tall local men appeared out of the bordering sugar cane plantation, heading towards me with loud whoops of joy and energetic gyrations to match. Cannibals! – my doubtless too vivid young imagination immediately concluded! In a blind panic I turned and fled back to the docks, by then convinced that I was being pursued as a prize for their cooking pot. Eventually, when all seemed quiet, I crept out of the hiding place I had found among a stack of large bales and slunk back up the gangplank, only to be confronted at the top by my parents who had earlier returned and had no hesitation in voicing their extreme displeasure.

I had the special pleasure of celebrating my tenth birthday in Sydney, a day I shall always remember with boyish satisfaction in that, having been asked what I would like for my birthday, I had pleaded for a day's excursion pass on the Sydney ferries. My hidden motive for this was that I was besotted with fantasies about sharks. It followed that I spent the whole day hanging over the edge of a ferry desperately trying to spot a shark, whether we were heading up the Parramatta River and on to Taronga Zoo or out towards Bondi. The only disappointment was that, as might have been anticipated, I never saw a single shark.

After that exotic tour lasting over six months, and with the ceremonial occasions in Johannesburg marking my father's retirement behind us, my parents decided to head to England, where they bought a small country cottage a few miles south of Canterbury. This lay in a valley known locally as Pett Bottom, a 'bottom' being Kentish rural-speak for a valley. Rather colourfully, the next valley, parallel to ours, was known locally as Madam's Bottom which could be reached by going down Man's Hill.

While the cottage was being renovated and extended, we lived with my grandmother in her seafront house at Hythe. There I attended my first English school, Seabrook Lodge, where I had the good fortune to discover Miss Rowe, the music mistress. Despite presenting a distinctly severe first impression with her mass of black hair giving way to a sharp fringe, Miss Rowe proved to be a stimulating and warm-hearted musical mentor. Thanks to her, I experienced my first opera, *Carmen*, given by the touring Carl Rosa Opera in Folkestone. I was completely bowled over by its wonderfully colourful melodies but not by the clearly makeshift and flimsy staging. I also remember Miss Rowe taking a group of us to the Leas Cliff Hall in Folkestone for a piano recital by the legendary Alfred Cortot, of which my most abiding memory remains one of fascination with his seemingly enormous hands and long fingers.

Once the cottage near Canterbury was ready, I was moved to another nearby rural prep school, Wootton Court, not far from Ealham. No sooner had I arrived there, however, than the owner and headmaster, Mr. Yates, decided that the Battle of Britain being fought overhead dictated a swift evacuation to North Wales where the school occupied what, pre-war, had been a flourishing large fishing hotel overlooking Lake Vyrnwy. One or two members of the hotel's domestic staff had been retained to help clean and run the school, one of these being chubby and cuddly Gwyneth. For some reason best known to herself, Gwyneth had evidently resolved that her immediate mission in life should be to help me confront the challenges of oncoming puberty. It was all delightfully and innocently playful, but also entirely novel and fun.

Inevitably, the hotel's facilities were scarcely geared to the requirements of a boys' school, least of all as far as sports amenities were concerned. There was one very small swimming bath and cricket could only be played by converting four adjoining tennis courts. But there were splendid compensations. I retain the happiest memories of expeditions and enterprise challenges undertaken on the heather- and bracken-covered hills of this part of rural Wales. Although we were not allowed access to the lake because it served as a reservoir for Liverpool, we did undertake competitive runs around it. The whole school would troop down to the local church every Sunday morning but the local vicar's sermons, being mostly given in Welsh, were largely unintelligible to us. Mr. Yates would determinedly compensate for this shortcoming by ensuring that we all took part in round-robin bible readings. Musical activities were similarly limited, my main excitement being when the headmaster would personally drive me over to Oswestry for the next in an ordained sequence of Associated Board examinations.

A more demanding school environment was clearly desirable and I was wholly delighted when I could move from Wales to Haileybury. There I immediately learned to play the bassoon (long since abandoned and replaced by clarinet) and to enjoy increasingly rewarding piano lessons with Kathleen McCurrach, the wife of the Director of Music, Hector. [Plate 2] She was a wonderfully sensitive and helpful piano teacher and my lessons, always given in the McCurrach's house, were a delight from start to finish, the enjoyment being enhanced by the family setting and the brief escape from the rigours of school life which an hour in their home represented.

Years later, after Hector's death, Kathleen retired to live quietly near some of her family in Scotland. She was destined to live to the great age of 106 and continued to play the piano until shortly before her death. Her hundredth birthday marked an unforgettably wonderful reunion. Some 200 of us assembled at the spacious Hydro Hotel in Peebles to attend a sumptuous lunch at which Kathleen spoke with all her characteristic and effortless elegance. However, this grand occasion was by no means the end of the birthday celebrations. After a short siesta we all forgathered in the ballroom which was proudly graced by a gleaming all-white grand piano. Kathleen then beguiled us with a beautifully sensitive performance of Schumann's *Kinderscenen*, this pleasure being followed by a group of Schubert Lieder in which Kathleen accompanied a good local baritone. When the music was over the doors behind the platform were flung open and in strode the Lord Lieutenant brandishing the Queen's congratulatory telegram which he presented to Kathleen with a suitably theatrical gesture.

The school choir and orchestra at Haileybury were always stimulating experiences. Hector was infinitely enterprising and it was not long before we were pounding out the *Polovtsian Dances* from *Prince Igor*. Turning to more recent repertoire, we all relished the then very recent *Rio Grande* by Constant Lambert and John Ireland's *These things shall be*. I also had many opportunities to participate in school music competitions and, from time to time, to try my hand at arranging – as, for instance, when I was charged with converting the waltz from Tchaikovsky's *Serenade for Strings* into a vaguely playable arrangement for wind band.

But my world was to come crashing down when, one June morning in 1943, my housemaster asked me to take a seat in the calm of his private sitting room in order to tell me that my father had died. The next day I was on a train to Canterbury for my father's funeral in St. Giles, a diminutive church at Kingston, a village a few miles south of Canterbury where he lies buried. He had died, I like to believe, as he might have wished – from a heart attack after returning from manoeuvres with his trusty old Home Guard colleagues.

Cloister Foibles

The times I spent in and around Canterbury Cathedral were at best irregular and often improvised. Since I was boarding at Haileybury during term time, such opportunities only occurred during the school holidays. Initially, they arose from friendship with another new boy, Malcolm France, who was destined for a distinguished career in the Church of England. His father, Canon William France, was then Warden of St. Augustine's, the theological college attached to Canterbury Cathedral. He had offered me a warm welcome, and it was thanks to his kindness that I was able to feel at home in the Cathedral Close.

During the early years of the war, Canterbury largely escaped direct damage, but all this changed in 1942 when a heavy bombing raid obliterated a whole area immediately surrounding the Cathedral. In the course of this raid, the Bell Harry Tower of Canterbury Cathedral was set ablaze by a German incendiary bomb. This disaster prompted the Fathers of St. Augustine's to take an unusual initiative by acquiring the services of a small manually operated but surprisingly mobile fire engine. We boys indulged in barely excusable revelry by 'exercising' this campus toy. Improvised fire drills were undertaken with unlimited enthusiasm during which the fire engine's hosepipes might just find themselves accidentally misdirected.

All this culminated in a somewhat startling moment during a service in the Cathedral. Another Canon of the Cathedral resolutely held that prayer should be regarded as a matter of thinking aloud with God listening. On this occasion we had reached an unforgettable point when, following the traditional prayer for the well-being of the Fathers of St. Augustine's, this same good cleric simply intoned the added words "and their new fire engine". So it was that the whole congregation, on their knees, found themselves offering a supplication to the Almighty for the welfare of the glistening red fire engine.

If that rather charming moment taught me anything it was that dedicated priests often retain a touching innocence and are mostly without guile. I was also to become aware of some rather less laudable characteristics, such as mortal vanity. This I derived from closer observation of Canterbury's Dean at the time, Dr. Hewlett Johnson. 'The Red Dean', as he was popularly known both in the town and far more widely on account of his passionately pronounced communist leanings, was also a man to whom modesty did not appear to come easily. When you entered the Deanery you were confronted by many visual reminders of its august occupant, particularly by a large and forbidding bust of the Red Dean frowning down upon you as you mounted the stairs.

As a small boy I once experienced the Dean's vanity at quaintly close quarters. I was sent for a haircut to Mr. Carr the barber, whose shop was in a small lane near the Cathedral. I seem to remember that I resented this obligation because it conflicted with some more desirable activity at that time. At all events the situation became still less agreeable when I found myself endlessly waiting in line while Mr. Carr went dutifully to work, painstakingly tending to the ring of white hair surrounding the bald pate of this gaitered divine. The process seemed to continue for an eternity, with each successive snip requiring close scrutiny in the mirror. Yes, I was probably intolerantly impatient but this irritating experience did at least teach me that however lofty may be a man's station, he can still be prey to an undermining measure of conceit.

If this particular Dr. Johnson's preoccupation with status and presentation taught me an abiding lesson about human vanity, and if I may have found the simple trust shown by the Fathers of St. Augustine to be somewhat beguiling, another experience brought home to me the raw side of adult hypocrisy in a way which, while initially entertaining, also left its mark. This was on the occasion of an evening concert given in the Cloisters of Canterbury Cathedral by the Boyd Neel Orchestra[5]. The great and the good of the Dean and Chapter were gathered right round the Cloisters with the orchestra playing in one corner. By tradition, the central sward remained unoccupied except, on this occasion, for the isolated form of a large lady in a heavy tweed suit who was to be seen throughout the first half of the concert reclining casually on the tombstone dedicated to the memory of Archbishop Cosmo Gordon Lang. A stream of hissed

---

[5] A pioneer string orchestra, founded in 1933 by Dr. Boyd Neel who, after the war, was to desert Britain for a life in Canada on appointment as Dean of the Royal Conservatory of Music in Toronto.

and muttered invective reached my tender ears from neighbouring concert-goers, complaining of the sacrilege that this represented and demanding to know who this disrespectful figure so abusing the dignity of the Cloisters might be. But then, during the interval, her identity was revealed as being that of Dorothy Sayers, the prominent and versatile writer who, at that time, was something of a national treasure on account of her dramatized history of the life of Jesus Christ under the title *The Man Born to be King*, presented by the British Broadcasting Corporation (BBC) Home Service in monthly episodes and produced by the legendary Val Gielgud. The muttering as we foregathered at the start of the second half of the concert had, by now, been transformed: "Isn't it wonderful? Dorothy Sayers, don't you know, *'The Man Born to be King'*. How marvellous to see her here." Not another suggestion of blasphemy or sacrilege.

One further memory of a Canterbury Cathedral event offered me delicious boyhood delight on account of it being perhaps the first instance I had ever encountered of a person of high authority being caused momentary embarrassment. The scene this time is the Chapter House, and the occasion a recital by the legendary Hungarian violinist, Jelly d'Arányi[6], partnered by the great accompanist, Gerald Moore. Every seat was occupied and a respectful hush fell while Archbishop Fisher, standing with his back to the platform, unwittingly delayed the proceedings by engaging in animated conversation with occupants in the front row. The succeeding minutes were periodically punctuated by the sight of Gerald Moore hesitantly peering round a door at the back of the platform but then hastily withdrawing as he saw the Archbishop still on his feet in conversation. This pantomime was repeated a couple of times by which point gentle ripples of mirth circulated each time that Moore was seen obviously trying to ascertain whether he and Jelly d'Arányi could come on stage. Finally, he evidently decided it was time to take some direct action and went to the piano to try out a discreet arpeggio, whereupon the Archbishop spun round and with a muttered apology quickly resumed his seat. Thereafter calm was restored and some captivating performances followed.

---

[6] Much admired pre-war violinist, grand-niece of the legendary Joseph Joachim and dedicatee of, *inter alia*, Ravel's *Tzigane*, Vaughan Williams's *Concerto Accademico* and, together with her comparably successful violinist sister, Adila Fachiri, Gustav Holst's Double Concerto.

Student Days

HAILEYBURY

My school years passed in a whirl of busy contentment. I played a lot of sport, notably cricket, which has always been a lifelong love, and fives. Naturally, I also spent endless hours making music, either arranging or playing. Thanks to the presence of a new director of music, Bill Snowdon (latterly arrived from Stowe), I not only discovered Debussy but found myself increasingly drawn to the whole French impressionistic school, whether portrayed on canvas or in music.

After some apprehension I found that carrying out prefectorial responsibilities was in itself quite satisfying, as was being Head of House and in this capacity helping to care for the welfare of some of the new boys. One of these was Rodger Doig, destined to become an enormously talented and successful rugby player, who was appointed Head of School in 1951 but who, tragically, was to die at the age of just 20 while serving in the Korean War as a Lieutenant in the Seaforth Highlanders.

It is perhaps mildly amusing in this age of glitzy celebrity status to reflect upon the pride we took in the many bright stars in the Haileybury firmament during our time, whether concerning distinguished parents or in relation to the achievements of a number of boys. One of our many conspicuous luminaries was Sir Gordon Richards, for many years champion jockey, whose son, Jack, was one of our better cricketers. A prominent figure in the entertainment world of the day was Henry Hall, another Haileybury parent, who brought his enormously popular dance band to entertain us one memorable Saturday evening, complete with a lady singer swathed in a full-length leopard skin coat over whom we boys swooned deliriously!

Mention of Henry Hall leads me to reflect upon some of the rising thespian talent of which Haileybury could boast at the time. Henry Hall's son, Michael, already destined for stage success, was one who made an early theatrical mark as a boy. So, too, did Gerald Harper, whose relaxed authority and calm personality became a familiar feature of many fine British films emerging as the second half of the century progressed. I could scarcely claim any comparable talents for myself but do recall hovering ineffectually over Ophelia's grave as the First Priest while Laertes (Harper) and Hamlet (Hall) vainly protested to the stubborn priest that the unfortunate lady should have been allowed to lie in sanctified ground.

When it comes to outright celebrity status, their successes on stage and screen, substantial though they were, could scarcely compare with the meteoric rise to fame which attended Stirling Moss, another contemporary. Within a few short years of leaving school he was to become the most prominent racing driver in the world. He was selected 'Driver of the Year' at the age of 25, became the first Englishman to win the Mille Miglia a year later, and was destined to be British Motor Racing Champion no fewer than ten times. A knighthood reflected his legendary successes, while the value of his influence throughout the motor racing world cannot be exaggerated.

The Haileyburian who without question remains to this day the school's most illustrious son, came to national and indeed global prominence during my fourth year at Haileybury. He was, of course, Clement Attlee, whose election to succeed Churchill as Prime Minister gave us particularly delicious satisfaction on account of the fact that this appeared to represent Haileybury supplanting Harrow in the national power stakes. Reports had it that as the bus bringing Haileybury's visiting cricketers disgorged its passengers, the Harrovian ranks were heard to offer rather revealingly half-hearted, "Three cheers for the Reds". Reviewing these events nearly seventy years later, it is interesting to reflect, in these days of sulphurously prejudiced political preoccupation with links between independent schools and elitism, how seldom politicians remind their listeners that Labour's greatest Prime Minster had, in fact, been just one more public school boy.

The demands of the war largely accounted for the rather elderly age range among the teaching staff at the time. Nevertheless, well-matured as they may have been, their teaching methods embodied many excellent and, in some cases, unusual features, such as conducting much sixth form work in Oxbridge-style seminars. For example, I recall that Dr. Parker would install the members of the German Sixth in armchairs in his capacious study. There we would explore the delights of Goethe and Schiller while Dr. Parker's oversized ginger cat slumbered peacefully in a carved out elephant foot by the fireside. Those of us who had the good fortune to move on to university were undoubtedly the better prepared to meet the striking difference in approaches between school teaching and university learning.

In my own case an application to Jesus College, Cambridge, was being prepared. The choice of college derived directly from the fact that my father had himself been a meritorious Jesuan. I was immensely helped in the application process by my housemaster, one Caleb Gordon Whitefield ('Whitters'), a battle-hardened survivor from First World War service in Mesopotamia, who offered me much wise guidance. Whitters also inspired in me an increasing interest and indeed fascination with history. Invariably, his approach was to ask five questions concerning each historical event: who? when? what? why? result? – all in all a practical and effective way of reaching a good understanding of any particular event.

As I prepared to leave school at the end of that winter term, I did so in a spirit of warm satisfaction and genuine gratitude for all that the school had given me during five very rewarding and happy years. Unavoidably, there had been ups and downs but many more of the former. Quite unintentionally I had made a lucky start to my career early in my first term. Practice at Haileybury at the time protected new boys[7] from punishment during their first fortnight at the school. For some reason which I can no longer recall, I managed to incur the displeasure of my House Prefects on my seventeenth day. The resultant public caning was apparently the earliest hitherto administered and the resulting record conferred upon me an entirely undeserved element of heroic status among my peers.

By comparison with current conditions, Haileybury during the war would have seemed positively Spartan, with few of today's creature comforts. I doubt if any of us felt in the slightest degree deprived. For example, the sleeping arrangements in my House, Bartle Frere, provided simply for the forty-eight of us to sleep in one long dormitory with twenty-four beds in small cubicles ranged on either side. But it is perhaps worth adding in the light of recent unpleasant press reports that none of us felt in any way insecure

---

[7] In those days, new boys at Haileybury were known as 'New Governors', a quaint historical reflection of the fact that Haileybury had been established in 1862 by the Dutch East India Company with a view to preparing young men to go out and govern Her Majesty's colonies.

and everyone, I am entirely satisfied, slept unmolested in his bed.

One evening ritual in our House was that, after lights out, Whitters, as Housemaster, would gather the House Prefects for a relaxed conversation round a table at one end of the dormitory. These convivial chats were immensely helpful in consolidating a good spirit between Housemaster and those managing the House. A delightful moment occurred one evening when Whitters loudly announced, "Ah, Manduell! I've had another letter from Jesus". The resultant ripple of mirth among the occupants of a number of neighbouring beds was palpable.

Eventually all was well and a place at Jesus was confirmed for the following autumn. At the same time I was able to contemplate the enticing vista of some nine months without designated activity, a prospect as bewildering as it was novel. The key question, to which possible answers had now to be sought, was how might the first part of 1947 best be occupied?

Strasbourg

In 1870 Bismarck's army stormed into Alsace. That first substantial Prussian invasion of France may not figure so prominently in today's history books as do the cataclysmic German sequels which were to follow. Nonetheless, the occupation of Alsace, and the subsequent annexation which lasted until the 1918 armistice, wreaked widespread havoc on life in what hitherto had been a quiet, slightly detached, part of eastern France nestling between the Vosges mountains and the Rhine. Social, cultural and economic life was cruelly devastated. Few would be spared from having their lives totally disrupted, certainly not the members of the Oberlé family.

The Oberlés had, for generations, farmed at Knoersheim [Plate 3], a village lying a dozen or so kilometres south east of Saverne. Throughout this rich wine-growing area the land had always yielded plentiful rewards. Until 1870 life had been good. But then, confronted by the Prussian assault, two young Oberlé brothers found themselves having to make fundamental decisions. The elder decided to endure the occupation and maintain the family farm; in due course he married and had a son, Joseph. The younger fled westwards into France and ended up on the island of Guernsey where he too started a family and had a son, Lucien.

Eventually, Lucien emigrated to South Africa where he was a

highly-regarded schoolmaster, in which capacity he and my father became close friends. The two families would share holidays even though their respective schools lay 500 miles apart. Sadly, however, each couple was destined to lose one of the partners during the course of the war. An initial exchange of correspondence between Lucien and my mother, conducted by 'aerogram' (the only authorised form of international communication conforming to prevailing censorship regulations), gradually led to an increasingly close degree of friendship. In due course the tone of their letters warmed sufficiently to encourage Lucien somehow to secure for himself a berth on a troopship sailing from Durban to Britain.

I was soon to discover that in Lucien I had, to my great good fortune, acquired a stepfather possessed of extraordinary kindness and wisdom. It was Lucien who most imaginatively suggested that an interesting and rewarding arrangement to fill the time between Haileybury and Cambridge might be for me to acquire an awareness of post-war Europe by capitalising upon his family connections with Alsace. In a very short space of time he had secured for me registration to undertake a one semester 'diplôme en lettres' course at the University of Strasbourg.

Accommodation had been reserved in a university hostel, jointly funded by Swiss interests and the Louis Pasteur Foundation. At the same time, cousin Joseph had kindly indicated that I would be welcome to visit him and his family in Knoersheim at any time. Final arrangements (such as acquiring a passport and securing a rail ticket from Boulogne to Strasbourg) followed with breath-taking speed. By the middle of January I was wheeling onto the cross-Channel ferry at Folkestone my brand new Hercules bicycle into whose panniers Lucien had, with cunning foresight, packed an enormous quantity of coffee beans.

The Strasbourg I discovered in January 1947 would be unrecognizable to those who know the international centre it has become today in order to accommodate the European Parliament with all the razzmatazz that its status at the heart of Europe brings to it. I arrived to find an essentially mediaeval town which, with its lopsided single spired cathedral, had largely remained unchanged save for mercifully limited damage during the 1940-5 Nazi occupation. A drab poverty was everywhere and the shock to one fresh from the comparatively cosseted world I had previously known was immediate and considerable.

The sheer extent of general deprivation was brought home to me vividly when, on my first morning in Strasbourg, I went for a walk along a canal close to the hostel. Working from rafts moored along the canal bank were a number of elderly washerwomen, struggling to break the ice in order to accomplish their depressingly cruel work. The bleak weather made their brutal task all the more challenging since 1947 was to enter the record books as one of the coldest European winters of the century. Having to work in ice-cold water was bad enough, but being obliged to use poor quality soap[8] which would not lather must have conspired to defeat their best endeavours. The raw poverty which this scene presented to me remains as vivid today as it did then.

Another considerable shock, for which I was ill-prepared, was to encounter an unexpected degree of difficulty in holding satisfactory casual conversations. I had arrived in Strasbourg as a reasonably fluent French speaker confident that I could also cope adequately in German if required to. What I had not anticipated was that so few people over the age of 50 actually commanded any French. This was simply because they had been at school before 1918 when Alsace was part of Germany, so no French was taught in the schools, the study of German being obligatory. At the same time, few people freely chose to express themselves in German in view of all that they had endured during the years of Nazi occupation. The *lingua franca* was a local Alsatian dialect[9] which derived to a certain extent from German.

Life was severely constrained by rationing. Normal foodstuffs were only obtainable by coupon. Somewhat surprisingly there seemed to be only limited black market activity. I was obliged to surrender all my coupons in return for the basic meals we received at the hostel. The few unrationed solutions available to satisfy one's gnawing hunger largely took the form of direct imports from

---

[8] A widely circulated rumour suggested that an ingredient in the only soap available derived directly from the erstwhile inmates of nearby Schirmeck concentration camp.

[9] One clue which I found occasionally helpful was to convert all 'A's in German into 'O's in Alsacien, and to slur syllables together. To take a few place names as examples: Place du Corbeau (Raven Square) Rabenplatz phonetically became Robeplots in Alsacien. Similarly, Wasselonne, a neighbouring market town, was known locally as Vossele – and so on.

Algeria, such as dried figs and dates. In addition, during that harsh winter, the roast chestnuts man was always a welcome sight waiting at the street corner.

This is where Lucien's coffee beans were my salvation. Coffee was in such short supply and of such poor quality that I found I could trade half a kilo for a slap-up restaurant meal, sometimes even in sufficient quantity to enable me to entertain a university friend. I also struck up a deal with a restaurant in the rather fashionable Place Kleber where on one occasion I was able to entertain a group of four friends for no more than one kilo of coffee beans. Eventually my supply of coffee beans was exhausted and I was in no position to negotiate any further deals.

One other location where I could count on receiving a very generous square meal was, as you might anticipate, cousin Joseph's table at Knoersheim. Every third or fourth weekend I would cycle out from Strasbourg, a journey of about an hour, to be rewarded with flagons of Joseph's own wine – white, rosé and red – which one could delight in drawing directly off the barrel. Joseph's wife, Mamam, was generosity personified and I would be encouraged to return to Strasbourg with the now vacant panniers packed full with all manner of rural produce such as the family's special salted bacon. The Oberlés' kindness was never-ending.

One particular weekend visit to Knoersheim offered me a first-hand opportunity to appreciate French partisan politics at their most strident. It happened to be when voting for the local elections was taking place. On the Saturday evening we were all royally entertained around the bar in Joseph's inn by the political agent visiting on behalf of de Gaulle's party. His generous hospitality appeared to know no bounds as the Amer, a local bitter beer, flowed without restraint. By the time the villagers dispersed they were all committed Gaullists and there was no question which way all would vote on the morrow. Or was there?

The next morning I dutifully accompanied Joseph to Mass only to find that the whole sermon turned into a hustings tirade on behalf of Bidault's catholic MRP[10] party. The cynic will not be surprised to

---

[10] MRP – Mouvement Républicain Populaire formed soon after the war by Georges-Augustin Bidault, a former foreign minister and prime minister in the Fourth Republic.

learn that a large majority of the congregation then headed straight from church to the voting booths, entirely forgetful of the Gaullist hospitality they had enjoyed the previous evening but now resolved to do their traditional duty as bidden by the Priest.

Another favourite out-of-town excursion which I enjoyed on three different occasions was to spend the weekend with a fellow student with whom I had formed a good friendship, Raymond Baer. His parental home was in Thionville, nestling in northern Lorraine and close to the Luxembourg border. The train journeys to Thionville taught me another delightful lesson about the French gift for taking advantage of a given situation. Raymond's father, who was employed by the state railways, the SNCF, explained that bonuses were offered to locomotive crews in two specific categories: the first, if they conserved precious coal, which was still in fairly short supply; the second, if they helped to preserve the SNCF's proud reputation for punctuality.

It so happened that our train from Strasbourg changed crews at Metz, a big industrial town in southern Lorraine and therefore near mid-way on our journey. We could confidently anticipate that the train would make only sluggish progress as far as Metz, whereupon the first crew would dismount and collect a bonus for so admirably conserving coal. Thereupon, the new crew would reinvigorate the burners with unlimited quantities of the painstakingly saved coal in order that the train could make up for lost time and arrive punctually in Thionville when another bonus would be available for collection. Needless to add, this convenient arrangement would be reversed on the return journey.

My visits to the Baer family also offered me another experience which today I recall with some amazement, if only for the fact that it did not seem unusual at the time. Raymond's sister was very beautiful but proved to be unapproachable because, as Raymond told me in great confidence, she had already been recruited to the French secret service as a potential German-speaking spy. Back in 1947, and with all of us still so closely attuned to the war, it did not seem to me in any way unusual that this should have been her chosen dedication. Hopefully she was never called upon to practise her skills, at least on the Eastern side of the Iron Curtain.

Two further excursions I made took me beyond national borders. The first was a visit to Freiburg in the French occupied zone of Germany. This came about when a Strasbourg rugby club I had joined went to play a match against the French occupying forces. After crossing the Rhine we travelled by train from Kehl to Freiburg, sitting on wooden benches in a pre-war third-class carriage. On arrival at the virtually obliterated Freiburg station we were obliged to stumble across a brick-strewn wasteland to show our passes to a ticket collector in what was, for all the world, just a sentry box.

By contrast, when we arrived at the ground we found we were to play in a large concrete stadium built by Hitler to the greater glory of the Third Reich. This had somehow escaped destruction. Since rugby has never been a German sport, it was perhaps inevitable that the only spectators in this concrete cavern should have been a few French regimental friends. This in turn meant that the players' voices echoed around the empty stadium in extraordinarily desolate fashion. The quite remarkable resonance which resulted was certainly powerful enough for the few spectators to acquire an extensive knowledge of French expletives as explosively exercised by our dominant captain, himself a former *maquis*[11] leader.

My other excursion out of France was also physically demanding but in a different way. For some reason I decided to set myself the task of cycling to Switzerland. The trip took a full week but was very satisfying and also revealing in that I was able to observe the stark contrast between war-torn France and neutral Switzerland. The largest town in southern Alsace, Mulhouse, had inevitably suffered extensive damage resulting from the advance of General Patton's Third Army as it stormed up the Belfort Gap. By contrast, Basel was immaculate, fresh and welcoming. The question in my mind as I cycled back northwards was to ask whether it was divine providence or devilish cunning which had ensured that Switzerland should escape the carnage and desolation suffered elsewhere.

I cannot easily exaggerate the surge of joyous relief which I experienced on arrival in Alsace through the realisation that now, and effectively for the first time, I could concentrate extensively on music without such pleasure being crowded out by other overriding demands. One result was that I located a quite excellent second-hand music shop where I could find scores to study with a greed and impatience which I had never previously enjoyed. Many of my early acquisitions were designed to follow up the interest in the French Impressionists which I had acquired during my last year at

---

[11] The French wartime underground resistance movement.

Haileybury. With still greater excitement I began to discover quite a lot of contemporary music, while at the same time, and with a growing sense of awe, I began seriously to explore the music of Wagner – for me at that time an experience almost akin to being submerged under a great tidal wave. In a virtually disused room on the ground floor of the hostel I had also discovered an elderly upright piano. To all intents and purposes I was able to adopt this room as a working studio, having found it largely free from interruptions except for the occasional visit from a portly *femme-de-chambre* with whom I had useful opportunities to practise the Alsacien dialect.

Strasbourg offered a wonderful ambience to anyone interested in music in that its musical activity was both historically reflective and adventurously explorative. At that time the city enjoyed considerable eminence through the spreading distinction, and indeed fame, of one of its leading citizens, Albert Schweitzer. Unfortunately, I was never able to hear Schweitzer play on his favourite organ in the cathedral, since he had chosen to continue, until the following year, working in the hospital he had founded at Lambaréné in the Gabon. Before leaving England I had, at the suggestion of my school director of music, dipped into Schweitzer's fine two-volume study of J. S. Bach, in the excellent translation by Ernest Newman. Now I felt it to be an infinite privilege to be living in the city which was home to this great man who, as an organ student in Paris, had confounded the great Widor and whose lifetime achievements in both theology and medicine were to bring him the Nobel Peace Prize in 1952 and who – and this, perhaps, I found most intriguing of all – had formed a close friendship with Wagner's widow, Cosima, after she retreated to Alsace.

If the music of Bach was Schweitzer's lifeblood so, too, was it the dominant feature of Strasbourg's musical life in 1947 on account of a large ambitious Bach festival. I lost count of the many examples of really fine singing which the festival promoted. It also enjoyed considerable panache through having as its artistic director the great French conductor, Charles Munch. He directed a number of fine concerts but was unfairly traduced in one or two organs of the press who seemed to resent his omnipresence.[12]

---

[12] Large posters around the town had proclaimed "Le Grand Festival Johann Sebastian Bach avec le concours de Charles Munch". One day a particularly sour review headline, however, read "Le Grand Festival Charles Munch avec le concours de Johann Sebastian Bach".

My nascent love of opera also flourished thanks to the fact that Opéra du Rhin, today so highly regarded in operatic circles, had quickly found its post-war feet. On my first visit, the company had presented a suitably opulent *Aida*, but perhaps my most memorable evening in the opera house occurred on the occasion of a performance of Charpentier's *Louise*. I had been invited to the performance by a local music critic and had, at one point, sought from my learned host some information about the composer who, I was given to understand, was long dead. Imagine, therefore, my youthful incredulity when a small and frail figure with flowing white hair appeared before the footlights to receive the acclamation of the house. It was Charpentier himself, who was to live another nine years until the age of 96.

An entirely fortuitous connection also linked Charpentier with aspects of the work I was undertaking at the university for my diploma. In order to ensure that my labours would not be unduly onerous I had, with a little bit of cunning, managed to persuade my kindly tutor that the university would accept a diploma thesis on the work of Théophile Gautier, concentrating in particular on his preoccupation with matters Chinese as these emerge in his *Chinoiserie* poems. However, Gautier was by no means only a poet, as my research into his life revealed. He had also been remarkably active as both music and drama critic reviewing in a number of important periodicals, notably *La presse* and the *Journal officiel du soir*. I was not a little intrigued by the fact that it was Charpentier who had chosen to collect Gautier's reviews and publish them separately under the title *La musique*.

High summer having arrived, it seemed logical to bring to an end what had been six extraordinarily revealing and rewarding months in Alsace by heading back to England to catch some of the best of that summer's cricket. The South Africans were touring, but their bowling was being summarily despatched to all corners of the field by the 'Middlesex twins', Bill Edrich and Denis Compton, who carried all before them that summer – except, I am glad to say, on the occasion of the traditional Middlesex match during the Canterbury Festival. To the satisfaction of all Kentish supporters, the highlight was surely the moment when Les Ames, having already taken heavy toll of the Middlesex bowling, played a majestic lofted off-drive to bring up his hundredth first-class century.

Cambridge

Viewed in retrospect I can only, in all honesty, regard my time at Cambridge as a forfeited opportunity – a non-event, if you like – when it should have been a significant character- and career-forming experience. This is a sad admission to have to make, the more so since the shortcoming was largely mine.

Too late, but only after I had embarked upon my first year reading French and German, did I come to the realisation that, whatever interest in languages I may have entertained at school, their study no longer represented a sufficiently satisfying option. While the mistake I had made may be all too familiar, it is one which many students arriving at university experience. They have failed to question whether a facility at school represents a more sustained motivation. In my case six months in Strasbourg had been more game-changing than I had realised at the time. Months had been spent with music as my engrossing priority but I had dismally failed to anticipate its ultimate consequence. I should have asked the obvious questions and perhaps in an insufficiently assertive way I may have done so. The fact remains that, failing to appreciate the need for an earlier decision, I allowed myself effectively to drift along one route when I should have been staking a firm claim to another.

Initially I felt obliged to justify the support of those who had helped me reach Cambridge, and indeed to warrant the College's decision in accepting me, by deciding to stick to the designated path and make the best of it. This resolution I seriously and conscientiously maintained for some months. My tutors were tolerant and encouraging, and no doubt I might have sustained a full three years and have emerged from the final tripos examinations with some credit. But it would all have been, in a sense, a deception on myself. When I eventually came to explore the options for changing to a music degree course, I received a scarcely surprising unhelpful response. I did not possess in music the credentials which had secured my passage to Cambridge to read languages, and I can hardly blame the authorities for their decision. All that I effectively knew, with increasing conviction, was that I was continuing to be confronted by unrewarding and increasingly unyielding challenges. In the end I felt compelled to take the only realistic decision apparently open to me: to withdraw from the university and then try to compensate for my misjudgment in vigorous pursuit of my musical ambitions and compulsions.

My arrival in Cambridge was also in various small ways dispiriting. I had been disappointed to find that I was among a small number of freshmen not given rooms in College. By contrast, I had been allocated lodgings in Jesus Lane where the landlady, Miss Smee, while doubtless well-intentioned, maintained a house which was consistently rather damp and cold. An atmosphere of some gloom also seemed to assail my two fellow Jesuans. One was a Chinese medical student whose room was dominated by a large human skeleton. He went to play tennis one spring morning shortly before his first year exams were due and later that afternoon hung himself. For a time we were all mystified by his absence until our landlady brought news of his tragedy with the words, "'E done 'imself in, 'e 'as. They does – can't take the exams, I s'ppose." The other resident, who hailed from Kenya and was reading agriculture, was to suffer a more dramatic and very different experience when he learnt, shortly before the first year was out, that his family farm had been overrun, torched and razed to the ground by Mau Mau insurgents.

Of course, it was not all doom and gloom. I was able to participate in a number of musical activities such as the performance of Purcell's *King Arthur* which we presented in the College cloisters. The College choir achieved good standards and it was a pleasure to sing in it, our rehearsals often being prompted by delightful quips from Anthony Armstrong-Jones. Tony was swiftly selected to cox the Cambridge Eight and I often wonder whether it may have been after the traditional ducking in the Thames at the conclusion of the Boat Race that the future Lord Snowdon may have caught Princess Margaret's eye.

Another dedicated oarsman was a fellow freshman, Paul Bourne, who stroked the Jesus Eight to reach Head of the River and who, in due course, was to exercise a key role in the Henley Royal Regatta. Paul and I were destined to become lifelong friends almost from the moment when everyone mustered for the traditional freshmen's photograph. A close friendship with the Bourne family was to ensue. In high summer 1953 Paul did me the honour of asking me to be his best man on the occasion of his marriage to Ruth in Cape Town. Two years later, in Paul's absence on Colonial Service duty in Northern Rhodesia, his brother David, a gifted painter, did me the complementary honour of being my best man.

What was perhaps my most arresting, if unexpected, musical

experience during my university days occurred not in Cambridge but in Bletchley. We had been over to Oxford for a traditional annual rugby match against the counterpart Jesus College there. As our return journey progressed, it began to snow heavily and a strong wind got up. By the time we had reached the edge of Bletchley we were in the middle of a violent snow storm, at which point our elderly chartered bus gave up the ghost. The driver, being unable to remedy the situation, suggested there was no option but for us to walk into town to find some shelter while we sought alternative transport. As we battled our way through what was now not just a snow storm but a raging blizzard some lights became apparent in a large building which, as we drew closer, turned out to be the local ABC cinema. As the storm outside raged, what did we find was showing but the then new and much lauded film *Scott of the Antarctic* with music by Vaughan Williams. In this improbable way I first became acquainted with the music which would be developed shortly afterwards into one of the grand old man's last great works, his *Sinfonia Antartica*.

My resolution in terms of my university course saw me through to acceptable first year results. But this only reinforced for me a feeling of growing irrelevance, since I no longer harboured even the faintest thought that I might in any way seek to use my languages for career purposes. It was at this point that fate seemingly intervened in a way which dealt a grievous shock to the whole of my family when my stepfather, Lucien, was killed in a climbing accident near Eshowe in Zululand.

As a direct consequence, the family's financial situation became somewhat acute. Acting on all these portents I concluded that the necessary course of action was to sell our cottage in Kent and for me then to take my elderly grandmother out to South Africa to join my twice widowed mother and my two younger sisters. I had not anticipated that it would take over a year for the sale to be completed but when it was I duly set sail and arrived in Durban with a profound sense of relief that a difficult chapter in my life was now over.

A few days before my departure, I was fortunate enough to obtain a ticket to Covent Garden for a performance of *Die Meistersinger*. It was an overwhelmingly glorious occasion, showing the Royal Opera House at its finest. The central role of cobbler Hans Sachs was sung by the incomparable Hans Hotter. Eva was the lovely Elisabeth Grummer, while Peter Anders presented a personable Walter, and Benno Kusche gave us an infinitely entertaining Beckmesser. Presiding over the whole occasion, and inspiring the orchestra to glow as it never did at that time under Karl Rankl, was Sir Thomas Beecham, appearing as a gala guest conductor. In a stimulating way I found myself invoking the axiom of the camel's hump as a repository for reserve resource; however limited I might be destined to find musical opportunities in South Africa, I came away from Covent Garden in the conviction that at least I would be taking with me a glorious memory which would never be dimmed and which it had been a rare privilege to experience.

Durban

There can be nothing quite like a long sea voyage to create an artificially protected bubble in which to review ravages and, hopefully, to compensate for these by assembling new ambitions and igniting fresh initiatives. Such were some of the thoughts uppermost in my mind as the 'Windsor Castle' sailed serenely on its three-week Atlantic journey from Southampton to Durban. Those last extended months in England, tying up various loose ends and endeavouring to look more realistically to the future, had been difficult. But now, although there could be, at that point, no certainty that I would ever be in a position to return to England, at least I was able to focus upon what possibilities Durban might yield. There was also the modest excitement of returning to the land of my birth after a gap of some eleven years.

From the outset, the decision to study and work in Durban proved to be the right one in all circumstances. It was also, incidentally, a wonderful place in which to make mistakes but to do so without being subjected to any confidence-crucifying spotlight. I was able to concentrate with limitless energy and optimism upon my largely self-taught musical studies, particularly, of course, in relation to composition. I would greedily devour Cecil Forsyth's book on orchestration to the point of memorising key information in as clear and concentrated fashion as I was able. At the same time I also embarked on a fairly rigorous self-imposed course of study drawing on selected twentieth-century models to improve my skills in given media: for example, Bartók for his string quartets, Prokofiev for his piano writing and, especially, Britten for his remarkable gifts in handling both voices and accompaniments. The other unarguable priority was to be personally solvent and almost from the point of my return, I found I could achieve this.

Fortunately I was able to start enjoying some realistic musical opportunities. An early lucky break at this point was that Edward Dunn, the chief conductor and music director of the Durban Civic Orchestra, happened to be looking for somebody to care for all manner of ancillary responsibilities which he found it understandably tedious to carry through personally. Recompensed I may only have been now and again, but rewarded by the hour I most certainly was. I gradually came to share a delightful spirit of camaraderie with members of the orchestra. They probably looked upon me as being unconscionably green and wet behind the ears but, time and again, a given instrumentalist would respond to my doubtless tiresome questions with generous practical demonstrations. On a couple of brief occasions Edward Dunn asked the orchestra to try out something I had been writing, such as when I had prepared a short orchestral fantasy based on the Christmas carol 'Ding Dong Merrily on High'. Unsurprisingly perhaps, it was deemed unfit for general consumption, but just discovering where it did not work, and why, taught me a great deal.

There were two professional orchestras in Durban: Dunn's some sixty strong, and a short distance down the road, the South African Broadcasting Corporation (SABC) which maintained a studio orchestra of some thirty-five players. Occasionally the two orchestras would combine for a special undertaking such as Stravinsky's *Rite of Spring*. The SABC's conductor was Leonard Pearce who was ever-ready with helpful advice. Both he and Edward Dunn had musical sons – Edward's a horn player, Napier, would become a seasoned horn player in America, while Leonard's son, Michael, a violinist, was destined to join the Royal Philharmonic Orchestra in London and also to be one of the first musicians publicly to undergo gender reassignment.

In parallel, I was able to pick up useful and modestly remunerative occasional work writing about music for the *Natal Daily News* whose features editor, Redvers Haines, seemed content to offer me periodic slots. A third source of income I was able to secure was as an unqualified but remarkably well paid lecturer in English and about life in England at the Natal Technical College. My class was largely composed of South Africans whose first language was not English but who proved to be a most convivial bunch of students.

These three strands, the orchestra, the newspaper and the college, together provided a useful if modest flow of income, while I was able to pursue the intensive course of composition study which I had set myself.

Edward Dunn also showed a generous degree of trust in two additional but very different ways. One was in taking a big risk by inviting me to rehearse the municipally sponsored amateur orchestra, the Durban Philharmonic, although I cannot believe this was to the unqualified benefit of the players. Invaluable experience of a very different kind which Edward Dunn also put my way was when he asked me to become his assistant in organising and running a special festival mounted to mark the centenary of Durban's foundation in 1854. Here again, considerable enthusiasm from the municipality was key to his being able to announce a Durban Centenary Festival embracing a wide sweep of arts events.

Among these our music theatre offerings ranged from *The Mikado* and Jerome Kern's *Sunny* to *Il Trovatore* and the then brand new Menotti opera, *The Consul*. As with so much in Durban, this festival proved a sharp and stimulating learning experience for me, not least in trying to learn how to accompany tap in *Sunny*. Our *Il Trovatore* was, can you believe it, in a special version for children which enabled us to harness the unbridled enthusiasm of youngsters from schools all over Durban. At one point, a sturdy team of youngsters were to deliver uninhibited hammer blows while the massed singers joyously celebrated in a roof-raising anvil chorus.

Some months earlier, I had by far and away the greatest stroke of good fortune ever to come my way. The SABC used to promote recitals and concerts before invited audiences and on one occasion I went to the studios to hear a recital by a young South African pianist who had been studying in Amsterdam and London, and who had briefly returned to visit her family in Durban. Her recital was principally of music by Schumann and included his too seldom heard *Faschingsschwank aus Wien*. As she played, I thought I had never heard a piano sounding more beautiful, with more depth and range of tone and with phrasing more beautifully shaped. Who was this divine artist who had suddenly appeared here in Durban?

At all events an introduction followed, and a lot else very quickly. It was not all that long before I and this gifted pianist, Renna Kellaway, who had played a key role in our children's *Il Trovatore* production, became at least informally engaged. She continues to remember with some understandable degree of horror the occasion when I subjected her to a lamentably incompetent demonstration of how not to press one's suit or even (sort of) pop a hesitant question. We had gone down to Amanzimtoti, a small seaside resort a few miles south of Durban. After a long evening walk along the beach we found ourselves seated on an upturned fishing boat, whereupon I started to bore the proverbial pants off Renna while she listened, apparently dutifully, to the extended exposition which I offered her regarding *The Ring of the Nibelungen* and that remarkable world of gods and giants, dwarfs and serpents, heroes and rivermaidens which Wagner had assembled. How she survived such a numbing experience I am not sure, but somehow we seemed to leave Amanzimtoti with a new understanding and with me feeling the happiest man on earth.

A life-changing stroke of luck, of ultimately career-changing benefit, was to follow from getting to know the Kellaway family, and from being warmly welcomed among them. Renna's mother, a mathematics teacher, happened to spot in one of her education journals a notice placed by the Performing Right Society (PRS) inviting applications from young composers for a postgraduate scholarship in composition tenable at the Royal Academy of Music in London. Suddenly a new vista opened for me, if only I could secure such a scholarship.

There was little over a month to go before the closing date. In that time I must have composed at a rate which I have never subsequently matched in order to complete a sufficient portfolio to submit to London. There already existed most of a massive four-movement symphony for the fullest of full orchestras, and this I completed sitting up late into the night. I had already written my *Belloc Variations*, a set of short movements for piano and orchestra intended to characterise some of Belloc's more pithy short poems, which I also included in my portfolio. To this I finally added a further work for full orchestra which I entitled *Overture to Activity*, a title which I hoped would prove prophetic. Happily it did so, and I learned to my uncontainable delight that I had been selected to receive this PRS postgraduate scholarship[13] at the Royal Academy of Music, tenable for three years.

---

[13] Previously held by John Joubert, so I had much to live up to.

Thus, after some short and improbably fruitful years in Durban, I could contemplate this heaven-sent chance to return to England and enjoy my first opportunity for professional study in composition, along with all the other benefits the Royal Academy of Music could provide. I could scarcely believe my good fortune. Whereas my voyage south to Durban had been at a time when, truth to tell, my confidence was certainly at a very low ebb, and while musically I was totally untested, the return journey north was one I could now undertake with impatience and boundless optimism for all that I hoped might follow.

LONDON

My arrival at the Royal Academy of Music in September 1954 could not have been more enjoyable or more helpfully organised. After a courtesy introduction to the then Principal of the Academy, Sir Reginald Thatcher, whose retirement the following year would, incidentally, lead to a somewhat fundamental disruption to my studies, the Warden of the Academy, Myers ('Bill') Foggin, immediately took me under his wing in a most supportive and friendly manner. Bill was destined, a few years later, to become Principal of Trinity College of Music, a move which, not unexpectedly, proved to be greatly to the benefit of Trinity's staff and students.

A typical example of Bill's thoughtful care for others was his concern for where I might live. He happened to know of a converted mill at Tring in deepest Hertfordshire and wondered whether renting this might constitute an attractive option. I did not feel that it would be realistic to adopt such an exotic proposition. For one thing, the rent seemed more than my scholarship could bear, while the consequence of living out in the country rather than in central London might well have been to deny myself all manner of interesting opportunities. As an alternative I found a one room flat in Belsize Park, North London. This was an altogether much more practical proposition, and in due course became Renna's and my first home after we married the following summer.

Prior to my arrival, the Academy had allocated me to William Alwyn for principal study composition. It could not have made a wiser choice. He was a wonderfully understanding and supportive tutor who immediately identified countless shortcomings stemming from my raw inexperience and set me a range of new work. This was principally designed not only to remedy my many deficiencies but to make a start in providing me with some essential composing skills. He had a judicious and forceful way of curbing my clumsy and ill-disciplined excesses. At the same time he would also pose stimulating new challenges for me by prescribing specific tasks calculated to oblige me to sharpen my inner ear. As a versatile musician of considerable professional experience, composer, flautist[14], and much else besides, all the advice which Alwyn gave me was precise, direct and unerringly beneficial.

I vividly remember an occasion when I brought to him for inspection a *scena* for dramatic soprano and large orchestra which I had written at the invitation of the well-known South African dramatic soprano, Cecilia Wessels. He turned to me with an immediate question: "What on earth possessed you to set Shelley? There's far too much music in his poetry already. You can hardly add to it." Perhaps only someone with Alwyn's remarkable skill with words, as was demonstrated in everything he wrote including his own libretti, would have offered such a spontaneously sweeping reaction. All his advice was invariably practical and to the point as, for example, when he would caution me by saying: "If tempted to write a *tremolo*, don't: instead devise a figuration." On a different level, I also remember him saying with a glint of playful mischief in his eyes: "Don't ever be afraid to ask a player to do something he has never done before."

Lessons with Bill were always full of surprises. For example, he would often introduce a visitor to our lessons. On one occasion, without warning, in walked Aram Khachaturian. Until that moment I am afraid I was entirely ignorant of his music except for the widely played *Sabre Dance*. He was a large bear of a man with a ready deep-throated laugh. Upon Bill telling him that I came from South Africa, he immediately asked to learn something about South African folk music. The best I could do on the spot was to quote the very popular South African folk song 'Sarie Marais', and it was not many minutes before anybody passing the studio might have chanced to hear an Armenian flavoured version of 'Sarie Marais' stemming from Khachaturian's deep bass voice.

One of the earliest works Bill had set me to write was one

---

[14] Alwyn had been, for some years, principal flute in the LSO.

modelled on a recent composition of his own for cor anglais and strings which Sir John Barbirolli had commissioned from him for the Hallé Orchestra. And thereby hangs a tale in that Barbirolli was a great supporter of Bill's and a great believer in his music. He had strongly recommended that Bill should succeed Sir Reginald Thatcher as Principal of the Academy. Indeed it seemed that Bill himself was quite convinced that his candidature was assured. Although we students naturally could not learn the details of what followed, the practical effect of the decision towards the end of the 1955 spring term not to appoint Bill, but to opt instead for Sir Thomas Armstrong, was that Bill, never the mildest or least head-strong of men, abruptly decided the Academy was no longer for him. I shall always remember the sense of pain with which Bill ended the lesson he was giving me immediately after learning of the Academy's decision. Without warning he suddenly said, with strangely cold dispassion: "I am sorry but that's the last lesson I shall give you. I am leaving the Academy."

As composer, performer, writer and artist, Bill was always the consummate professional. To my shame I knew all too little of Alwyn's music before I came to the Academy. I also only learned a great deal about him many years later when I came to appreciate his considerable skills in other fields both as a writer and as a visual artist, where his use of colour was never less than vibrant. Much of his most important music was for too long woefully neglected during the years preceding his death in September 1985. This occurred shortly before what would have been his eightieth birthday. To mark it, the BBC had originally planned a celebratory concert but this became, in effect, a topical memorial. For this concert, I had written, for recorder, my *Variations on a Trio Tune* based on a theme from Alwyn's own String Trio, commissioned by John Turner who also gave the first performance. Happily there has, more recently, been a reassuring surge of interest in Bill's music. Many listening to the fine broadcasts which the BBC have mounted will inevitably have been greatly impressed, not to say moved, by Bill's power and originality as a symphonist, while his film scores continue to delight cinema enthusiasts. It is also particularly welcome that in recent years an annual festival should have been established in Alwyn's name in East Anglia, in no small measure through the energetic enterprise of John Turner and the Trust founded in Alwyn's name.

From the start the Academy generously allowed me a wide range of essential experiences to strengthen and support my studies in composition. These included wholly enjoyable weekly clarinet lessons with John Davies, the Academy's senior clarinet tutor who gamely endured a serious war injury. I also much enjoyed energetic exploration of the nascent world of percussion with Eric Pritchard, timpanist with the BBC Symphony Orchestra. Most importantly, I was able to join the conducting class run by Maurice Miles, at that time conductor-in-chief of the late-lamented Yorkshire Symphony Orchestra and also conductor of the Royal Academy of Music (RAM) Second Orchestra. Conducting classes with Maurice were principally of the traditional kind using one or two pianos, but occasionally we were allowed time to work with the Second Orchestra itself. Every session with Maurice was carefully prepared and richly rewarding. For example, the depth of analysis and guidance which he offered us would always bear fruit in workshop preparation. We might spend several sessions preparing a major symphony and this would then be followed by a performance in which each movement would be conducted in turn by one of the four of us comprising the conducting class. I always felt that in Maurice Miles I had a true friend, who could be consulted at any time and who was ever-ready to support my career. Indeed he was to do just this in a very practical and positive fashion by playing a key part in opening the door to my entry into the BBC.

Back in the '50s, the RAM hardly enjoyed the community spirit to be found there nowadays. There were several reasons for this. Social amenities were minimal and largely restricted to a very primitive canteen in the basement. Because practice facilities were too limited, students were compelled, one way and another, to seek alternatives elsewhere, such as the nearby Dyneley Studios. Apart from groups which came together out of common interest, there were few amenities to improve students' social and corporate life such as universities traditionally provide but which the British conservatoires have only more recently begun to offer.

One particular example of group participation which I found especially rewarding and enjoyable was a weekly seminar occupying the whole of Thursday morning for which Professor Peter Latham[15]

---

[15] Then the City of London's Gresham Professor of Music, and the author of a fine study of Brahms.

gathered a group of four or five of us at his house in Frognal Rise, at the top of Hampstead. Each of us in turn would have been required to produce a 'learned' dissertation on a prescribed subject which would then be discussed in depth, always with stimulating leads from Peter. At the conclusion of these enjoyable sessions we would repair to the nearby Holly Bush pub to slake our thirst with large draughts of real ale served, in Peter's case, in his favourite pewter tankard which the pub reserved for his sole use. Once or twice we were joined in those lunchtime drinking sessions by a close friend of Peter's, Edric Cundell, who was then Principal of the Guildhall School of Music and Drama, and who also lived nearby.

Renna and I retain grateful memories of Peter and Angela, his ebullient and generous wife. More than once they invited us to tea. As impoverished students, surviving on just a few ounces of margarine a week, Angela's injunction to us to cover the teatime crumpets with "lashings of butter, my darlings, simply lashings", was a more than welcome invitation. Friends of the Lathams once provided us with a rather less appetising teatime experience when our hostess, proclaiming her delight in creating original recipes, served sandwich cake with a filling of compressed cold peas. Her husband had earlier secured nationwide prominence as a result of an unusual overnight initiative. The *Daily Express* had published a poem celebrating the heroic release of British prisoners from the the *Altmark* lying in a Norwegian Fjord in February 1940. Our host, after reading the poem, instantly set it to music; the song which resulted he then rushed up to Fleet Street. The outcome was that all readers of the *Daily Express* found the song reproduced as part of their breakfast reading.

To the limited extent that student composers were able to get together, this was often to participate in a New Music Club which met on Thursday afternoons for workshop sessions in a large room under the Duke's Hall platform. Although we could not help feeling we were consigned to some remote ghetto as far as the rest of the Academy was concerned, these workshops could throw up some particularly interesting music. One such occasion was when, word having filtered down the road from Manchester about a certain young Peter Maxwell Davies who had just written a stunning trumpet sonata, we unofficially introduced this work to London at one of our sessions. These were also notable for a number of student works for violin inspired by a clutch of particularly fine violinists whose years at the Academy happened to overlap and who included Ralph Holmes, John Georgiadis, Carmel Kaine, John Tunnell, Ken Sillito and Miles Baster. Which other conservatoire could boast such a roll call of prominent violinists coinciding in one institution?

I had been somewhat overawed on arrival to find that one composer whose music I had come to admire from afar in South Africa, Iain Hamilton, was still technically a student at the RAM when I arrived. His works were frequently being broadcast. Since he favoured very formal wear, complete with furled umbrella, he cut a somewhat detached figure amongst younger students such as the phenomenally precocious Richard Rodney Bennett and the consistently colourful Cornelius Cardew. Cardew never lacked for initiative and originality; years later, he was to set himself the task of learning the guitar well enough to appear in Boulez's *Le marteau sans maître* in one of the earliest BBC Third Programme[16] Tuesday Invitation concerts. My closest composing colleague, also a student of Bill Alwyn's, was Raymond Hockley who, somewhat regrettably, was to sacrifice much promise as a composer for his dedicated work for the church.

For me, Bill Alwyn's abrupt departure from the Academy was little short of seismic in its effect. For the authorities, the priority was clearly to reallocate all Bill's students to one of the other distinguished composers then on the Academy's staff. These included such notable figures as York Bowen, Alan Bush and Howard Ferguson. As far as I know these three largely accommodated Bill's other displaced students, with the exception of Richard Rodney Bennett and myself.

When Bill Foggin, as Warden, invited me to discuss the situation, I was entirely clear in my own mind that, if it could possibly be arranged, I would greatly prefer to study with Lennox Berkeley, whose music I had come to know not only with affection but with a strong sense of affinity. The early part of the Easter holidays passed before matters could be resolved. But happily, and to my intense delight, Bill Foggin was able to confirm that my dearest wish would be met. It followed that one afternoon, in late April, I made my way to that part of London known as Little Venice and up Warwick Avenue until I stood outside number eight. [Plate 4] Inevitably, I

---

[16] Now Radio 3.

was intensely nervous but, in another sense, even more excited. As I approached the big blue front door, I somehow sensed that this moment would mark the start of a very special and infinitely rewarding association. So it was to be.

From my very first moments in Lennox and Freda Berkeley's beautiful sitting room, which was also to be the setting for every lesson I was to receive from Lennox, I felt as though, by some minor miracle, I was always destined to enjoy the infinite privilege of their friendship and of Lennox's invariably sensitive guidance. Lennox derived only limited pleasure from teaching in the Academy and my good fortune was that every lesson during the ensuing years was given in their lovely home. Today, 8 Warwick Avenue proudly bears, for any passer-by to see, a plaque recording that it was once the home of Sir Lennox Berkeley.

Lennox's approach was totally different from that of Bill Alwyn. In fact, as I believe all other former students of Lennox would agree, his method was always to invite one to come to him, to invite questions and also to explore existing music together. This applied whether we might be looking at something I had brought, or a work by Lennox himself, or indeed, any of the models he would use by drawing on the works of composers he particularly admired, ranging from Palestrina to Poulenc or, with particular reference to opera, from Verdi to Britten. For instance we might be studying the last act of Verdi's *Otello*, when Lennox would excitedly point to the sinister effect of *Otello*'s approach to Desdemona's bed chamber being graphically drawn by the foreboding passage which Verdi, at that point, writes for the double basses. How often I was to find in Lennox's own writing that a very small alteration could be enormously significant.

I always found exploring Lennox's own music with him to be particularly helpful, especially when he was kind enough to allow me sight of a work in progress. Soon after I began studying with him he was completing a commission from the Cheltenham Festival to write a sextet for clarinet, horn and string quartet for the 1955 Festival. This was an early instance of the many occasions on which I found it particularly fruitful to observe, on a near weekly basis, one of Lennox's works in progress. Although his innate modesty seemed often to cause him to hesitate over features in his own works, I frequently found that, if he could be pressed, he would reveal the way in which some small adjustment to an initial draft had produced significant effect. The lesson for me was always that a matter of minute detail might prove to be powerfully influential if resolved in the right way. The other very basic guidance which Lennox frequently offered concerned the importance of silence: drawing on models from French music which he so admired, these examples underlined the virtue of economy and of knowing what to leave out.

After two short months, my first term studying with Lennox was over and the long vacation stretched ahead. For Renna and me this was to be a very special period, culminating on Thursday 1 September with our wedding in Pinner Parish Church which trembled to its foundations when our good friend, Cecilia Wessels, rose to deliver Elizabeth's greeting from Wagner's *Tannhäuser* as an uplifting operatic element in our wedding service. The ceremony was conducted by Paul Bourne's father, Percy, a parish priest in Wolverhampton, who very kindly agreed to come down to London to take the service for us. Percy used to delight in claiming that his was the most illiterate congregation in Britain, being largely composed of bargees for whom schooling was, at best, an occasional and intermittent pleasure. Their central base, if they had one, which lay within Percy's parish, was the large canal basin in Wolverhampton where the principal inland waterways converge.

I had been sufficiently petrified by the whole occasion to have turned up at the church in odd socks for which I was loudly as well as roundly chastised by my Aunt Elizabeth during the course of the delightful garden reception. We duly headed north for our honeymoon at Watendlath, the setting for Judith Paris' idyll in Walpole's *Herries Chronicles*. Two weeks of sheer joy followed in the little farmhouse at the edge of this small tarn, nestling high above Keswick and Derwentwater. Our welcoming hostess was Mrs. Tyson who clearly derived romantic pleasure from hosting a honeymoon couple, but whom we were unfortunately too often apt to confuse with her lookalike twin sister in the neighbouring farmhouse. *En route* we had been able to thank Percy Bourne by calling in to take communion in his own Wolverhampton church.

My second year at the Academy flowed smoothly with every week bringing me renewed confidence as a composer and ever-increasing benefits and pleasures deriving from my studies with

Lennox. Lennox and Freda[17] had become considerate friends, and early in the second year we were able to celebrate moving to a much larger flat in Antrim Grove by repaying some of their kind hospitality. Because all my lessons with Lennox were at his home in Little Venice, I was actually in the Academy far less than before, although participation in Maurice Miles's conducting class continued unabated, as did other practical studies. One further bonus which I came to value was that the new Principal, Sir Thomas Armstrong, was kind enough to take an interest in my endeavours, his goodwill continuing long after I had left the Academy. There can have been no-one who did not profoundly admire Sir Thomas, a fine musician and a great man whose contribution to the musical life of our country was richly reflected in his memorial service for which we all foregathered in Christ Church, Oxford. He was the father of Robert Armstrong, subsequently ennobled as Lord Armstrong of Ilminster, whose own countless services to music[18] should never be overlooked, however much his role as Cabinet Secretary during Margaret Thatcher's administration might inevitably enjoy far greater prominence.

It was during my second year at the Academy that somehow I began to feel I might be writing some music which could possibly be worth keeping. One such work, settings of French Renaissance poems by Ronsard, du Bellay and Marot, has survived and is now published and is occasionally included in recitals. Another, which was to follow shortly, was my String Trio. This became the first work of mine to be broadcast by the BBC when the Oromonte Trio gave its premiere in a Third Programme recording. All this while Renna's own career was developing in very encouraging fashion. She was about to pass her BBC audition, to begin broadcasting regularly and would shortly form an excellent duo with the violinist Brigid Ranger.

---

[17] Anyone seeking rewarding insight into the Berkeleys is warmly recommended to read Tony Scotland's absorbing and revealing *Lennox and Freda*, published by Michael Russell, 2010.

[18] Lord Armstrong also served as the Chairman of the RNCM Board of Governors, 2000-5.

A Few Domestic Byways

Some Elderly Allsops

My maternal grandmother, Annie Amelia Allsop, was born into a prosperous mid-Victorian family living in Lincoln. Their home, a fine house imposingly situated close to the cathedral, bore eloquent testimony to the success with which the engineering firm of Clayton, Shuttleworth & Allsop had forged ahead during the Industrial Revolution. I have no recollection of meeting any surviving Claytons or Shuttleworths but I have various childhood memories of some of the Allsops.

There were eight children in my grandmother's generation, three boys and five girls. The eldest was great uncle Tom, never to be seen without frock coat and stiff wing collar. He became effectively head of the family and, as will be seen, undertook his responsibilities with befitting Victorian severity. Annie Amelia delighted in the "triple-A rating" which her initials gave her, but would never divulge her age to anyone. All she would offer was that she was born after Shaw but before Elgar. This, however, did enable anyone with access to the relevant information to narrow down her birth to the eleven-month period separating the births of these two great icons of our island culture, both of whom she revered. She also had an endearing sense of fun, and I remember being both amused and puzzled as a child by her seemingly invariable capacity to shed tears in profusion whenever she laughed.

Since engineering was bringing considerable prosperity to the family, the girls seem to have enjoyed many of the pleasures and privileges which successful Victorian society offered. In my grandmother's case this included finishing school in Paris. All appears to have gone well for Annie Amelia as she explored the new delights about her until word reached Lincoln that friendship with a percussionist in the Paris Opera was growing disturbingly close. He may indeed have been the orchestra's timpanist rather than a percussionist; all I ever heard was that he was "a drummer in the Paris Opera".

There ensued a sequence vaguely reminiscent of the second act of *La Traviata*, or even *Manon*. Believing that imminent deflowering now threatened his sister, great uncle Tom resolutely set off for Paris to rescue both her and the family reputation. Within hours of his arrival he was escorting capricious young Annie Amelia to the Gare du Nord to catch an onward train to Calais. When he arrived home, the young percussionist was greeted by the concierge with a vivid description of the abduction. Thereupon he hurtled in pursuit to the Gare du Nord, arriving just as the train prepared to depart and in time, as it did so, to thrust through the open window an elegantly fashioned mandolin. While Uncle Tom had effectively extinguished the budding romance, the mandolin survived and I can still picture it with its decoratively embellished mother-of-pearl inlays.

No suggestions of comparable exuberance were ever, to my knowledge, made regarding great aunt Emily. When the time came for her to leave Lincoln and the security of home, she duly made her way to Hampstead where she applied herself with near saintly dedication to the welfare of her local parish church. When I was seven or eight my parents invited great aunt Emily to come and stay with us in Johannesburg. To this day I have a guilty memory of being severely reprimanded when, one afternoon at tea, I was unable to control my giggling as great aunt Emily's dentures fell out and cascaded down into the sugar bowl.

To visit us, great aunt Emily had sailed down the west coast of Africa but, as many did, returned to England via the east coast and the Suez Canal. It appears that when the ship docked at Dar-es-Salaam, the Bishop of Tanganyika came on board, heading for some leave back in England. There followed what may have been the closest approach to a shipboard romance of which the bishop and my great aunt might have been capable. At all events, they appear to have sustained a degree of amiable companionship until the ship docked in Southampton. As with so many shipboard associations, contact was lost once on land. According to family legend, great aunt Emily appears to have felt this keenly, since she confided her regrets to great uncle Tom. The only reassurance which he is recorded as having offered her inevitably sounds improbably archaic and rather severely Victorian to our ears today but was doubtless well-meant: "After all, Emily, you must remember that he was only a colonial bishop."

If great aunt Emily was, for most of her life, a model of sanctity, the same could not be said of the youngest of the sisters, Constance Ellen, known as Connie. It seems that at an early stage her maidenly devotion became attached to a swarthy member of a group of gypsies. So strong was this attraction that great aunt Connie in true Victorian fashion eloped and set up home for the rest of her life within a gypsy encampment in the New Forest. When, eventually, she was called to her maker, the leader of the gypsy company wrote to great uncle Tom to ask whether the family would wish to receive great aunt Connie's remains for Christian burial. Great uncle Tom's response was curt, to the point and true to his Victorian convictions: "In sin she has lived, in sin let her lie." As far as the family is aware, great aunt Connie's bones still lie undisturbed in some leafy glade deep in the New Forest.

Trams

I have to confess that as a boy I had no interest whatsoever in trains or aeroplanes. Indeed, I vividly remember being severely chastised for failing to show sufficient enthusiasm when an over-indulgent godfather generously gave me a Hornby train set. However, I do remember, in my Johannesburg days, becoming intrigued watching new double-decker red trams swishing silently along Roberts Avenue past my father's school. Later, when I was living in Strasbourg, I would experience a daily encounter with the No. 10 tram, heading to the university. There was a challenging double 'S' bend as the line approached the main university building. Periodically, the No. 10 would fail to negotiate this successfully, whereupon the obligation on willing students was to help driver and conductor heave the tram back on the rails.

Down in Durban many years earlier, my future father-in-law, Harold Kellaway, also enjoyed a close encounter with one particular tram when he was courting Renna's mother. Out late one night, they had missed the last tram home. Unfazed, Harold suggested they walk back to the municipal tram depot. Exercising his engineering skills, he succeeded in detaching a tram from its overnight moorings and driving it to a discreet distance from Renna's parents' house, leaving it there for perplexed officials to collect the next morning.

In 1950, as a penniless student, I paid my first visit to the Edinburgh Festival (itself then only three years old). This was, for me, a momentously memorable experience for including a visit from the La Scala Opera chorus and orchestra, under the inspiring

30-year-old Guido Cantelli[19] and the legendary Victor de Sabata, providing as a shattering climax to their visit a performance of Verdi's *Requiem* such as my young ears had never previously thought possible.

I managed to find cheap theatrical digs in an eastern suburb of Edinburgh, Joppa. A good tram service ran between Joppa and the city centre. Prominently displayed in each tram were two stern uncompromising notices. One read "DO NOT TENDER LARGE SILVER FOR CHANGE", the second "IT IS FORBIDDEN TO EXPECTORATE". Viewed in retrospect at a distance of over sixty years, these notices, if nothing else, collectively demonstrate three stark realities: the extent to which galloping inflation subsequently intervened; the degree to which the nation's social habits have improved; and, finally, the extent to which education has deteriorated. Today, the equivalence of large silver is to be found in paper or plastic, few spit in public, but fewer still can be expected to define "expectorate".

CRICKETING

It was not until I was about ten that the first seeds were sown of what was to become a lifelong love of cricket. My interest in the game originated in a slightly curious way and had a purely phonetic origin. The radio was on and a cricket commentary was in progress, although no-one, even myself, was paying particular attention to it. But a name kept recurring: Edrich. Somehow the name became lodged: Ed-rich? Rich Ed? I turned to my father for guidance. "Edrich," he told me, "is a young English batsman – Bill Edrich – and he is just in the process of making a double century against South Africa." For some reason his reply must have added to my interest, for I began listening more closely. Nonetheless, this was just a radio commentary and there was nothing to watch.

This coincided with the start of my schooldays when cricket became, for the first time, a part of my life. Like many with a passion for the game, I have to confess that I was never particularly good at it. Somehow, I too often would get myself dismissed through a rash stroke or send up a stream of half volleys, while failing to find

---

[19] Viewed by many as Toscanini's natural successor, Guido Cantelli was tragically killed in an air crash in Paris only six years later.

a decent bowling length. But none of these shortcomings in any way checked my increasing love of the game. By the time I was at Haileybury, cricket had become a rather frequent distraction from other supposedly more important activities.

Occasionally opportunities occurred when I could indulge my love of cricket without paying a penalty. One such chance unexpectedly came about in early May 1946 when my mother and stepfather were away on their honeymoon in Guernsey. A summons to appear at Faversham magistrates' court arrived at Haileybury. This originated from an incident during the previous Easter holidays when my mother and I had gone to hear Eileen Joyce playing the Grieg concerto in a concert conducted by Sir Malcolm Sargent at the Royal Albert Hall. Petrol rationing ruled out driving all the way to London. We therefore left the car at Faversham station and went on by train. Returning to Faversham in the evening, we found a large police constable standing by the car. After I had volunteered that I had been the driver, the constable reminded me that the law then required the use of side lights when parking on a highway after sunset. My particulars were then taken down with due solemnity.

When the summons arrived at Haileybury, I immediately took it to my Housemaster who gravely informed me that this was so serious a matter that I would have to take it to the Head, a particularly dry cleric seldom known to smile, let along laugh. He predictably, and at great length, advised me that he took a grim view of any boys finding themselves on the wrong side of the law. Notwithstanding, it was resolved that I should obey the summons and attend the magistrates' court in Faversham as required. Duly granted an exeat, and armed with both a train ticket and a modest cash float to pay any fine levied, I set off for this unexpected day back in Kent.

When the great moment arrived and the clerk to the court solemnly intoned, "Call John Manquell", I rose uncertainly to my feet. The magistrate asked, "Are you John Manquell?" "Well, not exactly, Sir." "Well, sit down then," barked the beak. The clerk tried again: "Call John Manquell." Once more I sought to respond. By now the bench was looking at me very severely. I managed to explain that I thought I was the person required but that my name was incorrect. I explained what it should have been and suggested that, in the dark, the constable's pencil must evidently have prescribed a *q* rather than a *d* in the middle of my name. The beak's evident irritation at this point switched from myself to the clerk. Scrutiny of the relevant documentation followed, whereupon the magistrate abruptly snapped, "Case dismissed."

After a few moments I began to realise that the constable's minor error meant that I was now a free man, with no fine to pay and a free day stretching ahead – gold, in any schoolboy's estimation. Instead of making my tracks back to school where, it being a Wednesday, we would have been occupied with such tedious obligations as corps parade, I made straight for Lord's where the school's cash for the prospective fine now paid for my admission to the cricketing holy of holies. The sun was shining, Middlesex were playing Somerset and Arthur Wellard, renowned for his six-hitting, enjoyed himself mightily at the expense of Jim Sims, the Middlesex spinner. Needless to add, I returned to Haileybury in a spirit of profound contentment.

As I have sadly acknowledged, I have never laid claim to being anywhere near as good at the game as I might have wished. But I was lucky enough, even while still at school, to witness some great cricket. There was Wally Hammond elegantly stroking two centuries for an England XI against a World XI, for whom the great Leary Constantine was still able to bowl at a vicious speed and for whom Keith Miller played an innings of peerless authority which included a lofted six straight to the old press box high in the pavilion.

Mention of Keith Miller's name brings to mind one occasion when I was actually able to rub shoulders with some test cricketers. This was in Eshowe, the capital of Zululand, of all improbable settings. The Australians, under Lindsay Hassett (who had succeeded Sir Donald Bradman as captain), were at the start of a tour of South Africa and were playing a one day warm-up country game against a scratch XI. I was holidaying in Eshowe at the time and was allowed, with several others, to give the Australians batting practice by bowling in the nets. The memory of Keith Miller striking my harmless slow left arm bowling back over my shoulder with a majesty and power seemingly sufficient to send the ball into the Indian Ocean many miles distant will never leave me.

Nor shall I ever forget the sight of Ray Lindwall's beautifully balanced run-up to the wicket – poetry in motion on which to feast one's eyes. Run-ups have always been, for me, a subject of particular fascination, none more idiosyncratic than Doug Wright's inimitable bounding kangaroo-like approach while bowling at the Nackington End during Canterbury Festival Week. Or again, can there have been a more stealthily terrifying run-up than that of Michael Holding as, with cheetah-like speed and in silence, he demolished his epic fourteen wickets during the Oval Test against England in 1976?

I have never participated in club cricket teams where a position in a given league conditioned the character of the play. Rather, like many, I have preferred more relaxed forms of club cricket or village matches. In Kent I was lucky enough to be invited to play for the itinerant Band of Brothers, while during years working in London I periodically turned out for Chiswick. This I much enjoyed since I managed to make a few runs as one of the opening bats. My partner in this was an Italian. In these days of mass immigration an Italian / South African partnership would raise no eyebrows, but in the '50s it evoked some cautious curiosity and it was just as well that we occasionally managed to make some runs.

Participation in the Lancaster University staff XI was both enjoyable and a wonderful way to form friendships with many different members of staff possessing variable abilities on the pitch. Our team boasted a pro Vice-Chancellor, who delivered cunning leg breaks and a Professor of Religious Studies whose language, when missing the ball, was seldom temperate. We benefitted from an archaeologically inclined classicist wicketkeeper and especially owed much to the Assistant Secretary of the University, Merton Atkins, who was the indefatigably enthusiastic secretary of the club.

In 1970, Merton had received an invitation from the governor of nearby Bela River open prison asking whether a fixture against the inmates might be possible. The author of the invitation explained, somewhat unnecessarily, that the prison team could only play home matches and would we therefore visit the prison? Merton promptly relayed our enthusiasm and a very happy occasion ensued, even if we were sentenced to battling with doorstop-sized cheese sandwiches in the tea interval.

The following year, Merton received an invitation to repeat the exercise, and we again responded with enthusiasm. What, however, was not revealed at that stage was that a 'guest' of the prison was one Roy Gilchrist. He had been a spearhead opening bowler for the West Indian team touring England in 1957. Word had it that he had been obliged to spend the whole of the team's sea-voyage to England learning how to hold a pen – something he had apparently never previously done – in order to meet the continual expectation that touring players should provide endless autographs. Following a short chance chat with him during the tea interval, I can vouch for the fact that Gilchrist would not deny that he had been involved in a number of spirited altercations during his playing career, both on and off the field. His custodial punishment at Bela River apparently arose from an attack on his wife, allegedly with a hot iron.

Perhaps mercifully, we were in ignorance that he would be in the Bela River side turning out for our fixture. Although he was many years beyond his prime, and no longer the danger to batsmen he had earlier been, I can personally testify that the velocity and intensity with which he delivered the ball was of an order that one would never normally expect to encounter in club cricket. Happily, I can record that, whether by chance or through arriving at a gentler disposition, he only pounded me during my innings in relatively soft areas. Nonetheless, I can bear witness to the fact that it was a very long time before three significantly black bruises eventually disappeared.

The BBC

Music Producer 1956-9

As my final year at the Academy dawned, I began to be conscious of a need to start looking a little further ahead. My principal tutors at the Royal Academy, Lennox Berkeley and the conductor, Maurice Miles, showed helpful interest in my future, Maurice in particular disguising the fact that a conducting career would not be a realistic proposition for me. He was, however, always of an optimistic disposition. At all events he had got wind of a temporary vacancy in the Music Division of the BBC which he was kind enough to draw to my attention with a phone call one October afternoon. Would I like to attend for a preliminary interview?

The upshot was that a few days later I found myself being interviewed in a small room in Yalding House, the Music Division's home in Great Portland Street. This encounter took the form of a relaxed one-to-one conversation conducted by Leonard Isaacs [Plate 5] who, at that time, was in charge of all music broadcasting on the BBC's Home Service[20]. He seemed flatteringly interested in what little experience I had of organising music events (such as the role I had played as assistant to Edward Dunn running the Durban Centenary Festival in 1954). The sequel, a few days later, was a more formal interview conducted by Maurice Johnstone[21], Eric Warr[22] and, once again, Leonard Isaacs[23]. I was initially reassured by the amiably relaxed manner in which the interview proceeded, although astonished at how short and simple were the questions I was asked: "How many quartets did Bartók write?" "Six, sir." "And Schubert?" "I'm not sure, but a great many." Such were the depths of musical knowledge plumbed at this interview.

I left thinking it could not possibly lead anywhere but, to my astonishment, a few weeks later I received a formal letter offering

---

[20] Now Radio 4.
[21] HMP(S) – Head of Music Programmes (Sound)
[22] AHMP(S) – Assistant Head of Music Programmes (Sound)..
[23] HSMO – Home Service Music Organiser.

me a six-month contract to replace one Bernard Keeffe, a member of BBC Music Division who had been seconded to work as a music producer in television (a rarity in those days). I was to present myself to Maurice Johnstone in his office in Yalding House, 156 Great Portland Street at 9.30am on Monday 12 November 1956. Wearing the only suit I possessed, and otherwise carefully prepared for my new working life by my long-suffering Renna, I set off for Great Portland Street with good time to spare. What I did not know was that 156 Great Portland Street only existed in the imagination of the General Post Office (GPO). This was because the entrance to Yalding House was in fact off a side road, Bolsover Street. Time was fast running out as I raced up and down Great Portland Street in a state of accelerating panic to find a non-existent number 156! Some kind passer-by eventually helped me and I found myself inside Yalding House where I was led to the office of one Mildred Holland[24]. Mildred was a redoubtable golfer who commuted daily from Reading and who patiently explained that it was unrealistic on my part to expect to find Maurice Johnstone in his office at such an early hour. Instead she said, "I think you had better go and see Harry Croft Jackson[25]."

Harry, a one-time Orcadian organist, was a good example of the young men who, pre-war, had found their way to the BBC, often by a circuitous route, and who then, with the war over, found themselves in middle age in possession of senior positions in the Corporation. One of Harry's principal contributions to BBC Music Division had been to compile the *Green Book*, a manual specifying in infinite detail the acceptable form for publication of names, and other processes such as catalogue identification, prior to publication in the *Radio Times* and elsewhere. Woe betide us young producers if, for example, we failed to observe the distinction between the term 'conductor' (which was used for the orchestra's regular conductor) and 'conducted by' (used for someone who was not the orchestra's regular conductor).

After a friendly introduction, Harry took me up to Bernard Keeffe's vacated office where, upon studying a desk diary, he suggested that I should "go down to Maida Vale and look after

---

[24] AAMus – Administrative Assistant Music.
[25] MPO – Music Programmes Organiser.

Taneyev." I had no idea where in Maida Vale Taneyev might be found or indeed why he or she needed looking after! Patiently, Harry explained to me that in Maida Vale there was a BBC studio complex and that Taneyev was a long-dead Russian composer of whom I certainly should have known more than I evidently did. I eventually found my way to Delaware Road and the BBC Studios which I was to come to know very well. I found five very distinguished musicians of the day rehearsing in Studio 3: the legendary pianist Julius Isserlis (Steven's grandfather) and the Hirsch Quartet all busy rehearsing a Taneyev piano quintet. Three hours later the recording was complete but I had played no useful part in it. It was then time to catch a 187 bus in the direction of Hampstead and so bring to an end a first day which had clearly been of no productive benefit to my new employers.

I should like to think that the succeeding days were more rewarding for all concerned. They were enriched for me by further meetings with Leonard Isaacs and a heart-warming encounter with Leonard's Third Programme counterpart, Peter Crossley-Holland[26]. [Plate 6] By a curious coincidence I had, two years earlier, brought with me from South Africa a letter of greetings from a Mrs. East, an aunt of Peter's, who kept a garage in Eshowe, Zululand. Among Peter's many gifts, were the significant explorations he carried out in various branches of ethnomusicology, notably Tibetan music. We were destined to remain friends until he died in 2001 when I was honoured to be invited to write a work for his commemorative concert.

My closest colleagues swiftly became the team of music producers then working for the BBC in Yalding House. They included Peter Gould[27], a most able pianist assisting Leonard Isaacs, and Robert Simpson[28], a fine composer working as assistant to Peter Crossley-Holland. Already at that time recognised as a rising composer of considerable note, Bob was destined to enrich the catalogue of

---

[26] TPMO – Third Programme Music Organiser.
[27] AHSMO – Assistant Home Service Music Organiser.
[28] ATPMO – Assistant Third Programme Music Organiser. A few years later Bob also invited me to participate in a new symposium on the symphony which he was preparing for Penguin Books. In response to his invitation, I contributed chapters on three French composers: Berlioz, César Franck, and Roussel.

symphonies and string quartets by British composers to a highly significant and often memorable degree. Bob and I developed an early, if uneven, friendship. We discovered that we had each long entertained a deep admiration for the work of Albert Schweitzer while we also shared a lively enthusiasm for cricket. On the other hand, I found Bob's strong pacifism uncomfortable, while the way in which he trumpeted his republicanism was prone to be downright vitriolic.

Other young music producers in our team included Julian Budden, who was to become an acknowledged authority on the operas of Verdi when he published his archetypal three-volume study of that composer's work. Three others to be mentioned briefly were David Stone, whose beautifully crafted arrangements for string orchestras should be enshrined in all repertoire explored by school orchestras, Hugh Middlemiss, a stickler for precision timing, and Allan Giles, a young Australian straight from the outback who could be relied upon to challenge orthodoxy wherever he encountered it.

A colourful colleague who was still a member of BBC Music Division when I first arrived was Denis Stevens. Sadly he was destined to desert us within a few short months. His broadcasts of early music were one of the landmark jewels in BBC Third Programme broadcasting in the mid '50s. Indeed it would be fair to say that the nation largely became aware of all the riches which Renaissance and Medieval music offered through some of the pioneering programmes produced by Denis Stevens.

One story of Denis will bear further repetition, although I cannot vouch for the complete accuracy of what follows. A short programme of early Portuguese *a capella* music – sacred or secular I know not which – had been scheduled for an early evening slot. In those days, when so much broadcasting was live and not pre-recorded, durations could vary, although producers were under instructions to take care and limit these to a manageable degree in terms of the overall schedule. On this occasion what should simply have been a 30-minute programme overran by more than twice its allotted time slot, thus throwing the timing of the whole evening's subsequent broadcasting into disarray.

When the Controller Third Programme, John Morris, arrived in his office the next morning and studied the record of the previous evening's broadcasting, he was understandably not best pleased. Reaching for an internal memo form, and summoning a BBC messenger, he sent a handwritten note to Denis Stevens demanding to know why the programme in question had overrun by so much. In response to this angry demand, Denis simply and calmly handed to the breathless messenger an annotated reply of five words: "because it was too long." As this little exchange demonstrated, Denis was adept at dealing with any emergency. History does not relate whether his response was received in high quarters with apoplexy or amusement.

Our little group only represented a very small part of Yalding House which was entirely occupied by the BBC's Music Division. On the ground floor was an extensive performance music library, the envy of all other music libraries worldwide. Within the further four floors were an excellent and conveniently placed canteen, which did much to enhance the conviviality of life in Yalding House, and three floors given over partly to a particularly distinctive reference library, to a large contingent of light music producers, and to various other essential groups such as the five staff accompanists which the BBC retained in those days, one of whom, Clifton Helliwell [Plate 7], was to play a valuable and influential part in the early development of the Royal Northern College of Music.

In addition to those colleagues I have named, senior to them all, was Richard Howgill[29]. Unlike his successors, Howgill did not appear to play any active part in the day-to-day conduct of Music Division, leaving this to Maurice Johnstone and Frank Wade, Music Division's Head of Light Music. In fact, the closest that many of us came to involvement with Richard Howgill was to record his daughter, Pauline, an able pianist. She had her own piano trio which was once engaged to record for the Third Programme a curiously improbable programme of three unlikely piano trios: by Malipiero, Dresden and Panufnik. On transmission, an unfortunate duplication occurred in that, by some technical mischance, reels 1 and 3, and therefore parts of the Malipiero and Panufnik works, were for a time played and transmitted simultaneously. Furious indeed was the assault on the ears of Tom Crowe, the senior announcer then on duty in Third Programme Continuity, when Pauline's father telephoned to exercise his outraged authority.

Around this time the corridors of Yalding House were momentarily enlivened by an amusing sequence concerning our

---

[29] CMus – Controller Music.

immediate hierarchy, Richard Howgill and Maurice Johnstone. It appeared that Bernard Herrmann[30], having achieved a position of prominence in America, was anxious to make his mark with the BBC and, to this end, had been sending letters to Howgill and Johnstone proposing a variety of programmes he might conduct. In response to these submissions he had received cordial letters assuring him that the BBC was very interested in his proposals and was giving them careful consideration. Shortly afterwards, Herrmann came to England and was dining one evening at the MM Club[31] in South Audley Street when his host observed that Howgill and Johnstone happened to be sitting at a nearby table. Excusing himself, Herrmann strode across to effect an introduction. Once his identity had been established, albeit after some initial hesitation, he was yet again assured of the BBC's abiding interest in his work and of its continued concern to give careful consideration to his proposals. To this Herrmann could only respond, "Jeez, that's what I admire about you British: masters of instantaneous indecision!"

Herrmann was never less than outspoken. On a subsequent occasion, when he was rehearsing one of his own works with the Philharmonia Orchestra, the principal flute, Gareth Morris, failed to notice that he was required, at a given point, to change from flute to piccolo. When Herrmann stopped the rehearsal to correct this, Morris apparently conceded the point but complained that the change was only very lightly marked in his part, whereupon Herrmann immediately flashed: "What do you want it in then? Neon?"

Richard Howgill was to leave us shortly, a characteristically quiet departure which we in the lower echelons of Yalding House scarcely noticed. William Glock [Plate 8], his successor, arrived

---

[30] Bernard Herrmann (1911-75) was by then at the forefront of music in the USA, both as a conductor and as a highly successful composer for the cinema. At that time he also enjoyed the unique distinction of being the only composer of a full length opera (*Wuthering Heights*) available in the gramophone record catalogues but never performed on stage.

[31] The MM Club (Mainly for Musicians) sadly no longer exists but was a very popular and hospitable haunt for musicians in the '50s and '60s. Its initials reflected a connection with the distinguished English cellist, May Mukle, who played a key role in its foundation. She was a friend of, *inter alia*, Casals, Ravel, Ireland and Vaughan Williams, who dedicated his *Six Studies in English Folk Song* to her.

like an invigorating blast of understandably impatient ambition to change much of the face of BBC music programming, notably at The Proms. Of course, he not only transformed BBC music-making but indeed in many other respects the whole face of music in Britain. This was notably true in respect of contemporary music where doors were opened for the first time to many challenging voices from Europe and beyond. To us in Yalding House he brought not only fresh inspiration but also a demand for professionalism and exacting standards which, to tell the truth, were probably much needed at that time.

Among the recitals I had the privilege to record during this period was one, scheduled for transmission as a star Easter Monday attraction, by the legendary Russian pianist Emil Gilels. The sequence which followed almost led to disaster, if not an international incident, as well as the distinct possibility of my abrupt departure from the BBC's ranks. Gilels arrived with his Soviet minder to record in the Farringdon studio, but did so clearly under orders to conduct an aggressive marketing ploy. He spoke not a word of English but through his minder, a heavy jowled and threatening individual, indicated that he would only proceed with the recording if I would undertake to secure a formal agreement for the BBC to purchase Petrof pianos from Prague in preference to Steinways from Hamburg. Eventually an uneasy peace prevailed, sufficient to allow the recording to proceed on the basis that I would write a formal letter – to whom was never quite established – extolling the virtues of Petrofs.

The near disaster to which I have referred was yet to occur, although mercifully Gilels remained blissfully unaware of this sequel. His mammoth programme consisted of five Scarlatti sonatas, followed by Beethoven's E minor sonata, op. 90; then came sonatas by both Scriabin and Prokofiev with, to conclude, some of Prokofiev's *Visions Fugitives*. Gilels' total dedication to perfection resulted in the whole recording requiring in excess of forty individual takes. As will be appreciated, very extensive editing therefore became necessary and this I carried out during long hours on Good Friday.

Once the editing was complete I arranged for a playback to assure myself that all was in order once we had added the announcer's contributions. However, to my horror, the playback revealed that the Beethoven Sonata had totally disappeared. The recording now proceeded without a break from the back announcement to the

Scarlatti group to the announcement to Scriabin's Fourth Sonata op. 30. Urgent enquiries revealed that reel 2 on which the Beethoven had existed was nowhere to be found. This was the position reached by the Saturday afternoon when a willing team of volunteers urgently searched through the large laundry baskets to which were consigned unwanted recordings designated to be 'washed' ready for re-use. The mercy was that some three hours into this increasingly frantic search we managed to unearth the missing reel. Had it not been for the usual processes being postponed on account of the Easter holiday weekend, this reel would almost certainly have already been washed. I shall never forget the delicious feeling of escape from a nightmare horror (and a probable sacking) which I experienced as Renna and I relaxed on my mother's houseboat in the upper reaches of the Thames at Chiswick while the transmission proceeded with no hint that the perfection of Gilels' artistry could ever have been put at risk through alien ineptitude.

Another legendary pianist of the day whose broadcasting recitals I took great delight in producing was the Dutchman, Cor de Groot. In my memory he remains one of the finest classical pianists I ever encountered. Indeed, I doubt whether his Philips recording of Beethoven's *Emperor Concerto* has been surpassed. He was also a pianist ever ready to explore contemporary music. For example, I remember one recital in July 1957 when he allowed himself to be persuaded to include major works by both William Alwyn and Alan Rawsthorne in addition to works by two contemporary compatriots, Willem Pijper and Henk Badings, in whose music he specialised. Not only did he include Badings' 1945 sonata in that recital, but a year later in a recital for the Third Programme in September 1958 he added Badings' 1947 sonata. One of our shortcomings in the ensuing years could be said to be that we seem to have entirely lost sight of Badings' music.

To our advantage, great artists periodically become closely associated with particular composers. Perhaps this was especially true of singers. For example, Richard Lewis, nearly everybody's favourite heroic tenor, developed a deep admiration for the music of Michael Tippett. Lewis was, of course, the unforgettable Achilles when *King Priam* was launched at the Coventry Cathedral Festival in 1962. But he had earlier already done much to champion the striking qualities of Tippett's songs. In particular, I shall always remember the startling impact he made in April 1957 with his memorable recordings of Tippett's two great song cycles: the cantata, *Boyhood's End* and his settings of the Great War poets Sydney Keyes and Wilfred Owen, the song cycle, *The Heart's Assurance*.

A remarkable and versatile musician – conductor, composer, teacher and so much more – who was often present in Yalding House during those early years was Mátyás Seiber. Quite frequently, he was simply in the building as one of the BBC's panel of score readers. This group would spend endless hours secluded in the small top-floor reference library assessing the multitude of new works relentlessly submitted for possible broadcasting. Among this team Mátyás was, in many ways, the wisest and most shrewd and his dedication never seemed to flag. A confirmed vegetarian, but with an indifferent constitution, he would occasionally open the door to my office at the end of an arduous morning spent score reading with the words "come and eat some grass", before leading me off to his favourite vegetarian restaurant nearby.

Small and slight, Mátyás as a conductor possessed an extraordinary ability to persuade singers and instrumentalists alike to do his bidding, however unfamiliar the music before them. I can readily recall a number of infinitely rewarding occasions when he was at the helm for concerts with his Dorian Singers. The programmes might range from his own distinctive choral works to folk-rooted music from his native Hungary or part songs by Michael Tippett, for whom Mátyás had a particular regard. One other concert conducted by Mátyás I particularly remember. In this, his Dorian Singers and the old Goldsbrough Orchestra recorded a programme which included works by some too infrequently heard composers such as Adrian Cruft, John Joubert and Anthony Milner in such a remarkable way as to convince us all that we were listening to masterpieces. Perhaps we were.

I do not believe that back in the 1950s such a term as 'world music' was in use, let alone the wider currency it has subsequently enjoyed. Nor, by the same token, were we generally alert to the charms and richness offered by traditional Asian, and for that matter Oriental, music. Yes, Debussy had, of course, much earlier distilled for us something of the distinctive world of the gamelan. But when, on 17 May 1957, Ravi Shankar came to the old Camden Theatre in Mornington Crescent to record for the Third Programme a sitar recital, the occasion constituted, at least in broadcasting terms, something of an historic breakthrough. I shall long remember the sense of both adventure and exploration with which I approached the prospect of this extended series of broadcasts which we had planned. It should be remembered that, in Ravi Shankar, we were not only recording a very remarkable young sitar player but were also welcoming a senior broadcasting colleague who had, for some seven years, been Director of Music for All-India Radio in New Delhi. So – a young star and a senior international colleague at one at the same time.

When Ravi Shankar died in 2012 at the age of 92, the many tributes paid to him afforded us an opportunity to recall just what an influential role this versatile musician played in later years when collaborating with leading musicians from other spheres, ranging from Yehudi Menuhin to George Harrison and The Beatles. He was also, of course, a gifted composer, as those who know Richard Attenborough's film *Gandhi* will testify. Not only did he also inspire many others but within his own family perpetuated a distinguished line of great Indian performers, not by any means the least of which was his brother-in-law, Ali Akbar, himself a world-famous sarod player. Back in 1957 so much of this still lay ahead of Ravi Shankar. But he was already widely respected and revered far beyond his ancestral home, in Benares, the Indian holy city on the banks of the Ganges.

In the Camden Theatre that day he recorded just two Ragas, an afternoon Raga and an evening Raga[32]. He was supported by the usual pairing of tabla and tambura, the tabla player being Chatur Lal, whose artistry would also become widely admired. Lal, sitting cross-legged in the traditional manner, was also unwittingly able to help us with the mechanics of the recording in a way which I hope the reader might find mildly amusing. In those days most of our recordings included presentation on the spot by the announcer. However, the problem with Indian Ragas is that no duration is pre-determined, the whole performance being a complex creative extemporisation. How, therefore, was the announcer, John Holmstrom[33], to anticipate the conclusion of a given piece? John concluded that a crafty way was to keep a careful eye on Chatur Lal's bare feet, having worked out that he was prone to screw up

---

[32] For the record, the *Raga Bhimpalasi* and the *Raga Charukeshi*.
[33] A contemporary of mine at Haileybury.

his toes in some semblance of orgasmic excitement as the climax was reached.

Back in 1957 I allowed myself a certain degree of pride at having been the Producer of the BBC's first purposeful initiative into Indian classical music. In fact, the Third Programme broadcast a considerable number of recordings of South Indian classical music which I was also privileged to produce during 1957 and 1958. In addition to Ravi Shankar, we also welcomed another very great sitar player from South India, Ustad Vilayat Khan, like Shankar destined for global adulation. In all this activity we were also much encouraged by the support of the Asian Music Circle founded and led by Ayana Deva Angadi, himself a very capable tanbura player. It was, therefore, an additional pleasure when we were able to record public concerts in which Angadi participated and where we could welcome members of his organisation. All in all, I hope that through the many recordings I was able to produce during those stimulating years we may have succeeded in helping the listening public of the day to embark on a voyage of discovery in which it could relish the distinctive world of Indian classical music.

In keeping with its support for Indian music, the Third Programme also provided periodic and no less enthusiastic support for Oriental music. I retain particular memories of two recordings, one Chinese and one Japanese, which I produced in the Concert Hall of Broadcasting House. The Japanese recording came first and featured a koto and sangen player, Shinichi Yuize, who was also an extremely colourful singer. He was supported by Hozan Yamamoto on the shakuhachi. What was particularly distinctive about this programme was that it included both seventeenth century works – two, for example by Yatsuhashi Kengyoin – and much more recent music by Tozan Nakao, who had just died, and Shinichi himself, still only in his thirties at the time. I concluded after this recording that if all exponents of Japanese music were as engaging and versatile it would win many friends among Western listeners.

If Japanese music and musicians were beginning to flow westwards in the 1950s this was not the case with the Chinese. At that time any musician coming from China represented a rare phenomenon. When, in May 1959, I found myself recording a young Chinese singer, Tchen Hsin-Ting, we were in a very different world. In this particular case, perhaps because the young lady had arrived unexpectedly through the portals of the Chinese Embassy in Portland Place as a Chinese Cultural Attaché initiative, security sensitivities were immediately activated. The consequence was that I received a stern memo from no less an authority than Frank Gillard[34] [Plate 9] requiring me to satisfy myself that none of the texts of her songs carried messages of political propaganda. Fortunately I was able to turn to a Mandarin-speaking colleague working in Bush House for the General Overseas Service (GOS), as the BBC's World Service was then called. To everybody's relief he was able to provide reassurance that the words of her songs contained nothing more inflammatory than delicate references to little yellow birds, lotus flowers and plum blossom.

One of the many privileges that any young BBC producer at the time enjoyed was that of being able to record or present live in the studio some of the great musicians of the day whose names are now legendary. I recall in particular vivid memories of two very great harpists. One was in December 1958 when I had the chance to record the great Spanish harpist, Nicanor Zabaleta. His recital also provided a unique opportunity for him to demonstrate with consummate artistry a broad historical range of harp music through the ages – sixteenth-century works by Antonio de Cabezón and Francisco Palero, together with seventeenth-century pieces by Lucas Ruiz de Ribayaz and Fernandez de Huete, contrasted in turn with a whole range of twentieth-century works. Apart from the music, what was particularly impressive was Zabaleta's totally unique sound: deeper, broader and I believe more brilliant than anything we had hitherto heard from any harpist.

Another great harpist who made a profound impact upon us all in a Maida Vale recital was Marcel Grandjany whose programme, in addition to Hindemith's telling Sonata, included two of his own distinctive works. Our exploration of the harp in those days also extended far beyond the traditional as, for instance, when Elena Polonska demonstrated the beguiling and distinctive qualities of the minstrel's harp in her fascinating recital of Italian, French and Breton music.

In parallel, one other activity similarly provided enriching experiences of music-making abroad. This was the opportunity to transmit music programmes on the GOS under the leadership

---

[34] DSB – Director of Sound Broadcasting, although the title was later changed to MDR, Managing Director Radio.

of David Cox[35]. David was a most convivial colleague and a fine composer whose works should certainly be heard more often than is currently the case. In particular, we were able to promote weekly prestige concerts before an invited audience in the concert hall of Broadcasting House. At one of these, the programme included a striking *Canzona for Brass* by Bob Simpson, which the composer charmingly dedicated jointly to David Cox and myself. Somewhat curiously, the scoring originally required three trumpets and four trombones, although I believe that the composer subsequently favoured the more conventional scoring for four trumpets and three trombones. Through these concerts we sought to bring interesting music broadcasts to listeners all over the world, whether they be tea-planters in Malaysia or Welsh ex-patriots in Patagonia, the recordings therefore being repeated several times at various points in the day. Another special feature of these GOS broadcasts was that they would make a point of featuring Commonwealth artists of indisputable pre-eminence – including such luminaries as the pianist Glenn Gould from Canada and the soprano Joan Sutherland from Australia.

Of all the programmes with which I was entrusted during these first years as a young music producer, the one which to this day carries for me the most starkly indelible memories in its challenging enormity, is the production I undertook for the Third Programme of Stravinsky's *The Soldier's Tale*. For this I had been fortunate enough to be able to assemble a remarkable cast. In the central role of the narrator was Christopher Hassall, distinguished actor, dramatist, librettist, lyricist and poet. That great Shakespearian actor Ernest Milton, originally from America, played the Devil opposite Charles Leno, a suitably gullible Soldier. We should remember that Stravinsky wrote *Histoire du Soldat* while living in Switzerland during the First World War. As a consequence he found himself limited to a mixed septet of instrumentalists, for which we assembled a suitably strong group to be conducted by Stravinsky's close professional associate, Robert Craft.

One reason for deciding to prepare this new production for the Third Programme lay in the then brand new translation provided for the publishers, Chester Music, by Kitty Black and Michael Flanders.

---

[35] XSMO – External Services Music Organiser.

It seems that this new translation had for some reason prompted particular interest on the part of Stravinsky himself, for on the Sunday morning preceding the start of rehearsals Renna received a phone call at our home in Hampstead in which a foreign accented voice (to this day we are not sure whose) asked that I should provide Stravinsky with sight of the new translation. The upshot was that a couple of hours later I was driving to collect the narrator, Christopher Hassall, from his home and bring him straight to Stravinsky's room in the Dorchester Hotel where Stravinsky, his wife, Vera, and our chosen conductor, Robert Craft, were already assembled.

There then ensued one of the most improbable and extraordinary sessions I have ever experienced. There we all were in Stravinsky's bedroom with the great man lying on the bed, while Robert Craft directed a run-through of those sections of the work where words and music are combined rhythmically. What emerged from this rather bizarre séance was that Stravinsky's concern was entirely with the syllabic stress of the new words, for instance in The Devil's couplet. When all was over he thanked us courteously, and Christopher and I left, somewhat bemused to say the least.

A few days later we were ready to convene in Maida Vale for the recording. Such equanimity as Christopher and myself might have regained was potentially undermined by the somewhat unexpected news that the great man intended to be present at the recording. There, indeed, he was. But whatever anxiety we may have had was swiftly soothed by the fact that Stravinsky remained discreetly quiet throughout, apparently pleased with the proceedings and enjoying a degree of affable good humour with all the participants. The point when all was finally completed was for many, I think, a moment of considerable pent-up relief. Certainly I have to confess that at that moment my nervous exhaustion was so completely overwhelming that the only course of action open to me was instant flight to the washroom.

Whilst only a few of the programmes that one was asked to undertake as a general producer were orchestral, two particular recordings stand out vividly in my mind. Both took place shortly after our recording in Stravinsky's presence of *Histoire du Soldat*. This was particularly appropriate since these recordings were to be conducted by Pierre Monteux, assuredly one of the twentieth-century's greatest conductors and destined to be forever associated with Stravinsky's music on account of having been at the helm for the riot-provoking first performance of *Sacre du Printemps*. Monteux had been invited by Beecham to work with the orchestra which was, in essence, Sir Thomas's own post-war creation, the re-formed Royal Philharmonic Orchestra (RPO). I was lucky enough to be asked to produce two programmes which Monteux recorded with the RPO in our Maida Vale studio. Each proved to be a memorable occasion.

During rehearsal of the first of these programmes word came that Beecham himself was on his way to listen. By this time the great man had been confined to a wheelchair, and it is necessary for me to indicate briefly the layout of the main studio in order to describe what followed on Beecham's arrival. The small gallery from which one looked down upon the main floor of the studio was, in fact, at street level. On entering the building, one could turn immediately left and progress through a sequence of three successive double doors in order to arrive at the gallery. Upon meeting Beecham at the main doors, I guided him as he was pushed progressively through each of these doors. As we emerged through the second, one could hear the orchestra quite distinctly. This prompted Beecham to turn to me and ask, "Is that my orchestra?" "Indeed it is, Sir Thomas", I responded. "Hmm," came the rejoinder, "I'd never have thought it!" What did that enigmatic response indicate? I am sure that it was, in fact, a spontaneous compliment to Monteux.

Throughout these two recordings Monteux could not have been more affable, relaxed and indeed genial. In breaks he would chat quite spontaneously about his life's experiences. On one occasion, having listened with fascination to the unusually leisurely tempo he was setting for Wagner's *Siegfried Idyll*, I was emboldened to comment on the interestingly broad tempo he had set. Monteux replied, "It may be slow, but I play it as Siegfried did when he was conducting an orchestra in which I played as a young man. But I must tell you, Siegfried was not a very good conductor!" In fact, Monteux's tempi always seemed perfectly judged; as Jack Brymer, the RPO's principal clarinet once said of him, "You can always feel the tempo before he starts."

During another break we were chatting about life in America where Monteux then lived in a rural retreat in Maine. Referring to a visit he had recently made to one of the southern states, he described how horrified he was when, lunching in a restaurant, he saw two black would-be diners being unceremoniously ejected from the building. Apparently, Monteux remonstrated with the maître d'hôtel who explained that the restaurant "did not serve coloureds". "But," replied Monteux, extending his arm, "I am coloured: see, I am pink! So, I shall not eat here!"

The presentation of BBC music broadcasting at that time hovered between the formal and explicit and the less formal and more convivial or, on occasions, no factual presentation to speak of. Two series of broadcasts with which I had the good fortune to be closely involved illustrate these points. On the one hand was a series of Home Service friendly orchestral concerts under the generic title *Music to Remember* when, each Monday evening, presenters who had cultivated interesting but less formal ways of introducing music were invited to replace the formal BBC announcer. One who carried this art to a considerable degree and won many adherents was Robert Irwin. Another was Maurice Hardy, who would step out of the ranks of the Bournemouth Symphony Orchestra's cellos to present a concert in an entirely personal and very persuasive manner. Maurice was something of an original for, during the summer and in his free time, he and his violinist wife would offer alfresco concerts touring the New Forest and other localities in the vicinity of Bournemouth in a gypsy caravan. Their programmes would even extend to Haydn piano trios in which they were supported by specially made recordings of the piano parts to which they could then add the violin and cello lines live.

Another series which I was lucky enough to be invited to produce was entitled *Music in Miniature.* Both the title and the format had been invented by Basil Douglas who left the BBC to establish his own inimitable and widely admired artists' agency. *Music in Miniature* simply consisted of a 30-minute sequence of carefully interlinked short pieces of music, uninterrupted by any presentation and performed by a variety of individual performers or groups. For example we might, and indeed did, in one programme enjoy contributions by Janet Baker, Julian Bream, Clifford Curzon and the Aeolian Quartet. To make this recording we would convene in the Farringdon Studio while running the aural gauntlet created by the rumble of Metropolitan line trains below.

Two factors about music broadcasting back in the '50s should perhaps be remembered. One is that, unlike today, the great majority of broadcasts were not recorded but were transmitted live. The other is that virtually all broadcasting before the '60s was in mono, or should I say monophony. But in the late '50s we were, to a limited extent, beginning to experiment in stereophony. I was fortunate enough to be quite closely involved with these experiments, as distinct from others conducted with striking originality in the BBC's electronic workshops by pioneers like Ivor Walsworth and Daphne Oram.

Within the field of domestic broadcasting recording techniques were being developed in various interesting ways by the strong team of BBC recording engineers working under the leadership of Raymond Suffield and his able lieutenant, Eric Dougherty. To create some potentially spatial listening a team of three of us were invited to pool our imagination. I have, for instance, vivid memories of a broadcast of scenes from *Alice in Wonderland*. The listener, sitting at home, would then be invited aurally to trace the movements of the Cheshire cat as it wandered about the tree.

Occasionally, we did even attempt quadrophony as, for instance, when we took over St.. Andrew's Hall in Glasgow to position, within its generously proportioned rectangle, four groups of horns and strings to make a quadraphonic recording of Mozart's *Notturno* in D K286. This may well have been the last music ever to have been heard in this wonderful hall for, just two or three days later, it was burnt to the ground, a tragedy which destroyed one of Britain's greatest concert halls but for which, mercifully, our primitive quadrophonic recording could in no way be held responsible.

My principal colleagues in these experiments were the very gifted Drama Producer, Raymond Raikes, and the pioneering Features Director, Douglas Cleverdon. The reader will not need to be reminded that it was Douglas who inspired the commission and production of Dylan Thomas's *Under Milk Wood*, of which to this day no greater single achievement lies to the credit of the old Third Programme. Many older listeners will also recall remarkable drama productions directed by Raymond Raikes.

For my part I shall long remember one delicious moment in particular. Raymond had invited me to look in on the preparation of a new play for which a glittering cast had been convened in Broadcasting House Studio 5A, a curiously constructed suite with the control channel one floor higher than the studio itself, thus enabling one to survey the work of those in the studio below. In the control room I found Lewis Casson looking down upon the assembled cast which included his distinguished wife, Sybil Thorndike, taking a leading role. At this point the cast was simply reading through the script, but it seemed to Lewis that Sybil's voice was unnecessarily faint. Depressing the talk-back key he tactfully suggested, "Sybil, I think you should sit a little nearer the table." She took absolutely no notice but, a few minutes later, having accidentally turned two pages at once, and after reading a line or two which clearly did not follow, held up a hand to declare with commanding nonchalance, "I think I shall sit a little nearer the table!"

BBC Symphony Orchestra 1959-1961

In the summer of 1959 Michael Whewell, bassoonist, fellow BBC Music Producer and a good personal friend, was invited to move to Belfast. Up to that time such national patronage as the arts in Northern Ireland enjoyed had been conducted under the umbrella of CEMA[36]. Michael's job was to prepare for the creation in due course of the Arts Council of Northern Ireland, which was to assume responsibility for the arts in the province when CEMA was closed down. The position that he left was that of Producer to the BBC Symphony Orchestra to which I was fortunate enough to be appointed in September 1959.

This was the start of two very absorbing and stimulating years for me, packed with many experiences still vivid in the memory after more than fifty years. It was to be a matter of real regret that I found myself leaving this particular job two years later when the BBC found a new perch for me in Birmingham.

As you might expect, close association with an orchestra such as the BBC Symphony carried many rewards. Prominent among these was the opportunity to work with some of the remarkable people who were members of the orchestra at that time. For example, the orchestra boasted an outstanding quartet of immensely gifted players who constituted the woodwind principals. The flautist, Doug Whittaker, was a fairly laid back Australian with an imperishable silvery tone and a passionate devotion to both photography and fast Jaguar cars. I shall never forget an exhilarating evening drive as his passenger when, after a concert in Coventry, he drove me back to London in just one hour, scarcely for a moment ever leaving the fast lane of the M1. This was at a time when the new M1 was still

---

[36] CEMA – Committee for the Encouragement of Music and the Arts.

very lightly used and when the whole experience of fast motorway travel was something of a novelty.

Sitting next to him in the orchestra was Janet Craxton, possessed of a most beautiful and distinctive tone, who had, in the estimation of many, inherited the mantle of Leon Goossens as the country's premier oboist. The oboe repertoire has been infinitely enriched by works written specifically for Janet by so many distinguished composers, especially British ones, and I well remember how enthusiastic she was about Lennox Berkeley's works for oboe such as his Quintet and Sonatina.

Joining the orchestra at virtually the same time as I took up my own appointment was Colin Bradbury. He was to occupy the principal clarinet's chair with unfailing distinction for more than thirty years. He has brought untold strength to British music-making in so many ways: as a performer, as a teacher at the RCM and (by no means least) as the father of John, an equally fine clarinettist. In various prominent ways he has also set goals for us all to emulate, as he did when, in his capacity as President of the Incorporated Society of Musicians, he joined forces with Sir Peter Maxwell Davies publicly to challenge recurrent failure on the part of government to nurture the arts. The orchestra's remarkable woodwind quartet was completed by Geoffrey Gambold, whose own individual bassoon playing blended so beautifully with that of his colleagues, as did the assured and elegant playing of the principal horn, Douglas Moore.

Throughout the other ranks of the orchestra were to be found characters whose contributions to the life and pulse of the orchestra were no less distinctive. Paul Beard was still its accomplished leader, as he had been for many years although, truth to tell, he now often appeared more detached than wholehearted. I shall long remember a particularly difficult rehearsal when Rudolf Kempe[37] was our guest conductor. Throughout the session Paul had appeared less than positively engaged, sitting back with legs fully extended in front of him. When the break came, I endeavoured to find some appropriate words of explanatory regret but Kempe, gentleman that he was, simply shrugged his shoulders and said, "I often wonder why some

---

[37] Rudolf Kempe was destined to become Chief Conductor of the BBC Symphony Orchestra in 1975, only to die within a few short months of his appointment on 11 May 1976.

players do not just go away and dig in their garden."

Principal viola, Harry Danks, was endlessly resilient and enthusiastic, even when a well-aimed toilet roll fell on his very valuable instrument during the riot which followed the premiere of Luigi Nono's opera, *Intolleranza*, for which the BBC Symphony Orchestra had been engaged by the Venice Biennale. The principal cellist was Alexander Kok, a natural revolutionary by nature and the complete antithesis of his gentle brother Felix, who for many years led the City of Birmingham Symphony Orchestra (CBSO). Gerald Drucker was, as in everything he undertook, the most musical of double bass principals.

Adorning not only the strings but indeed the whole orchestra was the endearingly indestructible Sidonie Goossens, our principal harp. She had, in that capacity, been a founder member of the orchestra by invitation of Adrian Boult. She was dearly loved by us all and wonderfully admired as a member of that distinguished family among whom she could count brothers Eugene, the conductor, and Leon, the oboist – to say nothing of her younger sister, Marie, who would also grace the orchestra whenever more than one harpist was required. She only retired in 1980 having therefore served the orchestra for a full fifty years. Sidonie was destined for a long, distinguished and much lauded retirement, only dying in December 2004 at the age of 105.

The ranks of the brass players contained members who were seldom hesitant to express concern regarding their own and the orchestra's wellbeing. Wesley Woodage, second trumpet, was the orchestra's spokesman, ably supported in many respects by trombonist, Jack Pinches. Jack was one of the outsize characters in the orchestra, who also taught trombone and doubtless other brass instruments at Eton, but whose domestic value to his colleagues was to be observed in the break of any rehearsal. Then he would open up a large, shining brown leather case to reveal an intriguing array of smokers' requirements. He was, in effect, the orchestra's travelling tobacconist with a ready supply of brands which he knew to be those favoured by the pipe smokers, in addition to a range of preferred cigarettes, never forgetting a few Havanas discreetly reserved for visiting conductors who found favour with him.

The two years I had the good fortune to spend with this fine orchestra also marked a time when its crusading programmes meant that the percussion section found itself meeting endless fresh new demands as composers made increasingly prominent and original use of percussion instruments. At the heart of this key group within the orchestra, and imperturbably ready to confront these varied challenges, stood the incomparable Gilbert Webster, for whom no innovation was too complicated or demanding. Some fourteen years later, he was to leave the orchestra and join the RNCM in order to develop a pioneering percussion studio at the College. Whatever may have been my limited powers of persuasion in inducing Gilbert to join us in Manchester, they had been fortuitously reinforced by the consequences of a severe accident which Gilbert had experienced when falling off high rostra at the back of the orchestra. The outcome was to hasten his departure from the BBC, after receiving a substantial settlement in damages from the Corporation.

I should say a word about the status of the members of the orchestra. This had a bearing on how our union consultations were conducted. By the nature of the contracts, they were not simply appointed as musicians but also as broadcasters, like all other members of BBC staff at the time. They enjoyed all the benefits open to staff members such as pensionable entitlements. Needless to say, this advantageous situation led to very settled communities within the BBC's orchestras – some thirteen of them all told at that time. It is reassuring, and infinitely to the BBC's credit, that in these days of economic restraint five of these orchestras still flourish to this day.

The orchestra was managed by George Willoughby who, on account of some wartime injury, walked with an unnaturally stiff and rigid back, but whose approach always commanded respect. He had a gift for winning the spontaneous support of players and I shall long remember an occasion when he saved the day in delightful fashion. A young South African mezzo-soprano, Sybil Michelow, was scheduled to make her first appearance with the orchestra, conducted on this occasion by Sir Malcolm Sargent. She had been engaged to sing Brahms's *Four Serious Songs*. In the way of these things, the booking had gone to her agent using the original German title, *Vier ernste Gesänge*. Not unnaturally she had assumed that she was booked to sing them in German. There had evidently been no prior piano rehearsal, for it was only when she began the first song that Malcolm Sargent stopped the orchestra and turned to her in a rather patronising way to say, "No, no: in English." The poor girl was understandably thrown and close to tears. Sargent, trying to mollify her, added, "You see, my dear, if you sing it in English the whole orchestra will be so moved." George Willoughby, spontaneously drew from his pocket a small notebook and, with pencil poised in policeman fashion, declared, "Now then, anybody I see moved: I am taking his name!" Sybil Michelow, being the trooper she was, recovered her poise, sang it in flawless English at the next rehearsal and was promptly engaged to appear at the Last Night of the Proms.

I have written initially something about the players who brought such character to the orchestra during my time with it. But the central figure was, naturally, our chief conductor, Rudolf Schwarz [Plate 10], a musician of extraordinary sensitivity and depth. His instinctive humanity, coupled with an infallible stylistic authority, were traits immediately recognised by all those members of the orchestra who could appreciate that he also brought with him rare qualities which had been born of both suffering and compassion.

One of Vienna's countless gifted Jewish musicians, Rudi had trained as a viola player, in which capacity he became a member of the Vienna State Opera orchestra. Moving to Düsseldorf and then Karlsruhe, his early opera experiences in Germany saw him emerging as a Wagner conductor of unusual ability. Inevitably though, the shadow of Nazism overtook him. He was imprisoned for a period and then released. By 1941 he had been rearrested and deported to Auschwitz, and it was only thanks to the intervention of Zitla Furtwängler[38] that he was released. An illusory breath of freedom was swiftly cut short by a fresh arrest which led to extended prison periods first in Sachsenhausen and ultimately in Belsen, until release by the Allies came in 1945. At this time Schwarz was suffering from typhoid and was sent to convalesce in Sweden; there he was lovingly restored to health by Greta, who then became Rudi's second wife.

While Rudi was preparing to chance his arm as a conductor in America his brother, who lived in London, spotted an advertisement placed by what was then the Bournemouth Municipal Orchestra, seeking a chief conductor to rebuild the orchestra after its own war-time ravages. This fortuitous development allowed Rudi to establish a successful and rewarding career in Britain. He was welcomed with enthusiastic unanimity in Bournemouth where the orchestra prospered significantly for the next four years. This

---

[38] The great conductor's wife.

auspicious period was then followed by six rewarding years in Birmingham as Chief Conductor of the CBSO, before he moved to the BBC Symphony Orchestra in 1957.

His lack of a discernible beat was often the subject of ill-judged critical comment, expressed in ignorance of the fact that while in Auschwitz he had, like so many others, suffered infinitely cruel physical treatment, leading in his case to a severe injury to his right shoulder blade which seriously limited his capacity to command unrestricted arm movement. Rudi would never speak about the war years or his experiences but instead expressed his gratitude for all the joys and support which had subsequently come his way, first in Sweden and then, for so many happy and rewarding years, in Britain.

In thinking of Rudi I shall always retain memories of one of the most sensitive, kind and wise people I have ever had the good fortune to know. His concern for the welfare of other people was legendary, and I know communicated itself to many members of the BBC Symphony Orchestra. These qualities were richly reflected in the way in which Rudi made music. He was always concerned for what he termed 'the true message' which meant, of course, the character of the music, its idiomatic and stylistic authenticity. He always lavished infinite care on matters of detail; for instance, he might be rehearsing a Dvořák *Slavonic Dance* as a short filler to complete the programme for a prescribed broadcasting slot, but the contours and the detail of the music would receive as much affectionate concern as might any larger piece. In fact, Dvořák always seemed to me a composer to whom Rudi responded with particularly personal affection; it was a good example of the special qualities which the conductor Simon Rattle is on record as having discerned in Rudi when he wrote that "he never gave any interpretation that did not have a real truth about it."

Planning programmes with Rudi was always, I found, an intriguing occupation in that he was the most accommodating and uncomplaining of colleagues for which any nervous young producer could have asked. This particularly applied to repertoire choice in that, whatever may have been his inner sentiments, he seldom showed any reluctance to undertake works asked of him. On only one occasion that I can recall did he come forward with an emphatic proposal. This was on behalf of the music of Hans Gál, with whom he had studied as a young man in Vienna.

The rhythm of the orchestra's life was dictated by the broadcasting requirements which it existed to fulfil. At certain times of the year, such as during the Proms, the orchestra's workload became very concentrated. It should be remembered that at that time, over fifty years ago, it was not uncommon for the orchestra to appear at the Royal Albert Hall on consecutive nights, even three or four times in a week. This inevitably necessitated as much prior rehearsal as could be accommodated during the summer months, notwithstanding appearances at festivals or other exotic engagements, such as the excursion to the Venice Biennale which I have mentioned.

The pattern during the winter months was rather more settled and centred upon the broad expectation that the orchestra would generally provide a Wednesday evening concert, either in the Royal Festival Hall or live before an invited audience in the orchestra's Maida Vale studio. This would be broadcast on either the Home Service or the Third Programme according to the programme content. The Wednesday concert might then be followed at the weekend by a Third Programme Saturday evening broadcast of a fairly taxing and challenging nature and / or a Home Service Sunday afternoon broadcast relying more on central repertoire.

Occasionally, these twin demands of weekend broadcasts for both the Home Service and the Third Programme could create interesting situations when potential collisions were all too evident. I shall long remember one particular week when two guest conductors were with us, one for the Third Programme broadcast, the other for the Home Service concert. Otto Klemperer had been engaged to prepare a Bruckner programme consisting of the Sixth Symphony and the *Te Deum* with the BBC Singers. In parallel, Sir Malcolm Sargent was to present a rather more traditional programme though I do not remember the content in any detail. Since Klemperer had made it very clear that he would only rehearse once a day we devised an arrangement whereby the morning rehearsal would be given over to Bruckner with Klemperer, while Malcolm Sargent would take the afternoon rehearsal.

This arrangement worked remarkably smoothly except for the way in which Klemperer shaped his Bruckner rehearsals. He did not so much rehearse as simply play through, then play through and even play through again. So picture the scene on Monday morning in Studio 1 at Maida Vale. The orchestra and the BBC Singers are assembled, and Klemperer is given a rapturous reception. "Erste

Teil." The orchestra embarks on the first movement of the symphony. The BBC Singers listen attentively. "Zweite Teil," calls out Klemperer. The orchestra continues with the second movement. This is then followed by "Dritte Teil." Klemperer then announces "Pause", and shuffles off his creaking chair. Everybody disperses to the canteen, and eventually reassembles. Klemperer returns: *"Te Deum."* The singers are in good voice. It goes well. "Gut." "Vierte Teil." That's Monday morning! On Tuesday, the first movement, Erste Teil, is again followed by Zweite Teil, is followed by Dritte Teil, is followed by coffee. The *Te Deum* is then run through and the finale then played with suitable devotion. So everybody is content. A pattern has been set and we all know where we are going.

However, on Wednesday this arrangement is again followed, but only up to a point. Yes, the first movement is followed by the second but Klemperer, with a wicked smile, since he has observed that the ranks of waiting singers have been thinned by the evident expectation that they would not be wanted, calls out *"Te Deum."* Instant consternation. Search parties are sent out to bring back stray singers from the canteen and eventually the rehearsal of the *Te Deum* can begin but not until Klemperer himself has hugely enjoyed the confusion that he has provoked. German humour, one might say!

Indeed, that incident rather reminds me of another which I believe to be true; it relates to when Klemperer was in the Royal Festival Hall with his own orchestra, the Philharmonia. The programme allegedly included a variety of works ranging from Mozart's *Eine kleine Nachtmusik*, simply for strings, to Janáček's *Sinfonietta* which, as many will know, is an extraordinary work involving twelve trumpets. Allegedly, at this Philharmonia rehearsal, Klemperer played the same sort of trick when the orchestra assembled and it was found that the twelfth trumpeter was missing. Outwardly patient, Klemperer calmly waited until the errant trumpeter appeared and was seated. At this point Klemperer playfully dismissed the whole orchestra except for the strings and proceeded to rehearse *Eine kleine Nachtmusik*.

Klemperer stories abounded at this time, as when he was preparing a recording of Beethoven's *Missa Solemnis*. Dietrich Fischer Dieskau, one of the soloists, found himself becoming increasingly uncomfortable with Klemperer's propensity for slow tempi. In exasperation, he was moved to call out across the orchestra: "Lieber Meister, I must tell you that God came to me in my dreams and he said, 'The *Credo* is too slow'." Without a moment's hesitation the great man responded: "Lieber Dietrich, I must tell you that the good Lord also disturbed my sleep last night, but just with a short question: 'Who is this Fischer Dieskau?'".

Sir Malcolm Sargent, who had shared this week's conducting duties with Klemperer, could often be difficult and was always conscious of his own dignity. But he could also be very kind, as I personally experienced when he turned to me one day and spontaneously invited me to lunch with him at London Zoo, an organisation to which he was devoted. Why he should feel a wish to be so kind to a young 30-year-old BBC producer I could not judge, but he extended this generosity to me further when, at the conclusion of the same lunch, he then suggested that he might make me a member of his London Club. Knowing that I could not possibly, at that stage, afford the annual subscription, I found some way to hesitate about accepting, and I hope that he did not think ill of me for this.

Not all conductors were so accommodating or considerate towards those of us in 'the box', that is to say the control channel. I shall long remember a rehearsal with Sir Thomas Beecham in the Royal Festival Hall when the studio manager responsible for producing a quality sound was one of the BBC's finest SMs, Jimmy Burnett. Satisfied that he had secured a perfect balance, Jimmy had turned down the speakers in the box when he suddenly became aware that Beecham was calling to him from the podium. "BBC", came the stentorian summons. Jimmy responded through the glass panel with two upraised thumbs. "BBC", repeated the stentorian voice: "Come out here please." Jimmy made his way out onto the platform to stand by Beecham whose little goat beard was quivering with amusement. "BBC," (he of course knew Jimmy Burnett's name perfectly well, but mischievously declined to use it) "would you please explain to the ladies and gentlemen of the orchestra what you meant to convey by that gesture with your thumbs?" Jimmy, with great presence of mind, responded: "Simply, Sir Thomas, that, as usual, you have achieved a miracle."

As is well known, Beecham was never averse to engaging in a little waspish humour when the mood suited him. This sense of mischief could periodically return when he was conducting the music of Vaughan Williams. Two little vignettes come to mind in this connection. One was during an early Royal Philharmonic Orchestra

(RPO)[39] rehearsal of Vaughan Williams's Sixth Symphony, with its long, quiet epilogue. Beecham, to the consternation of the orchestra's leader, David McCallum, went on quietly beating after the music had, in fact, finally died away. McCallum, after a short hesitation, and momentarily concluding that Beecham's attention might have temporarily wandered, whispered, "Sir Thomas, it has finished", to which Sir Thomas quietly responded, "Has it, indeed? I must say I thought it never would!" On another occasion we were in Studio 1 at Maida Vale preparing for a performance of Vaughan Williams's *Pastoral Symphony*. As the final sounds died away, Beecham turned quietly to the cellos and murmured, "I don't know about you gentlemen, but a city life for me."

While reflecting on the many distinguished musicians who came to conduct the BBC Symphony Orchestra during my two years with them, five in particular spring to mind. One of these was Rudolf Kempe who, had the fates been kinder, should have enjoyed a long tenure as chief conductor of the BBC Symphony Orchestra but who, very cruelly, left this world prematurely. His gentle manner and all-embracing musicianship swiftly won the loyalty of every orchestra.

A second was Lorin Maazel, who spent the first fifteen minutes of his very first rehearsal meticulously tuning and retuning sections of the orchestra, in particular the brass and the double basses, which did not go down too well. A third was Hans Rosbaud, whom we had invited to conduct the first performance in England of Messiaen's *Chronochromie*. I had been present at the Donaueschingen Festival when Rosbaud gave the world premiere of this remarkable work. At that time, he had appeared frail but now, when he came to us in London, he was, very sadly, a visibly sick man.

Two other guest conductors, who first and foremost were composers, also come to mind. One was the Italian composer Bruno Maderna who, in addition to conducting his own second *Serenata*, had passionately wanted to conduct Berlioz's *Symphonie Fantastique*: this he certainly did with great enthusiasm, until the rehearsal of the waltz teetered alarmingly on the precipice on account of his exaggerated rubato.

Possibly the BBC Symphony Orchestra's most endearing guest conductor during these two years was Zoltán Kodály. He enabled

---

[39] Beecham had personally recruited and formed the RPO after the war.

us to hear his *Háry János* played as never before. How he achieved this was something of a mystery. But a miraculous recording of the work was achieved on one single straight play-through, as though somehow each member of the orchestra, catching the mood of the moment, knew precisely where everybody was heading. Yes, this was one of those rare moments when perfection occurs quite spontaneously, but I do still vividly recall that performance had been preceded by a seemingly endless moment of stillness throughout the studio, while, in quiet meditation, Kodály rested the tip of his baton motionless against his chin.

MIDLAND REGION 1961-1964

On a spring morning in 1961 I was working in the control room of Studio 1 in Maida Vale when Daphne's telephone call came through. The BBC Symphony Orchestra was in mid-rehearsal and the call was from Daphne Smith, Secretary to William Glock, Controller Music. This was in the days before PAs had been invented and Daphne Smith was an incomparably wise and understanding secretary who smoothed the way for all of us who had the pleasure of working for Glock in whatever capacity. On this occasion her cheerful chirpy message was simply to ask if I would "call in to see William" as soon as I was next back in Yalding House, the home of BBC Music Division.

I was to discover that this interview was to herald a fundamental change in my career at the BBC, since the summons to William's office was to tell me that the BBC would now like me to move to Birmingham as HMRM[40]. This would be to succeed John Lowe, who had been appointed Artistic Director of the new Coventry Cathedral Festival due to be held in mid-summer 1962.

This was, of course, totally unexpected and something of a shock for both Renna and myself. We had been living in our first purchased house for only a year. We were happily finding our feet among new friends in Potters Bar, where little Helen had just started nursery school all decked out in a pretty fawn dress with dark brown blazer. Moreover, Renna was pregnant with David and, understandably enough, wished that this pivotal point in our lives

---

[40] HMRM – Head of Midland Region Music

had not occurred just then.

1961 was also a fundamental year for us in another way. Henryk Verwoerd, then President of South Africa, had suddenly underscored his violent dislike for everything British by withdrawing South Africa from the Commonwealth. Renna and I, being first generation South Africans, that is to say born in South Africa of British parents who had emigrated there, carried dual British and South African nationality. Following upon Verwoerd's decision, such automatic entitlement to dual nationality was to cease.

A crucial question arose: would being a South African national without British nationality have any effect on my employment at the BBC? I felt I should send a formal internal memorandum of enquiry to the BBC's then Director of Personnel, John Arkell. It was an indication of the wonderful club-like spirit of support which in those days so characterised the BBC that, almost by return of internal post, I received back my memorandum with a handwritten annotation on it from John Arkell himself. This simply read "Don't worry, we'll treat you as Irish!".

Thus reassured, we began to make ready for our new life, although John Lowe was not due to move until late summer. This allowed me time to complete a second full year working for the BBC Symphony Orchestra. The move to Birmingham then followed naturally and smoothly.

During the '60s it could be said that the four principal BBC regions were loosely modelled on all that London represented. Each of the four larger regions, being those with headquarters in Birmingham, Cardiff, Glasgow and Manchester, was very broadly a tenth of the size of the London operation, if viewed in terms of personnel, buildings, diversity and so on. The other two regions, based in Belfast and Bristol, were quite noticeably smaller, although they retained their own validity and special responsibilities, such as West Region's Natural History Unit in Bristol. Thus Birmingham, Cardiff, Glasgow and Manchester all boasted a range of specialist departments including, in each case, a strong music department with resident musicians and staff, and good studio facilities.

To someone coming to Birmingham from London in 1961 the first impression was inevitably of a significantly smaller operation, but one conducted within measurable proportions. Each region presented a wide range of distinctive radio and television programmes, typified in Midland Region by its concentration upon agriculture which had recently become popularised by the creation of the long-running rural saga, *The Archers*.

In Birmingham there also existed a warm family spirit. One way, for example, in which this showed itself was that, thanks to relaxed relations between BBC Midland Region and the Warwickshire County Cricket Club, we were, each year, allowed privileged use of the Edgbaston test ground in which to indulge our sporting fantasies by staging a knock-out tournament between cricket teams representing the BBC's North, Midland, West and South Regions. Similarly, the Birmingham Club House would witness spirited indoor sporting encounters such as our regional table tennis tournament won each year with dispiriting ease by Les Cawdrey, second clarinet of the MLO[41].

There was one striking difference between broadcasting in the regions and in London. Whereas in London radio and television were, for the most part, mutually exclusive, in the regions radio and television largely proceeded to mutual advantage in double harness and with an invigorating absence of the rigid divisions so prevalent in London.

From the day I arrived in Birmingham I instinctively knew this to be the start of a singularly happy and very rewarding period. Whereas I had left London to the predictable chorus of mischievous good humour, expressing hope that I might somehow survive life in the wilderness, in practice Birmingham and all that the region stood for could not have been more warmly welcoming from the start. Nor was this so-called 'wilderness' unduly impoverished musically. Within the arbitrary ways in which the BBC's boundaries were drawn, Midland Region ranged from the Welsh border to the North Sea. This meant that, in addition to everything Birmingham itself offered in terms of fine music-making and traditions, the region included at least four of the country's most important and influential music Festivals – those at Aldeburgh and King's Lynn in the east and at Cheltenham and Three Choirs in the west. The region's boundaries also embraced both Oxford and Cambridge with the many musical riches they represented. All these delights fell within BBC Midland Region's aegis. Therefore, in addition to the CBSO itself, and everything in and around Birmingham, we

---

[41] MLO – BBC Midland Light Orchestra.

could also all look forward to the stimulating prospect of making music in the new Coventry Cathedral in 1962.

Some years were yet to pass before the BBC built its glamorous Pebble Mill studios in 1971. When I arrived in Birmingham the region's headquarters were still housed in a former sanatorium on Carpenter Road in leafy Edgbaston. Notwithstanding the institutional character of our converted surroundings, these years were characterised by a sense of common purpose and camaraderie, such as it was not always possible to experience in London. The building only comprised two floors and the music department just occupied a small sequence of some half dozen offices in addition to our orchestral studio on the ground floor.

Down the passage from us were to be found *The Archers* offices, bursting with new-found confidence as the jewel in Midland region's crown. Indeed it was hard to move into the real world without encountering comments concerning the lives of Dan and Doris Archer up at Brookfield Farm, to say nothing of the night when this fantasy world engulfed the nation through the tragedy of the fire which killed their daughter-in-law. It was remarkable that within such a relatively small community so dramatic an event as the Brookfield Farm fire could have been contained in complete secrecy until the moment when it devastated the millions who regularly listened to *The Archers*.

At this time it was probably true to say that each region represented the BBC in miniature. Thus Midland Region had a number of small units concerned with such diverse activities as religious broadcasting, local television and agriculture. At the head of this team was John Dunkerley, CMR[42], the epitome of an old style broadcaster who had joined the BBC in its very early days and who was then nearing retirement. White-haired, he presided over us all with genial fatherly benevolence. While most encounters with him could be described as convivial rather than directly professional, the more senior of us were required to attend upon him for our annual interview. It became traditional for such interviews to be timed for 12 o'clock, when one would be greeted most affably with enquiries after one's health and the welfare of one's family. The occasion would otherwise be limited to Dunkerley satisfying himself that you had no problems, whereupon

---

[42] CMR – Controller Midland Region.

he would courteously suggest a glass of sherry prior to lunch.

John's abiding enthusiasm lay in the prize herd of Jersey cattle which he ran on his farm near Broadheath. He had been widowed for some years and we all welcomed the signs of growing affection between him and his secretary, Thelma Couch. Though a few unavoidably ribald remarks may have been benevolently aired, we all greatly rejoiced when the Dunkerley Couch wedding was finally announced and we were all invited to a splendid party to celebrate the event in Studio 6, the MLO's studio in Carpenter Road. At the climax to the proceedings the high doors at the end of the studio were thrown open and the staff's gift to John and Thelma was ushered in – a prize young Jersey heifer.

It was one of the endearing features of life in a rural region, and I'm sure Midland Region was no exception here, that domestic celebrations could occasionally be informally accommodated alongside professional priorities. This same Studio 6 was annually the scene of a Christmas party for all staff and their families. I shall never forget one such occasion to which I had taken our daughter Helen, then aged four or five. At a given moment those same large doors opened to admit a swarm of daleks straight from the set of *Dr. Who*! Not alone among the children, Helen was absolutely terrified out of her wits by the robotic realism of the invaders, complete with flashing lights and their repeated gravelly instruction, "Exterminate! Exterminate!". There was no way Helen was going to allow herself to be consoled or remain at the party, and she tells me that she can remember her terror to this day.

Supporting John Dunkerley was David Porter, HMRP[43], and the head of administration, Bill Roberts. Porter was an Irishman of whom the legend of an earlier escape from drowning was widely circulated. It appears that, while swimming off the Dalmation Coast, a strong current had drawn him inexorably away from the shore to the point where exhaustion overtook him and he could do no more than float with the current. By a measure of good fortune he had been dragged close to the stern of a luxury yacht riding at anchor. As David opened his eyes he discerned that a flag flying from the yacht's mast bore the familiar design of a harp, immediately recognisable as the Guinness company symbol. David's exhausted call for help met with an instant

---

[43] HMRP – Head of Midland Region Programmes.

response from Irish compatriots on board. In no time he was hauled to safety, thereby endorsing the proverbial adage concerning "the luck of the Irish".

David was supported by two other senior colleagues: Peter Cairns, AHMRP1[44], overseeing the region's television output, who had come to the BBC following a distinguished flying career; and my immediate superior, David Gretton, AHMRP2[45], Peter Cairns's counterpart for the region's radio broadcasts. Only rarely was the music department enabled to play any part in the region's television work but, by contrast, we were naturally one of the region's primary consumers of radio time and resources. I speedily came to count it one of the joys of my new job that I should be directly responsible to someone so understanding and at the same time supportive of music. David had a remarkable mind and was undoubtedly one of the most widely read people that I have ever had the good fortune to encounter. Renna and I will long remember an occasion when David Gretton held what I can only describe as a quotation dinner party, the central idea behind which appeared to be that the conversation should proceed by invoking one quotation after another, however inexpertly at times. All that I can recall is an extended failure on my part to make any useful contribution to what was, by any standard, a diverting if unusual amusement.

The music department had good reason to be grateful to David as, for instance, when I asked for a weekly one hour slot of air time on the Home Service to enable us to broadcast a series of chamber concerts on Monday evenings from various centres around the region. Some of these concerts would occasionally be given by the Delphos Ensemble, a group drawing on dedicated freelance players in Birmingham or selected members of the MLO which we 'reinvented' as a regional counterpart to the well-established Melos Ensemble in London. These weekly Monday evening concerts rejoiced in the title of *Musicale*. They could feature a group, a mixed bag of contrasting artists, or anything we felt reflected the many examples of vibrant music-making then to be found throughout the region. To our delight, this series quickly established a secure niche for itself in the broadcasting schedules and even began to attract

---

[44] AHMRP1 – Assistant Head of Midland Region Programmes Television.
[45] AHMRP2 – Assistant Head of Midland Region Programmes Radio.

invitations from various clubs and organisations throughout the Midlands and East Anglia. At the same time we also actively sought to place these concerts in venues where they could, as we hoped, nourish new audiences.

To be realistic, whatever we might initiate from the BBC could only embellish the many significant enterprises which already abounded. One such was the Barber Institute at Birmingham University where could be found Anthony Lewis[46], widely admired both as a scholar and for his pioneering role in the revival of interest in Handel's operas. Until then, Handel's unique gifts as an opera composer had still to be adequately appreciated. Professor Lewis revealed something of their infinite richness with the help of a far-sighted producer in Brian Trowell and some remarkable singers, notable among them the young emerging Janet Baker.

Throughout this time we were all looking forward with eager anticipation to the Coventry Cathedral Festival, to be directed by my predecessor in Birmingham, John Lowe. Although it was not to become the annual feature some hoped it might, this 1962 Festival reflected with true distinction Basil Spence's remarkable building it was created to celebrate. Few who enjoyed the privilege of attending some of the outstanding events during the Festival will forget the various moments of imperishable distinction which ensued.

Outstanding among these was Benjamin Britten's deeply moving *War Requiem*, with its telling use of wartime poets and entirely novel use of two conductors, two orchestras, large and small, and the wonderful singing which so enriched the whole experience. Comparable, if very different, was the wholly distinctive sound which the Berlin Philharmonic Orchestra under Eugen Jochum brought to its playing of Bruckner. By contrast, no one in the Belgrade Theatre on the occasion of the world premiere of Michael Tippett's opera *King Priam* will forget the blood-curdling moment as Richard Lewis's Achilles took wing.

Prior to the consecration, much speculation not unnaturally existed as to how the new cathedral's acoustics would play out. How would they complement the visual splendour offered by

---

[46] Later Sir Anthony, co-founder/editor of *Musica Britannica* and Principal of the Royal Academy of Music from 1968, in succession to Sir Thomas Armstrong.

Graham Sutherland's remarkable 'Christ in Glory' altar tapestry or John Piper's masterpiece windows? I shall long remember finding myself high up in the roof of the cathedral and looking down on a mass of diminutive figures who were, in fact, the members of the Berlin Orchestra. It was particularly interesting to discover that the quality of orchestral sound reaching us up there in the rafters was the nearest you could imagine to pure perfection, whereas it had seemed disappointingly diffuse on the ground.

More precise concentration on the floor of Coventry Cathedral was something I had witnessed a few days earlier in an entirely different way. The beautiful marble floor had been formed of black and white squares with a newly struck 1962 one penny piece glistening brightly at the corner of each of these squares, the whole being protected by heavy polythene sheeting during the final days before consecration. Some workmen, wearing heavy hobnail boots, had inadvertently roughed up some of this protective sheeting. Joseph Poole, the tall and distinguished Cathedral Precentor, who had noticed a workman unintentionally allowing his boots to make direct contact with this pristine marbled splendour, called out "Do not walk on the floor, my man", whereupon Bishop Bardsley, as luck would have it passing at that moment, remarked quietly "Pray Joseph, for what is the floor but to walk upon?"

While opportunities for music programmes on television were few and far between, I was able to have a hand in a short feature programme about St. Michael's Tenbury Wells, an unusually distinguished prep school in the heart of Worcestershire, but sadly no longer in existence today. It was notable for one special treasure in its possession – Handel's personal copy of *Messiah*. To give the programme added distinction we had invited Sir John Betjeman to come and 'front' the programme.

I retain two vivid memories of this particular undertaking. One was that I had given myself the pleasure of going to meet Sir John's train from London. In those days, before the electrification of the line between Euston and New Street, steam trains travelled from Paddington to Birmingham's Snow Hill station. But nowhere could I find the Poet Laureate. As it transpired, this was because he had taken an earlier train and, on arrival, had decided to explore the station's immediate surroundings – in particular a nearby canal, on the banks of which he had harvested for himself, as he told me with great delight, a tasty collection of wild strawberries.

My second memory of our television recording at St. Michael's is simply of the opening sequence where the director had arranged, at great expense, to hire a helicopter in order to enable us to open with an overhead shot descending upon Betjeman as he stood alone on the school's cricket pitch. The disappointment of this occasion was that the wind currents swirled around in such a way that Betjeman's broad-brimmed dark hat was unceremoniously swept out of shot and the whole effect largely lost in confusion.

After two years in virtually daily contact with the BBC Symphony Orchestra, I naturally found life involving the BBC MLO very different in that the orchestra basically existed to provide broadcasts of two strata of light music: either traditional fare ranging from Eric Coates to Franz Lehár or programmes of a somewhat jazzier character. To meet these two contrasting requirements we retained two joint resident chief conductors. One was Jack Coles, who had enjoyed great success in the entertainment world and who owned both a palatial house in St. John's Wood and a scarcely less splendid waterfront home in Positano. By contrast, the other, Gilbert Vinter, represented the more traditional repertoire, and was a very fine musician and composer in his own right. I believe that his bassoon quintet remains a premier example in that particular medium.

To cope with the ambidexterity which this mixed repertoire demanded, the permanent instrumentation of the orchestra, while slightly less than that of a full symphony orchestra, nonetheless called for players possessing good technical and stylistic versatility. While the orchestra's studio commitments ranged widely, so too did their more public activities. These included an annual tour of East Anglia and occasional symphonic jamborees such as when the MLO joined with the BBC Welsh Orchestra to shatter the peace of rural Wales by presenting Stravinsky's *The Rite of Spring* in the unlikely setting of a disused aircraft hangar in Newtown, Montgomeryshire.

Throughout all these years the CBSO was, as you would expect, the jewel in Birmingham's musical crown. While in later years it was to achieve fresh lustre under Sir Simon Rattle, the orchestra earlier scaled many distinctive heights under successive conductors, Hugo Rignold and Louis Frémaux. The BBC would regularly make recordings of the orchestra, broadly on a monthly basis. But only on one occasion, as I recall, did we enter into a significant new project with the orchestra. This was when I conceived the idea of promoting an international competition for wind players in which the common ground would be the performance of concertos by Mozart. Sir Adrian Boult was persuaded to lend his patronage to the project by agreeing to chair the international jury. The competition attracted a remarkable range of particularly talented soloists, and was finally won by that most gifted French oboist, Maurice Bourgue. Among the other finalists were a fine Romanian horn player, Paul Staicu, while from Belfast came the irrepressible flautist James Galway.

It is perhaps regrettable that Birmingham never repeated what was undoubtedly a competition with a distinctively original format. It drew fresh attention throughout Europe to the city as a musical centre. Even Nadia Boulanger, the legendary composer, conductor and teacher, allowed herself to be tempted to serve as a member of the jury, one of the last public assignments she ever undertook in England. One of the greatest joys that Renna and I ever experienced was that of having Nadia to stay with us as a house guest during the competition. A cherished domestic memory will always be of the way in which she hit it off with my very elderly aunt who had been closely linked to London theatrical life. These two frail but resolute octogenarian ladies appeared to experience no difficulty in comprehensively putting the world to rights in engaging harmony.

While the year 1963 had been enriched with many delights, also informing new friendships, it brought us an additional cherished blessing. Our second son, Jonathan, had arrived in the early autumn and proved to be a most contented baby, endlessly and happily gurgling his way through every day. These were relatively relaxed times which offered more opportunities to enjoy babyhood than had been the case while I was working in London. On one occasion Renna and I took young Jonathan to have some of his immunisation jabs. On the wall of the Doctor's waiting room was a large poster stressing the importance of all babies being suitably immunised. At its head it carried the bold injunction: "Remember, the first year of life is the most dangerous." Beneath it, some wag had scrawled "and the last one's not too hot either!"

The Music Programme 1964-8

Regrettably, our euphoric days in Birmingham were not to last. 1963 marked a period of enormous change and exhilarating opportunity for the BBC. We need to remember that up to that point the BBC had only been authorised to provide a single television channel. At this same time commercial television now began making its mark up and down the land, with important independent companies starting in London, Birmingham and Manchester. Commercial radio also made its mischievous first appearance with the arrival of Radio Caroline, a pop radio station broadcasting from a small ship bobbing around beyond territorial waters in the North Sea. Hitherto, listeners in Britain in search of commercial radio had mostly tuned to Radio Luxembourg, the now distant precursor of today's Classic FM.

Into this melting pot of far-reaching change, the BBC found itself with fresh opportunities which, under the inspiring and shrewd leadership of Director General, Sir Hugh Carlton Green, it was fully ready to seize with apparently unlimited enthusiasm. Securing for the first time the availability of a second television wavelength, the moment was now ripe for the arrival of BBC Two. This was where David Attenborough first made his indelible mark at the BBC. Invited, just a few short months after its initial launch, to become Director of BBC Two, David was able to reflect his own love of music and the arts in the programmes which the new service now offered and which had not easily found space when only a single BBC channel existed. As all the world knows, BBC programmes were soon thereafter to become significantly and beautifully enriched when the natural world ensnared him.

In the circumstances, one might have expected the spotlight on radio to be less compelling. No limelight comparable to that shed by a whole new glamorous world of television would brighten the landscape of radio as we knew it. Rather, radio's job was not to compete with television but to provide fresh complementary opportunities for listeners. One way in which many favoured bringing this about was to launch a good quality all-day music channel. A suitable wavelength was already available in that the Third Programme only broadcast in the evenings (preceded by occasional adult educational programmes grouped under the title *Study on Three*). So an untenanted wavelength existed and Music Division was expected to put it to good use.

This is where a personal role for me then appeared in that William Glock invited me to prepare and devise working schedules for an embryonic all-day music channel. In theory all should have been plain sailing at that point. But we had not sufficiently anticipated the enormous contractual difficulties which would be encountered in relation to both the MU[47] and the MCPS[48]. It might have been expected that all who stood to benefit would welcome the prospect of vast stretches of additional broadcasting time devoted to music. In particular, it was self-evident that significant new employment opportunities for musicians would exist. However, fundamental concerns emerged between interested parties. In a nutshell: the issues centred upon conflicting interests among those who stood to enjoy these new opportunities and responsibilities.

Leadership of BBC radio at the time principally rested with Frank Gillard[49] and Richard Marriott[50]. They favoured a broad formula whereby the BBC was to provide some seventy hours of new music broadcasting daily from 7am with some variable timings at the weekends. However, the plans foresaw extensive need to use what was then called 'needle time', the playing of gramophone records. The negotiations which had to be undertaken centred upon the requirement to reconcile the relative interests of making new programmes with using records to fill the remaining hours. In practice, this basically boiled down to a formula whereby forty of each seventy hours would be new material while gramophone records would fill the remaining thirty hours.

In today's much more flexible climate it may, at first sight, seem strange that the process of reaching a balanced agreement between newly contracted programmes and the use of gramophone records should have been as problematic as it proved. Protracted discussions ensued for many months in late 1963 and into 1964 before the long and tortuous process of negotiation could be completed.

Ultimately, this particularly hard-shelled nut was partially cracked by William Glock's imaginative proposal to form an entirely new orchestra to help sustain the live broadcasting load. Moreover, this orchestra's programme would be distinctively different in that it would include a specific training role to help strengthen the nation's young instrumental talent. The central concept here was a belief that to provide a one-year intensively structured and professionally directed training programme would materially enhance the quality of young

---

[47] MU – Musicians Union.
[48] MCPS – Mechanical Copyright Protection Society.
[49] DSB – Director of Sound Broadcasting shortly to be retitled MDR, Managing Director Radio.
[50] ADSB – Assistant Director of Sound Broadcasting.

instrumentalists emerging from our colleges and conservatoires. In due course the BBC's undertaking to provide new opportunities for young musicians in this way ultimately secured the support of the MU. Thus was born the BBC Training Orchestra, some seventy strong young musicians working and broadcasting from Colston Hall, Bristol, under the leadership of that great violinist and quartet leader, Leonard Hirsch.

Sadly, this project did not, in reality, flourish as strongly as we all hoped. Although the programmes by this young orchestra provided useful broadcasts, as well as a new dimension to the musical life in and around Bristol, the quality of the orchestra's playing seldom reached really acceptable levels. Ultimately the BBC Training Orchestra gave way to two other short-term BBC-funded schemes, one in London and one in Manchester. Both fulfilled useful training programmes but neither proved strong enough to continue beyond a few years.

Once the various complications had been resolved, it was decided to introduce the Music Programme in three specific phases. The first of these would be a weekly broadcast on Sundays. Our first day on the air was Sunday 30 August 1964 during which I vividly remember monitoring the whole day from the control channel and heaving a thankful sigh of relief at 5pm when all had gone well. Some weeks later we introduced morning broadcasts running from 7am until lunchtime, and the full Music Programme was finally implemented in the spring of 1965 when afternoon broadcasts completed the service.

Just as our spirited little Helen lit up our lives during my early days as a producer in London, while David's arrival presaged our move to Birmingham and Jonathan duly brought his invariably sunny contentment into our home, so it might be thought to have been timely that, just as the Music Programme launched its full daily schedule, our youngest son, Julius, followed Jonathan at a distance of a mere sixteen months, to start the vigorous and purposeful life he has always lived. Thus, just as the Music Programme established its full dimension so, too, came the joy and blessings our now complete family shared. [Plate 11]

The way was now clear for key decisions to be made as to how the vast tracts of seventy hours weekly new air time were to be filled. Some one-off decisions were universally welcomed and helped to strengthen character expectations for the new service. We resolved, for example, that we could open each Sunday's broadcasting with a Bach cantata, although such a concept in no way addressed the question of what was to be the general character of the new service.

There had been comfortable expectations in certain quarters that we would only broadcast 'agreeable' music which people could enjoy without undue effort. Naturally, within BBC Music Division such limited assumptions were resolutely contested. The broad agreement which ultimately emerged effectively led to a general understanding that our programmes would avoid undue provocation at a time when an otherwise diligent listener might cut himself whilst shaving. The watchword came from Frank Gillard in a memo to me which I cherish and which bore the heading: "NO BARTÓK BEFORE BREAKFAST". I doubt whether Frank himself expected that rule to remain unbroken for long.

As might have been anticipated, particularly spirited debate centred upon the place for opera in the new programme. It is amusing to reflect that there existed initially (but never within BBC Music Division) an assumption that extended opera broadcasts would drive listeners away. These curious reservations, vigorously entertained by Dick Marriott and others, led to a brief, but thankfully short-lived, compromise when it was suggested that we should 'serialise' *La Bohème*, capitalising upon Puccini's convenient foresight in having constructed his masterpiece in four quite compact acts. To general relief, these growing pains and reservations swiftly subsided and were soon cast aside. Before long the Music Programme was devoting each Thursday afternoon to a complete opera, with other operatic broadcasts at different points during the week.

As broadcasting throughout the week developed, so the Music Programme was able to feature a number of slots specifically devoted to such areas as very new music and very old music, with titles such as *Music In Our Time* swiftly becoming well-entrenched in the weekly broadcasting schedules. Much of what was heard had often not been broadcast previously, even in the Third Programme. Similarly, request programmes began to proliferate under such titles as *Your Midweek Choice* and these proved a popular way of filling the necessary tracts of needle-time.

The extended new hours available for music naturally meant that orchestras, groups and individuals up and down the land now found themselves with welcome opportunities for additional broadcasting engagements. Needless to say, the BBC Music Programme was very popular within the music profession on account of all the new opportunities it could provide. In addition, thanks to good relations with the European Broadcasting Union (EBU), we were also able to offer listeners more colour and diversity through repeating interesting programmes made available to the BBC by a wide range of European broadcasting organisations.

Magazine programmes devoted to music also featured strongly. We had inherited from the Home Service a hallowed Sunday feature entitled *Music Magazine*, traditionally presented by the well-loved team of Anna Instone and Julian Herbage. Meanwhile, those responsible for producing gramophone record programmes under the leadership of John Lade became ever more adept at creating themed listening to enhance the interest of increasingly attentive listeners.

As the Music Programme found its feet, so we introduced new activities designed particularly to bring the existence of the Music Programme more directly to the attention of the music-loving public. Two of these new enterprises, which we devised as we increasingly moved out of the studios and into selected public arenas, proved particularly popular and successful.

The first was to promote a competition for the performance of Mozart's piano concertos, something which also reflected William Glock's passionate concern to bring about improved stylistic assurance in the performance of Mozart's piano music. To this end we organised the BBC Mozart Piano Concerto Competition, held in Cardiff with the support of the then BBC Welsh Orchestra (now the National Orchestra of Wales). However, before reaching the concerto finals more than two hundred competitors from all over the world were first required to play Mozart's imperishable A minor *Rondo* which, as you might predict, effectively ruled out some eighty per cent of them. The forty-one competitors who survived that first round in London were then required to give a short recital to include one of five prescribed British piano works. These included piano sonatas by Alun Hoddinott and Michael Tippett.

Another piece in the selected list was Alan Rawsthorne's *Ballade*. Disappointingly, in the event, only one candidate was to choose it. She was Anne Pickup, a young girl from Blackpool, married to Gordon West, the Everton goalkeeper of the day. She gave a convincing performance of the *Ballade* which seemed to please Alan whom we had invited to be with us. At the reception we introduced Anne to Alan. He was, as usual, laconic and self-deprecating. Wine glass in hand, he thanked the young Anne for playing his piece and then asked her why she had selected it. Without a moment's hesitation, and in a broad Lancashire accent, she replied, "I just thought it were best o' bunch!" Alan smiled in his inimitable way, turned to me and said, "I have never in all my life found myself best o' bunch. It's a good feeling."

An impressive international jury, including Nadia Boulanger, assembled in Cardiff for the concerto stages of the competition. It was ultimately won by Oswald Russell, the son of the then newly independent Jamaica's Ambassador in Geneva. Inevitably, as with so many piano competitions, there was a less than rapturous response when the final result was announced. But what had undoubtedly been immensely beneficial for the profile of the Music Programme was that we had shown ourselves in Cardiff in a way which had attracted strong international attention.

One other distinctive competition, which did much to enhance the profile of the Music Programme, was the BBC Beethoven Competition held at Dartington in 1969. The competition was open to young teams playing Beethoven duos and trios. It was ultimately won by somebody destined to play a distinguished role in British music-making throughout all the succeeding years and one who is today still widely revered in chamber music circles: Levon Chilingirian whose partnership with the late Clifford Benson excelled in the Beethoven violin and piano sonatas.

Another important and effective way in which we were able to strengthen public awareness of the BBC Music Programme in face-to-face fashion was by organising a series of concentrated weekend celebrations (effectively mini festivals) in chosen university towns. These new events enjoyed increasingly enthusiastic support. We launched our first such university weekend in Cambridge in 1968 and in a fashion which gave these university weekends invaluable initial impetus. This first festival enjoyed many distinctive and distinguished features such as participation by, among others, Elliott Carter, Luigi Dallapiccola and Roberto Gerhard, whose own *Libra* we commissioned for first performance during the weekend. I am only sorry that the BBC did not choose to continue this stimulating series.

Within the BBC there existed a generous tradition to mark the departure of retiring or resigning members. This generally took the form of a small autograph book widely circulated in advance of each departure. I shall long cherish the one which BBC colleagues presented to me on my retirement. Two entries gave me particular pleasure. One, which I happily repeat here acknowledging the subtlety with which the author gently scored a neat goal against me, took the form of an inimitably ambiguous comment by Hans Keller, who wrote: "I am sure we will not be less in touch than we have been." Another, which I greatly valued, came from Frank Gillard, who was generous enough to write: "Congratulations on your first BBC career. I hope it will not be long before you start your second."

That was not to be. But I was invited, a few years later when Sir William Glock's retirement was approaching, to come and discuss the position of Controller Music with Ian Trethowan, by then Frank Gillard's successor as Managing Director Radio and shortly himself to become Director General of the BBC. The prospect was obviously very alluring, but I was only one year into my time at the RNCM, with our building programme incomplete and our new courses yet to start. Therefore, I could not, in all conscience, consider taking matters further.

```
01-580 4468                              BROADCASTING HOUSE
Broadcasts London-W1
Telex 22182                              LONDON W.1

                                         7th January 1969

    Dear Manduell,

        On the occasion of your resignation I am
    writing to express the BBC's great appreciation
    of your valuable services to our music output,
    regional and national, over the past twelve
    years.  Our special thanks are due to you for
    your contribution to the development of the
    Music Programme from its inception.

        I wish you every success and happiness as
    Director of the new Music Department of the
    University of Lancaster.

                    Yours sincerely,

                    Hugh Greene

                    Director-General


    J. Manduell, Esq.,
    c/o Barclays Bank Ltd.,
    67 Sandgate Road,
    Folkestone,
    Kent.
```

Letter to John from the Director General of the BBC.

Prague Spring

In 1964 I was delighted to be able to accept an invitation to represent the British Council at the Prague Spring Festival. I had never hitherto had any opportunity to penetrate the Iron Curtain and was conscious of being woefully ignorant about twentieth-century Czech music and musicians. The opportunity to remedy both these shortcomings and enjoy the exhilaration of sponsored travel and exploration was irresistible.

Arrangements for my journey to Czechoslovakia were conducted by the Foreign Office with all the protocol-driven precision attaching to such official visits. These even extended to the point where, to Renna's and my amusement, I found I was being insured against disappearance for two years in the sum of £10,000. This led us to think that it might prove advantageous if I could slip off to a cave in the Tatra Mountains, write music for a couple of years and then emerge once she had collected the compensation pay-out. As I was to discover, however, many aspects of conditions in Czechoslovakia would have hardly been conducive to enjoying any such form of exile.

Armed with an array of official documentation, including much advice on the exercise of due discretion in Communist territories, I duly prepared for this mission. But it began, not only badly, but most alarmingly. My plane for Prague was due to leave late on a given morning. I had therefore arranged to drive to Heathrow from our home in Solihull, making an early departure. Getting up before dawn, I took my little green mini (affectionately known as "The Bomb" after its registration number 109 BOM) out of the garage and placed in the boot my document-laden briefcase, newly purchased for the purpose. I then returned to the house for a nourishing cooked breakfast which Renna had prepared, only to find when I emerged that 'Bomb' had disappeared from the drive.

Stupidly, I had left the ignition key in place and there was I, about to undertake my first government-backed overseas mission, visualising all the necessary official papers being now in the clutches of someone who had been bright enough to see me bring the car out of the garage and who had then seized what must have seemed an attractive opportunity for an unexpectedly easy theft. As a consequence, and hours before any official might have reached his desk in London, I not only found myself alerting the police, but also preparing to advise the relevant authorities of my folly and the resulting situation. The police were wonderfully helpful, while my masters in London took a reassuringly calm view of the situation, refraining in polite restrained Whitehall fashion from explicitly telling me what an idiot I had been. Once all the alarm bells had been rung there was little to do but accept that this was now a case of mission terminated and to resolve that, at the very least, I would never again leave a car with the ignition keys in place, even in the supposed privacy of one's own drive.

To my relief and surprise, my despondent mood was interrupted towards lunchtime by a call from the police to say that 'Bomb' had been found in the car park of Birmingham's Elmdon Airport. Any reassurance I may have felt then speedily gave way to visualising a situation in which the car thief, after examining the contents of my briefcase, had decided to impersonate me and take a trip to Prague. Urgent fresh phone calls to London met with the same calm response and also an indication that the emigration authorities at Heathrow would be alerted in case anyone seeking to board a plane to Prague should present my passport.

Once 'Bomb' had been recovered some two hours later I found, on opening the boot, that my briefcase was apparently untouched and precisely as I had left it. It seemed that the boot had never been opened while an examination of 'Bomb's' interior suggested that the joyrider(s) had been fairly juvenile in that the most indicative clue they had left was that the steering wheel and door handles were smeared with the kind of mustard generally served with Frankfurter hotdogs.

While still consumed with mortification, I now had the task of advising my minders in London that all was apparently well again, which of course led to fresh signals being sent to Prague and, to my delight, agreement being given that a new booking for a flight to Prague the following day should be made. It was with considerable relief that Renna and I downed a couple of gins before retiring for what would necessarily be another short night, prior to my driving to Heathrow the next morning as originally planned.

On my first full day in Prague I was invited to join a luncheon given by the British Ambassador, Sir Cecil Parrott[51], and his charm-

---

[51] Two years later, in 1966, Sir Cecil would be appointed Professor of Russian and Soviet Studies at the University of Lancaster.

ing Norwegian wife, Ellen. In his youth, and up to the outbreak of war in 1939, Parrott had been private tutor to King Peter of Yugoslavia in Belgrade. Joining the diplomatic service at that point, he held successive posts in Oslo, where he met Ellen, and subsequently in Stockholm for the remainder of the war. Thereafter he enjoyed progressively more prestigious appointments in Brussels and Moscow before moving to Prague in 1960 as our Ambassador. He was also a very capable amateur pianist. According to Foreign Office legend he sometimes employed an ingenious and original way of charming official guests in that, prior to them being shown into his office, he would be installed at the far end, playing a fine grand piano. After feigning for a few moments to be unaware that his guest had been shown in, he would abruptly break off to offer his guest a warm greeting. In this way he would often establish from the outset an agreeably relaxed and cultured atmosphere in readiness for the encounter to follow.

An unusual feature of the British Embassy in Prague is that, being built on a steep hill, its spacious lawned garden at the back is effectively some floors above street level. It offers a wonderfully peaceful separation from all the urban bustle below on the other side of the building. Foregathered at a long table to enjoy Embassy hospitality were several important musical luminaries. They included the great Czech violinist, Josef Suk, son of his namesake father, the composer who had married Dvořák's daughter, and Suk's pianist partner in an untold number of great recitals, Jan Panenka. Another distinguished pianist also present was Shura Cherkassky, who had just arrived in readiness for his scheduled appearance at the Prague Spring festival a few days later. He had been accompanied on his flight from London by the redoubtable Emmie Tillett, doyenne among London's concert agents, who managed Cherkassky's affairs. The other guests included the inevitable representatives of Pragokonzert, the all-encompassing controlling body for music throughout Czechoslovakia, to whom, given the official nature of my visit, I would necessarily have to turn in order to develop desirable contacts.

At one delightful moment, the senior Pragokonzert representative turned to Cherkassky and, speaking across the table, suggested that Cherkassky might care to accompany him to select the piano he would play at his forthcoming recital, to which the official added that he could choose between Petrof[52] and Steinway models. Without a moment's hesitation Cherkassky, who had a curious habit of speaking through his teeth, apparently without moving his jaws, unhesitatingly grated, "Steinway, of course." Thereupon, I was aware of a sudden movement by Emmie, sitting next to me, followed immediately by a convulsive jerk from Cherkassky sitting opposite her. I could only conclude that Emmie had administered a sharp diplomatic correction under the table. At all events smiles then ensued when a visit to the Petrof showroom was agreed.

Diplomatic observance, as I was speedily to learn, was a dominant and inescapable factor in so many aspects of Czech life under President Navotny's hard regime at the time. This could even be reflected in such relatively mundane contexts as hotel arrangements, something brought home to me quite vividly by Wesley Woods, our cultural attaché who had only recently arrived in Prague and was waiting to be joined from Canada by his wife. He had suffered a very disagreeable experience on arrival at his designated hotel when he had discovered that his bed was actively occupied by attendant bedbugs. This had driven him to sleeping on the floor. During the night a telephone call had come through from his wife asking him, "How is the hotel?" to which a drowsy Wesley murmured, "Seriously flawed – I've even been floored!" At a reception a few days later, Wesley found himself in conversation with a Czech official who revealed himself to be a member of the country's security apparatchik. As their chat developed, the official, voicing pride in his organisation's capacity to deal with coded messages, then actually asked him if he could explain the 'flawed / floored' conundrum. He was much relieved to be given a simple explanation to resolve his homonymic confusion.

A revealing domestic sequel to this exchange followed sometime later. After Wesley's wife had arrived in Prague and a new bed had been installed, she complained to Wesley one night about the hardness of the hotel towels. Within the hour, and without any direct request having been made to the hotel management,

---

[52] Petrof – acknowledged as the premiere Czech-built piano, also widely respected and played abroad. Celebrations in 1964 marked the centenary of the firm's foundation by Antonín Petrof.

a chambermaid arrived bearing new soft towels. 'Gromek'[53] had clearly done his stuff.

It was common knowledge that counterpart Gromeks were installed not only in all apartments occupied by visitors of any importance, and in selected hotel rooms, but also in the homes of a great many Czech citizens. An American diplomat working in Prague at the time told me how the inevitable Gromek, residing in his dining room chandelier, tended to divert guests with a persistent hissing – conceivably, it might fancifully be thought, in response to the contents of the conversation to which that particular Gromek had been listening. When this became too irritating, the American occupants had found that, doubtless due to some questionable wiring, the only way to pacify Gromek was to walk down the length of the apartment and slam shut the door to the washroom at the end of the corridor. Apparently this was always effective.

A comparably ridiculous pantomime was also enacted whenever our military attaché set out. His Embassy car would invariably be followed by a black Czech limousine which the attaché's driver was instructed to keep under observation in his rear mirror. If, as had been known to occur, the pursuing security vehicle were to stop for a mechanical reason or to change a tyre, diplomatic courtesy demanded that the Embassy driver should get out and, with due ostentation, appear to study a map until, with order apparently restored, the cavalcade could proceed.

Much more frustrating were the obstacles I was to encounter in pursuing meetings with, or sight of works by, leading Czech composers, contact with whom was part of my own mission while in Prague. Responses to questions I might ask during visits to the Czech Composers' Union offices could prove as contradictory as they were perplexing. For example, Petr Eben[54], a leading Czech

---

[53] Gromek – the identity ascribed to the omnipresent listening device, of which everyone was constantly aware.

[54] A Czech composer whose music I was able to introduce to Britain when I arranged for his Piano Concerto to be played by the incomparable John Ogdon at the Cheltenham Festival. Years later I was fortunately able to persuade Charles University in Prague to release Petr Eben in order that he could spend a year at the RNCM guiding Anthony Gilbert's composition students while the latter was on sabbatical, bringing Australia the benefits of his inspirational teaching.

composer, might well not have been regarded as persona grata had it not been for the fact that his works were being played quite widely in the West. He was somebody who consistently refused to become a card-carrying Communist Party member, as had all his three gifted sons, and a distant relative, Ilja Hurník, a prominent satirist. Eben was also a committed Catholic, writing fine religious music which, needless to add, was rigorously excluded by the Czech authorities whenever possible. [Plate 12]

Because the Czech Composers' Union was entirely staffed by loyal party officials, I frequently found that enquiries I might make about this or that composer were unhelpfully received, even to the point where the very existence of a composer might be denied. This, for example, extended to affected ignorance of music by Miloslav Kabeláč, even though he was known to have some eight symphonies to his credit. To circumvent these difficulties I was guided in the direction of a restaurant quite near St. Vitus' Cathedral. This restaurant took its name, The Living Wood, from its very attractive timber construction, with artificial branches sweeping through the main hall and curling round individual tables. Good music was constantly played through speakers placed within this attractive woodwork, which conveniently prevented any stray Gromeks from overhearing confidential conversations. More than one meal in this restaurant proved very helpful in achieving the contacts I was seeking to establish.

Just as Petr Eben's situation was eased by the relative popularity of his music abroad, so the interests of another composer, Victor Kalabis, were protected in a different way. He enjoyed official approval not because he was a particularly good or interesting composer – frankly, I felt he was neither – nor was he protected by being a prominent and faithful Communist Party member. In his case his good fortune derived simply from the fact that he was married to the harpsichordist, Zuzana Růžičková. She enjoyed a worldwide reputation as a harpsichordist of undeniable distinction and was also loyally supportive and protective of her husband.

By contrast, the position of another Czech composer presented an altogether different case. This was Václav Dobiáš who held high rank within official circles as effectively Czechoslovakia's Minister for Music, if not Minister for Culture. Automatically, in view of the official nature of my visit, formal arrangements had been made for me to meet with Dobiáš, whose music I had taken the opportunity to study. I had been genuinely struck by an accomplished octet he had written, on which I had no hesitation in complimenting him. This clearly afforded him great pleasure and led to an immediate invitation to visit him at his home in the country a few days later in order that he could play me some more of his music.

It was agreed that he would call for me at my hotel, which he did. Rather to my surprise, I found that his official driver had apparently been laid off and that he was going to drive me himself to his private home in a village quite distant from Prague. This was to be a journey to remember on account of the fact that he proved to be one of those drivers who can never maintain a constant speed. His foot would alternately depress and release the accelerator pedal, and it was in this convulsive way that we then proceeded, never very fast and often quite slowly, until we reached our destination. However, for some inexplicable reason, this pattern was altered whenever we passed through a village. Then the accelerator would be strenuously depressed and we would roar through the streets, scattering poultry and children alike.

I wondered if an explanation for such erratic behaviour might be that some officials in vulnerable positions of authority may be prone to rising blood pressure when finding themselves in too close proximity to the proletariat. These alarms apart, Dobiáš and his wife proved to be delightful hosts, and the dinner I was served was distinctive in that succulent slices of venison were served with a variety of fresh vegetables replacing the apologetic pickled gherkin which, for most Czech people denied any imported out-of-season produce, represented the only green vegetable then available at the end of a long winter.

Lancaster University

During my later years at the BBC I found myself feeling more and more dissatisfied with what I increasingly came to see as the ephemera of broadcasting. Yes, we could devise wonderfully original, stimulating, even extraordinary programmes and, yes, we could repeat them frequently. But, in the final analysis, their life was limited. This led me to feel progressively drawn towards exploring alternative musical avenues. Indeed, it was often said at the time that if it was difficult to secure appointment to the BBC, it was still more difficult to secure release. True or not, these sentiments were somewhat reinforced for me by the rather depressing example set by senior BBC officials who had swiftly risen in the ranks but then found themselves unable to progress further.

One day, a visitor unintentionally set my thoughts heading in the direction of academia. John Clegg, a contemporary Cambridge Jesuan who had read mathematics, also displayed remarkable fluency and technical strength as a pianist. After coming down he had successfully maintained a dual career as both mathematician and musician. His life as a pianist took wing and periodically he was able not only to give recitals in Britain but to undertake a number of overseas tours as a British Council envoy. It was in this capacity, therefore, that our paths had crossed again. One of the principal responsibilities of the British Council's Music Department, whose advisory committee I was later to chair, was to pursue a dedicated policy of disseminating British music and musicians abroad. As part of this programme John would be invited to undertake overseas tours, and it was in order to plot such a visit to East Africa that he had come to see me. He mentioned that he was moving, as a Senior Lecturer in Mathematics, to Lancaster University where, he told me, some discussion about establishing a music department was also in train.

What initially for me was only idle interest concerning Lancaster, grew to the point where, when I had the pleasure of welcoming John back from his tour, I asked him to keep me informed about possible developments at the new university. This he duly did. It appeared that Professor Sir Cecil Parrott, whose hospitality in Prague I had enjoyed a few years previously, had, on his retirement from the

Foreign Office, assumed the Chair of Russian and Soviet Studies at Lancaster University. According to Clegg, Parrott was keen to bring music to the University, and had extended an invitation to Vladimir Ashkenazy[55], whom Parrott had known while serving at the British Embassy in Moscow, to undertake a recital for the University.

It was not long before the University took the step of agreeing, in principle, to move towards establishing a department of music. It should be remembered that, at that time, the University was very young. Indeed, it only obtained its Royal Charter in 1964 and therefore was a mere four years old when I had the pleasure of attending an interview with the Vice-Chancellor. Lancaster was, in fact, one of a small clutch of universities established in the early '60s, well before polytechnics began to aspire to university status. Another member of this group, the University of York, also received its Royal Charter at this time, and this was to herald a stimulating new Roses rivalry between these latter-day representatives of the Houses of York and Lancaster.

Lancaster had made a shrewd choice in appointing as its first Vice-Chancellor a man who was both a Quaker and an Economist – surely an ideal amalgam for such a task. Though naturally quiet, reticent and even shy by nature, Sir Charles Carter, as he became when duly knighted, proved to be a wonderfully wise and effective leader. [Plate 13] Exercising clear and decisive judgement, he made a number of strong appointments of fine scholars to establish and lead those disciplines in which Lancaster soon excelled, among them physics, mathematics, engineering and languages.

A number of the University's early leaders were also soon to become good friends, notably Philip Reynolds (Politics), destined to succeed Carter as the University's second Vice-Chancellor, together with Emlyn Lloyd (Mathematics), Austin Woolrych (History) and Tom Lawrenson (French). These four, and several others, were enormously encouraging and helpful when we came to set up the music department. So, too, were several key members of the University's senior administration, such as Stephen Jeffreys, Merton

---

[55] Sir Cecil Parrott's initiative had brought about what was effectively the University's first music promotion, although necessarily held in the town's Ashton Hall because this was shortly before the University moved from a temporary location in the town to the rural site it now occupies.

Atkins and Michael Forster (collectively heading the University's academic secretariat), together with Graham Mackenzie and Michael Argles (Librarians). With many of them friendship was also delightfully consolidated through our shared endeavours on behalf of the Lancaster University staff cricket XI.

Unassuming and gentle as Charles Carter may have been, he also had the capacity to respond with prompt and clear advice when any of us had need to consult him. Although inevitably obliged to devote enormous time and energy to representing the University's interests at large, he consistently maintained concern for every separate cog in the University wheel. One knew that if one sent Charles an internal memo seeking advice, one could be assured of a very prompt, clear and helpful reply. I shall always regard him as being one of the two men – the other being Sir William Glock – for whom I have worked and from whom I have learnt the most, especially regarding the challenges and trials of leadership. In particular, Charles once gave me some advice which I enormously valued when he cautioned against the difficulty of delegating comprehensively to a single deputy[56] if such delegation could more advantageously be spread among two or more.

I arrived in Lancaster to take up my appointment in November 1968. John and Marcelle Clegg kindly invited me to stay with them until my College flat was ready. The University had just moved to its site at Bailrigg, formerly a large farm on the west side of the M6 motorway, occupying a beautiful raised position which allowed for a sweeping view of Morecambe Bay and the Cumbrian Fells beyond. Indeed, the very presence of this glorious landscape could create a taxing distraction during the course of a Senate meeting. One could sit there marvelling at nature as the sun gently sank below the ocean horizon. At the same time, any natural inclination to slumber might be rudely challenged by the need to wrestle with tortuous wording attaching to a plethora of statutes governing the University's procedures. Inevitably, as befitted a young university, we were obliged to draft many provisions from scratch: happily, we were largely able to do so with good humour and a merciful absence of concern for established tradition.

---

[56] Ironically, Glock himself was to discover this difficulty after Professor Gerald Abraham was appointed ACMus (Assistant Controller Music).

Among Carter's many convictions, as he prepared to mould the University's structure, was a firm belief in the collegiate system. This encouraged the architects, Gaby Epstein and Peter Shepheard, to prepare their plans for the new university on the basis that there would be both college buildings and departmental buildings. All the colleges were conveniently sited within the campus and enjoyed locally derived names, the first clutch being Bowland, Lonsdale, Cartmel, County[57], Fylde and Furness. Each member of academic staff was designated to a college, in my case, Furness. One of the many attractive but practical features of Epstein's designs was the overhead protection provided for many of the campus walkways – no small advantage given the unfriendly elements all too prevalent in the north west of England.

Another example of fortuitous timing was that, shortly before I arrived, the University's extensive and ambitious building programme actually saw completion of the music department. It provided for a small square galleried recital hall, a separate library, half a dozen tutorial rooms and a comparable number of practice rooms, together with an attractive open air Roman-style well and one or two other rooms with useful potential. Such early progress in constructing the music department had only become possible on account of a very generous gift from the band leader, Jack Hylton. Without his munificence we certainly would not have been endowed with either the recital hall or some of the other facilities. Naturally, because it had been completed so promptly, I had had no opportunity to influence the plans, but they had been prepared with some good understanding of the professional requirements and also, at the same time, with much imagination.

The University generously allowed me a free hand in preparing more detailed plans of the ways in which we would occupy and develop these glistening new premises. When our competitive counterpart in the University of York had started life a year or two before us, its first Professor of Music, Wilfrid Mellers, had decided to found the work of his new department upon the appointment of a gifted group of rising young composers. I concluded, therefore, that it might be logical for Lancaster to mirror York by concentrating

---

[57] County College: its title reflected the fact that the entire building cost was borne by Lancashire County Council.

upon the development of skills in performance, but with a clear measure of emphasis on the music of our time. While the availability of resources would inevitably always be key, I was able to establish with the Vice-Chancellor an understanding that if I could raise significant support externally for this or that project the University would then endeavour to complement that funding.

One of the first steps I took was to seek the goodwill of Alexander Schouvaloff, then Chief Executive of the North West Arts Association (NWAA)[58]. As was characteristic of Alex throughout a long and distinguished career, eventually culminating in his appointment as Founder Curator of the Theatre Museum in Covent Garden, he was immediately responsive to the approach I made. The outcome was that NWAA generously agreed to fund fifty percent of the salaries to enable us to move swiftly towards creating the Lancaster Ensemble, a chamber group consisting of pianist and string quartet, with specific performance and teaching obligations.

We were able to persuade the gifted British pianist, David Wilde to join us. David was already a national figure after winning the International Bartók Competition in Budapest as well as an important national competition in Liverpool. For the string quartet we held auditions in London at the Wigmore Hall and found ourselves faced with a difficult decision in choosing between two young quartets, both of which were bursting with a stimulating sense of zeal and mission to bring exciting music-making to a new university. We ultimately settled upon a quartet formed by the violinist, Harry Cawood. Harry made his mark in the University with a demonic performance of the Bach Chaconne for Solo Violin. Tall, dark and lean, he seemed to some to offer a mesmeric reincarnation of Paganini himself.

Thus was formed the Lancaster Ensemble. To develop the department's faculty further, I approached the Granada Foundation for help in establishing a post for a composer. Here again, good fortune smiled upon us in that the rising young English composer Anthony Gilbert proved enthusiastically ready to sail into our new and uncharted waters as the University's Granada Fellow in

---

[58] NWAA – at this time the Arts Council of Great Britain, having abandoned a policy of regional departments, had established a group of self-governing and largely independent area Arts Associations.

Composition. Several other interesting but part-time appointments followed.

Turning aside from more traditional areas of study, I was also particularly concerned to establish within the music department an electronics studio. To this end we were fortunately able to secure a National Research Council grant. This timely award allowed us to commission Tristram Cary to mastermind the installation of a studio such as he had earlier established at the Royal College of Music. At that time, Tristram enjoyed a position of unchallenged prominence in the burgeoning world of innovative electronic music but, to Britain's misfortune, he was shortly to devote his initiative and inspiration to work in Australia. While use of our studio as a laboratory facility was not developed to its full potential before I left the University to head to Manchester, sufficient progress had been made to prompt the distinguished American composer, Professor Milton Babbitt, to pay us a visit.

One of the most forbidding challenges confronting us in establishing a brand new music department was that of building from scratch a good music library. Here again we were greatly assisted by a stroke of fortuitous timing. Hans Redlich, the distinguished Austrian music scholar, who formerly occupied the Chair of Music in the University of Manchester, had recently died. It was known that Redlich possessed a particularly fine personal library. Without hesitation, the University Librarian, Graham Mackenzie, agreed that he would support our initiating enquiries, whereupon the University's Assistant Librarian, Michael Argles, a committed music enthusiast, became directly involved in a project to acquire the Redlich collection.

While taking care not to be insensitive to anyone sorrowing in widow's weeds, Michael actually contrived to talk to Redlich's widow before his funeral had taken place. This revealed confirmation that her husband had not bequeathed his extraordinary library to the University of Manchester or to any other institution. It was then agreed that we could visit her a few days after the funeral to pursue the matter further. To our great delight we were able to return to Lancaster having secured her agreement in principle to the University acquiring this outstanding collection. The necessary legal processes were completed with uncharacteristic speed and encountered no difficulties or complications. The result was that Redlich's library arrived with remarkable rapidity to adorn the beautiful oak shelving with which the department had been provided. To this day the Redlich Collection remains one of the University's most distinctive acquisitions.

While these developments were proceeding, another very important new project was in progress: the building of the University's Great Hall. Happily, I was invited by the architect, Gaby Epstein, to participate in some of the deliberations and to make suggestions from a musical standpoint. All concerned were keen to obtain sufficiently good acoustic results to provide us with an effective 1,000-seater concert hall. From the start musicians, and indeed broadcasters, took a positive view of the sound the hall offers, and it was not long before it found itself in regular demand from the BBC and other users. Apart from formal occasions such as large scale degree congregations, the hall remains to this day a centre for regular term-time concerts. Fine as it became upon completion, the hall presented a very different picture during the early stages of construction when only tall steel girders could be seen rising out of the winter mud. I remember a delightful occasion when Alan Rawsthorne was with us to hear a recital by Renna and Brigid Ranger in which they played his violin sonata. I took him over to see how the building was progressing. There we were, in our gumboots, surveying the quagmire site when Alan was prompted to remark in his own inimitable laconic style: "Well, I suppose it could turn into a hanger big enough to hold a Zeppelin."

Building progressed with sufficient speed to enable me to believe, with a measure of confidence that, to coincide with the start of our course work, we could introduce, from the autumn of 1969, an ambitious series of weekly concerts. Quite apart from wishing to establish a strong initial impact for music at Lancaster, I was also much encouraged to think in appropriately broad-ranging terms by the realisation that no regular music-making of more than local significance was then to be found anywhere in rural England north of Liverpool and Manchester. It was therefore entirely reasonable to conclude that encouraging results could follow from attempting to plug this large geographical gap. Our concerts would not only proclaim the arrival of the Music Department, but would, at the same time, provide a glittering shop window for the whole university, still only six short years from foundation. The outcome was that by the spring of 1969 we were able to announce a series of subscription concerts starting in October under a broad generic title, adapted from the traditional three Bs but now reading "BARTÓK, BEETHOVEN AND BRITISH".

To launch our first season we were able to invite the Ulster Orchestra, then touring Britain under its widely admired Hungarian conductor, János Fürst. The orchestra's visit enabled us to mark the occasion in two distinctive ways. One was to express our appreciation to John Clegg for all that he had contributed to the establishment of music at Lancaster by inviting him to appear as soloist in Beethoven's C minor Piano Concerto. The other was that the Vice-Chancellor had also generously agreed that a new work I had written to launch the concert, my overture *Sunderland Point*, could also serve as my personal introduction to the University, thus sparing colleagues the necessity of listening to yet one more inaugural presentation lecture!

I was very keen that this overture, written during August, should carry an appropriately Lancastrian flavour. To this end, I headed to Cecil Sharp House in London where I was delighted to unearth a number of traditional folksongs which had been collected in the Lancaster area. Three of these appealed to me in particular and, by a happy coincidence, all three had been sung to the intrepid Anne Gilchrist[59] during her visits to Sunderland Point and Overton village in Easter 1906, and again to Sunderland Point and Grayrigg three years later. The overture makes no pretensions to being anything more than a melodic mix of three traditional songs with local associations. The work was dedicated to my friend and erstwhile colleague, Michael Whewell, who had left the BBC to become Director of the Arts Council of Northern Ireland, where the Ulster Orchestra was the province's indisputable jewel.

If the initial concert had been true to two elements in our tripartite Bartók / Beethoven / British billing, the second concert in the series underlined the Beethoven theme with early and late piano sonatas played by David Wilde. The following week, Sir Peter Maxwell Davis and his Pierrot Players ensured that we should not be thought insular in a programme of Berg, Berio and Schoenberg. This strong European blast was reinforced two weeks later by the

---

[59] Anne Gilchrist dedicated her life to collecting, indexing and publishing English folksongs. Recognised internationally, and awarded an OBE in 1948, she died at Lancaster in 1954, aged 90.

Budapest Chamber Ensemble, which, under András Mihály, brought works by Kurtág, Székely and Stravinsky.

The next Thursday the Netherlands Chamber Orchestra, under Szymon Goldberg, still further emphasised our belief in music from our own times with works by Stravinsky and Webern. This concert also reflected a few features in which, as a new organisation, we could perhaps take some particular pride. The Netherlands Chamber Orchestra was the third major international ensemble to visit us within six short weeks. This concert was also notable for being the first occasion on which we enjoyed sponsorship from both the University Arts Trust and the Arts Council of Great Britain. It was also the first occasion on which we raised the price of a programme from sixpence (five pence) to a shilling (ten pence)!

Our first Bartók celebration occurred when the Vegh Quartet brought us not only playing by one of the most outstanding quartets of the day but, when performing Bartók's fifth quartet, also demonstrated authentic colour deriving from direct study with Bartók himself. In turn, a concert of works by the Master of the Queen's Musick, Sir Arthur Bliss, featured both the first performance of his then new song cycle, *Angels of the Mind*, together with his Clarinet Quintet. This was a particularly happy occasion in that when we were planning these new concerts, I had asked Bliss if he would honour us by becoming President of Lancaster University Concerts. Characteristically, he had agreed by return, in a letter written from home in his own meticulous neat script. His presence and his new work therefore brought additional lustre to this concert.

We started the New Year with a particularly exciting concert by the London Sinfonietta, whose visit was only made possible through being generously sponsored by the Arts Council of Great Britain. Clarinettist Alan Hacker gave a riveting performance from his wheelchair of Alexander Goehr's *Monteverdi Paraphrase*. This was then followed by Roberto Gerhard's recent *Leo* before fun and games returned with Walton's *Façade*. Our concentration on living British composers was next enriched by a visit from Richard Rodney Bennett. He won many new friends among our students with his engagingly relaxed style in a programme devoted to his chamber music.

In February the BBC promoted a stimulating concert by the Philip Jones Brass Ensemble. The following week a hushed Great Hall, full to its distinctively decorated rafters, was spellbound during a recital by Julian Bream in sublimely intoxicating form. Just two days later such calm intimacy was invigoratingly dispelled by a challenging concert in which Bartók's extraordinary Sonata for Two Pianos and Percussion was contrasted with Stockhausen's *Zyklus*.

In March we were treated to some spectacular large ensemble playing by the legendary Czech Nonet. Their imaginative programme expanded progressively from Beethoven's Septet via Alun Hoddinott's *Octet* to Martinů's Nonet. The Spring Term ended with the first national symphony orchestra to grace the Great Hall when Bryden ('Jack') Thomson conducted the BBC Northern Symphony Orchestra (now the BBC Philharmonic) in a programme which sustained our Bartók theme in particularly exciting fashion, with a performance of his second piano concerto by David Wilde.

Three events of extraordinary distinction marked a short experimental season during May. In the first of these Victoria de los Angeles, in pristine voice and accompanied by her dedicated compatriot, Miguel Zanetti, gave a wholly memorable recital. The glamour of the occasion was signalled by our raising the price of a programme to two shillings (20 pence)!

The following week the legendary Nadia Boulanger honoured us twice: first, by presenting a riveting study of French song, illustrated by Janet Price and David Wilde, and, two weeks later, by generously chairing the jury for the final of the BBC's Composers Competition. Incidentally, this was effectively the last broadcast event for which I had been able to sow a few initial seeds before I left the BBC.

If our first season had proved invigoratingly successful and had attracted gratifyingly large audiences, this only threw down a clear challenge to us to match it in the second. This task seemed all the greater when we reflected that there remained an all-important area of music which had yet to feature. This, of course, was opera. Happily, we twice found distinctive ways to remedy this defect in the course of the second season.

Our first programme, in October 1970, encouragingly demonstrated the extent to which a year working together had sharpened the skills of our resident Lancaster Ensemble. It also sustained our fidelity to living British composers by including the first performance of *Nocturnal* for piano quintet by John McCabe. The printed programme underlined the arrival of the new era of decimal currency in which we were now living, by being charged at precisely five pence. This concert was matched a fortnight later when we had the pleasure of welcoming another university ensemble, the Cardiff University String Quartet who, at the wish of the BBC, included a quartet I had been commissioned to write for first performance at that summer's Cardiff Festival.

Beethoven and British were again to the fore the following week when the Kellaway / Ranger duo launched a series of seven recitals devoted to all Beethoven's violin sonatas and piano trios. Their programme on this occasion also included a new sonata by Cardiff University professor, Alun Hoddinott, which Brigid and Renna had premiered a few weeks earlier in their Purcell Room, London, recital.

Two days later a concert of rare distinction excited much interest within the University since it featured the poet laureate, Cecil Day-Lewis, along with the gifted young poet, Chrys Salt, and the BBC Northern Singers under Stephen Wilkinson. They came together under the title *The Turning Year*, a seasonal miscellany of verse and music. The Vice-Chancellor generously undertook to host the occasion and the poet laureate's visit, while the cost of printing a fairly elaborate programme justified us in stimulating inflation by doubling the programme cost to the princely sum of ten pence! Distinction of an altogether different order ensued the following week when, to another hushed full hall, Alfred Brendel gave a recital of no fewer than five Beethoven sonatas, culminating in the great E major, op. 109.

If the visit of the Czech Nonet during our first season had been an occasion for quite outstanding music-making so, too, was the visit now of the Melos Ensemble, whose concert paired two immortal masterpieces of Schubert: the string quintet and *The Trout*. Melodies of a very different order then followed when Cleo Laine and John Dankworth came to give one of their matchlessly intimate concerts, an occasion which also attracted BBC microphones. During the first season we had introduced a plebiscite scheme whereby our audiences had been invited to vote for works which they would particularly like to hear the Lancaster Ensemble repeat. Predictably perhaps, this exercise in family favourites yielded more Beethoven, but Bartók and British now gave way to Brahms and Dvořák.

As Christmas drew near we were able, for the very first time, to offer our audiences opera. Thankfully it proved possible to do so by presenting a memorable concert performance of Beethoven's *Fidelio*. The occasion represented a carefully prepared and long-planned celebration to mark Beethoven's bicentenary. Our concert took place on 10 December 1970, just six days before the anniversary of Beethoven's birth in Bonn on 16 December 1770.

Our *Fidelio* presented a glittering cast of Pauline Tinsley as Leonora and Ronald Dowd as Florestan, supported by a galaxy of leading singers of the day such as Richard van Allan, Teresa Cahill, Raimund Herincx and Robert Lloyd, together with the Royal Liverpool Philharmonic Orchestra, our own University Chorus with additional choruses drawn from Liverpool University and St. Martin's College, Lancaster. All were guided through this great masterpiece with majestical authority by Sir Charles Groves. Needless to say, none of this would have been remotely possible but for the remarkable generosity of the Arts Council of Great Britain in providing a significantly handsome degree of sponsorship.

The outcome of the whole event was also both dominated and threatened by national circumstances over which we could exercise only limited control. This was the period during which Edward Heath's government was battling through its three-day week torment. One consequence was that power cuts occurred with tiresome frequency at unpredictable points. Opera devotees will recall that, at the beginning of act two, the first words uttered by Florestan in his deep dungeon cell are "how dark it is down here". What steps could we take to anticipate and guard against the threat of the hall suddenly being plunged into murky darkness? With some cunning the University authorities had managed to establish with Norweb[60] an agreement whereby they would try to give us limited warning of an imminent cut. As another precaution we brought in gas fired lighting generators which could have been used, albeit after some delay, had the worst occurred. However, it did not, Florestan remained in view and a performance of great power and eloquence proceeded without further hazard.

Our first concert in the New Year reflected another fraternal University gesture, in that we had invited the Orion Trio from Southampton University to bring us performances of Beethoven piano trios and Alexander Goehr's quite excellent trio. Two days later David Wilde, ever a glutton for punishment, gave a recital which embraced within a single evening four of the most monumental works in the whole solo piano repertoire. Within two concentrated

---

[60] North West Electricity Board.

hours he gave breath-taking accounts of Chopin's B flat minor sonata, Mussorgsky's *Pictures from an Exhibition,* Bartók's 1926 Sonata and the great Liszt B minor Sonata.

Within the ensuing month the shape of our concerts quite fortuitously assumed a pattern of matching pairs. John Williams arrived to complement Julian Bream's earlier guitar recital with a programme which included Stephen Dodgson's remarkable *Fantasy-Divisions.* Alexander Young (*Die schöne Müllerin)* and John Shirley-Quirk (*Winterreise*) gave us wonderfully poetic accounts of Schubert's two great song cycles, while in successive weeks in mid-February we were privileged to receive two of the greatest international string quartets of the day, the Smetana from Prague and the Amadeus from London, the latter including Tippett's second quartet in their programme.

In a concert by the Lancaster Ensemble we included a new string quartet by Anthony Hedges from the University of Hull. This represented our first initiative in commissioning new repertoire, a policy to which I attached considerable importance. For Hedges's quartet we secured funding from the PRS. I was particularly glad that he agreed to undertake this commission because I knew he had long been cautious about writing for string quartet lest any result were to be unduly influenced by the masterpieces of Bartók which he so admired.

While song recitals and quartet concerts were unfolding we were also busy in the University's newly established Nuffield Centre rehearsing and preparing for the first opera that we would present in full production at Lancaster University. The Nuffield Centre provided a wonderful flexible space in which a producer could exercise his spatial or choreographic imagination to his heart's content, it being effectively a large dry swimming bath within which any set could be constructed while the audience could be positioned around or above the performing area, as required. The work we chose for this production had enjoyed a curious, not to say improbable, origin. The music was by the Australian composer, Malcolm Williamson, for which he had drawn on Strindberg's *A Dream Play* in order to fashion an opera, now given the title *The Growing Castle.* His choice of title owed not a little to the way in which the work had originated.

Richard, Earl of Dynevor, had invited Malcolm to write a work for first performance as part of a new arts programme he was planning to present in his South Wales seat at Llandeilo, Dynevor Castle[61], once the home of prominent Welsh mediaeval leaders. Richard Dynevor's original request to Malcolm Williamson had been for a song cycle for voice and piano. Malcolm, never hesitant to capitalise upon a promising situation, decided to develop a work using four singers, piano and percussion. This concept then gradually grew until it found its final form as a chamber opera involving some dozen characters though played by a total of only four different singers – soprano, alto, tenor and bass – but with the soprano clearly carrying the dominant role. Eventually this larger concept grew until it enjoyed Dynevor's personal support, despite the steep cost implications. Sadly Dynevor's broader concept of an arts centre in the castle was not destined to flourish. The title has passed to his son, Hugo, and the castle is now in the keeping of the National Trust.

For our production in Lancaster we were fortunately able to secure all the original cast together with Malcolm's enthusiastic participation as pianist and mentor during rehearsal. The cast was led by the irrepressible Jennifer Vyvyan, supported by Ailine Fischer, John Barrow and Robert Bateman. After a dress rehearsal before an invited audience we gave two public performances. Perhaps the most telling comment after it was all over came from Kenneth Parrot, the first Director of the Nuffield Centre, who said with some understandable relief, "Well, after that this place will never be the same." Not only were Malcolm Williamson and all concerned on something of a justifiable high, but we had recreated in our own brand new twentieth-century castle a realisation of Richard Dynevor's original ambition of which, I believe, he would have been proud.

We ended our second full season with the largest professional orchestra yet assembled on the Great Hall stage, playing one of the most exuberantly explosive symphonies, Shostakovich's tenth. The orchestra was the City of Birmingham Symphony under its gifted permanent French conductor at the time, Louis Frémaux. After Berlioz's joyous *Carnaval Romain* overture, David Wilde completed two years of remarkable pianistic achievement in Lancaster with a

---

[61] Dynevor Castle: its earliest authentically recorded origins date back to the twelfth century and in particular to Rhys ap Gruffydd who, utilising both Dynevor and other neighbouring castles whilst also withstanding an assault from Henry II, succeeded in securing a position of considerable power in the area.

tellingly idiomatic performance of Rachmaninov's *Paganini Variations*. That it was feasible for one of our foremost symphony orchestras to travel half way across England for a one-off concert in a northern university prompted, as you might expect, no small measure of curiosity, and even incredulity, among my University colleagues. How had the considerable cost been met? No, Lancaster had not suddenly found itself imbued with the spirit of Prometheus, arguably the world's first philanthropist. Rather, a shared determination on the part of all concerned, especially the CBSO management, to ensure the success of the project, also reinforced by ever-generous support from the Arts Council and a substantial anonymous donation, combined to help us achieve this ambitious goal.

In a comparable situation in London any of our major orchestras would almost certainly find themselves turning to business and industry in search of support from a major sponsor. On such occasions, members of the orchestra might be expected to enliven conversation during the post-concert reception by circulating among the sponsors' guests. My son-in-law, Patrick Harrild, for many years principal tuba in the LSO, once told me of a delightful exchange he happened to overhear at one of these receptions in the Barbican. Gary Kettel, a virtuoso young London percussionist, found himself in conversation with one of the sponsors, a suave City industrialist: "What d' you do, then?" Kettel asked. "Well, a-a-a-ctually, I'm in Oil," flowed the smooth response. "Cor," rejoined the irrepressibly irreverent Gary, "What's that make y' then? A bleedin' sardine?"

Just a very special vignette remained for us to savour when exams were over in June. I had for some time been seeking to acquire a really fine harpsichord for the University. To our delight the Musicians' Union[62] handsomely agreed to donate a beautiful bespoke instrument, made for us by the much admired Robert Goble in his works at Headington, near Oxford. The presentation recital was given by the incomparable George Malcolm who, through his brilliant playing, provided me with some wonderful final music-making before I headed for my new job in Manchester.

---

[62] To its eternal shame, the University, a few years later, advertised the MU's generous gift for sale, and thereby incurred the enduring wrath of the Musicians' Union, which understandably took a censorious view of this proposed disposition.

Some Music Competitions

SEGOVIA

It has been my good fortune to be involved in a great number of very interesting international music competitions. These have been experiences offering never-ending pleasure in discovering new and exciting musical talent. They have also provided comparable and parallel rewards in meeting and working with a number of remarkable international colleagues.

One unusual competition, held only once and never to be repeated, could hardly have been more distinctive. Improbable as it may seem, it was initiated by a senior director of the Sherry Shippers of Jerez, anxious to associate the name of his organisation with that of Andrés Segovia as their most distinguished musical compatriot. Fortunately, they had had the good sense to share their idea with Bill Kallaway, a dynamic and inventive concert promoter in London who approached me in order that we might together set the wheels in motion.

Our first task was to interest Segovia in the project. This necessitated an evening flight to Madrid and then, immediately on arrival, a taxi ride into a rural suburb where we duly found Segovia thoroughly enjoying himself at a colourful Spanish nightclub, with an exotic beauty on either arm and clearly relishing every moment. At first sight these may have seemed less than promising circumstances in which people unknown to the great man could make any significant progress, particularly if the negotiations proved to be difficult. However no problems arose. Segovia seemed to be immediately enthusiastic about the whole project.

This was just as well as it would involve his coming to England for a sustained period to chair the jury for the competition which was to bear his name. Bill Kallaway, with characteristic skill and flourish, had secured exclusive use of Leeds Castle[63], near Maidstone in Kent, for

---

[63] Leeds Castle: an early example of its use to further world peace was the high-powered but, at the time, entirely secret meeting held at Leeds Castle between Israel's Moshe Dayan and Egypt's Mohammed Ibrahim Karmel in 1978.

the competition. Henry VIII transformed the castle as the dedicated retreat of Catherine of Aragon, and it was subsequently used as the home of several successive queens before being privately acquired. After its last owner, Olive, Lady Baillie, died, the castle was bought by the nation as a charity with several principal purposes, among which were the promotion of medical research and the interests of world peace.

Bill's skill in persuading the Trustees to allow us exclusive use of the Castle for the competition led to a wide range of privileges which we all greatly relished. Jury members, competitors, broadcasters and others closely concerned with the competition were enabled to live in the castle throughout its duration. It was indeed a strange feeling to be there for ten days without ever moving out across the surrounding moat and without ever needing to have recourse to handling money or any of life's other recurring necessities. Everything was provided in sumptuous fashion and every moment was a sheer delight.

The jury naturally included guitar specialists but also other musicians, some selected by Segovia and others, with great skill, by Bill Kallaway. Collectively they endowed the whole event with a remarkable panoply of colourful authority. Among those specifically invited by Segovia was someone he clearly revered and valued and from whom we all learned much. This was Alexandre Tansman, a composer and pianist of Polish origin living in Paris; by now elderly, he retained enviable vitality and as much good humour as anyone could wish to encounter. I remember one evening at dinner when the conversation turned to touring and he described a piano recital tour of India which he had undertaken during the 1930s. Tansman's whole account colourfully illustrated both the leisurely days of the Raj and the way in which touring musicians could, at that time, follow a wonderfully broad and relaxing timetable.

At one point during the tour a break of several days existed. The local agent in Dehli thoughtfully asked Tansman if there was anything of particular interest he would like to do or see during this gap in the programme. "Yes," said Tansman, "I would very much like to visit Mahatma Gandhi." "I'm sure that can be arranged," responded the agent and it duly was. A local taxi driver arrived at the hotel one morning with instructions to drive Tansman to Gandhi's country home, some hours distant. They arrived just in time for lunch, to be greeted by Gandhi with quiet dignity after which it seems that an extended and relaxed conversation was begun. As the hours ticked by, Tansman became increasingly conscious of his taxi driver hovering in the distance. The conversation continued without interruption but supported by a ready flow of refreshments. "But you will, of course, stay with us here tonight." It was clearly an invitation which brooked no refusal. It also avoided a return journey to Delhi in the middle of the night.

The next day the conversation between Gandhi and Tansman resumed as though it had never broken off, and continued with pauses only for refreshment. Periodically, the taxi driver could be seen still hovering attentively in the distance and no move was made to end this tranquil but absorbing visit which extended into a second night. It was only after a leisurely breakfast on the third day that Tansman finally bade farewell to his host and rode back to Delhi, resigned to the probability that profits from his tour would be significantly reduced by this three-day excursion. When they eventually arrived, the taxi driver resolutely refused any suggestion of payment whatsoever, sweeping aside Tansman's protestations with the words: "Any visitor from overseas who wishes to see the Mahatma is our honoured guest."

As a jury chairman Segovia was nothing if not unpredictable. In fact he would allow his enthusiasms to be so engagingly transparent that any attempt at studied objectivity on our part was extremely difficult to sustain. I call to mind, for example, an occasion in the course of the opening reception when jury and candidates were all gathered together to enjoy plentiful glasses of Jerez. At one point a young American competitor, Eliot Fisk[64], was warmly greeted by the Maestro saying "Ah, I know this young man. I expect he will win!" All this from the chairman of the jury at a public reception before anyone had met or played a note.

Because Bill had succeeded in selling recording rights quite widely, many broadcasters were there apart from the BBC. One such was a representative from the RTF channel, France Musique. He was constantly wrestling with a complication stemming from the fact that Britain, even in its historical castles once in the ownership

---

[64] Eliot Fisk was to be Segovia's last student, a position which subsequently led to his acquiring, as a gift from Segovia's widow, authority to hold all Segovia's reproduction rights.

of royalty, uses 3-pin plug sockets. Our French friend had brought with him a mass of sophisticated recording equipment but all of it with 2-pin plugs. "Where," he would despairingly ask, "can I make the plug in?" He became known as 'Monsieur Plug-in'. Although we always endeavoured to help him, he continued to complain that he had never been obliged to ply his trade and make recordings in such primitive circumstances, remaining apparently unmoved by the setting of historical splendour which Leeds Castle represented.

The whole competition was characterised by the greatest good humour, not unnaturally in view of our wonderfully hospitable surroundings. The sheer joy of so much excellent music-making in such sumptuous settings inevitably resulted in something of a cold shock as we left the Castle for the modern world without. Unquestionably we had all enjoyed a remarkable and privileged experience, enhanced for all of us by the wise, benevolent and generous personality of one of the greatest musicians of our age.

BBC Young Musician of the Year

No more dramatic contrast could exist between the unchallenged supremacy of Segovia as an artist and the first burgeoning of a young musical talent such as that of Caroline Dale. I call her to mind as a precocious prodigy who emerged playing the Elgar Cello Concerto in the finals of the first BBC Young Musician of the Year Competition in 1978. It was also of some significance that in this first year the competition was won by a candidate offering one of the less usual solo instruments: Michael Hext, playing the Gordon Jacob Trombone Concerto.

The competition has, of course, subsequently become one of the key public competitive peaks to which gifted young British musicians now nearly all aspire. But back in 1978 it constituted a fresh, attractive opportunity for school age musicians to come together in a friendly competitive spirit. It was also an entirely new departure for music on television. I was very excited to be associated with this remarkable competition from its very outset.

Lasting credit should forever be accorded to Walter Todds, whose original concept the competition was, particularly for the fact that all competitors had to be under the age of 19. Walter was a remarkable man and it was very sad that he did not live to see his wonderful conception flower and flourish. It was meticulously run during those early years by Roy Tipping and benefitted enormously from the encouragement of Humphrey Burton then in charge of the BBC's music on television.

The choice of the RNCM as the setting for that first competition in 1978 (three more were to follow biennially in Manchester) came about quite fortuitously at a BBC gathering in London at which I happened to be present. So, too, by good chance, was the Chairman of the BBC Board of Governors at the time, Lord Swann[65], who expressed spontaneous enthusiasm for the scheme and who came to Manchester to present the prizes at the conclusion of that first competition. Wind players were in the ascendency during the first years of the competition for not only was the winner, Michael Hext, a trombonist, but the much admired clarinettist Michael Collins also first made his mark. Two years later that distinguished oboist Nicholas Daniel would win the second competition.

Whilst all the stages in the competition were held at the RNCM, public interest demanded that the Concerto Finals be moved to the larger Free Trade Hall. At the same time I believe it was of real benefit to the competition that from the outset it should have been associated in the public mind with a music college. Unquestionably that association certainly brought considerable benefits to the RNCM and the association was only broken after four competitions had been held at the College up to 1984. After this the BBC understandably favoured endowing the competition with a more national public perception by moving it around the country, as it has subsequently done.

The finals of that 1984 competition were significantly revealing in that the evening dramatically demonstrated the difficulty of securing a fair equation between big time popular concertos and those for instruments less prominently associated with the concerto world. It was clear that there were two pre-eminently gifted finalists: pianist and guitarist. The question was, could they be matched on even terms? As it turned out the challenge became one between Rachmaninov's Third Piano Concerto, played by Anna Markland (a most versatile musician now more closely associated as a singer with the immensely popular and distinctive Fagiolini group), and

---

[65] Lord (Michael) Swann – previously Principal and Vice-Chancellor of the University of Edinburgh.

Rodrigo's Guitar Concerto, played by Paul Galbraith. No matter how one evaluated the merits of these two young performers, the contest inevitably became one in which the heavyweight Rachmaninov out-pointed the lighter-weight Rodrigo.

By exercising the machinery of the European Broadcasting Union, a complementary Europe-wide competition was also established in which youngsters from various countries could pit their skills against their counterparts. In 1984 the international rounds of this European competition were hosted by Danish Radio and held in Copenhagen. Arising from the need to coincide transmission dates and times internationally, a gap of a day or two often had to occur between the physical performance of the semi-finals and finals and their transmission. As a member of the jury, this involved me making a number of return visits to Copenhagen. On one occasion I was not a little unnerved when, on landing at Manchester airport and passing through the blue corridor with only hand luggage, I was beckoned over by the customs official. Impassively he asked, "Where have you come from?" When I indicated Copenhagen, he allowed himself a hesitant smile. "I thought I recognised you, Sir. Are you allowed to tell us who has won?"

The Competition has also now, I think, survived a number of growing pains that it had to endure such as when, in a misplaced pursuit of glamour, it was decreed that all female competitors should appear in Laura Ashley dresses, generously provided by the BBC. But viewed in retrospect the balance sheet for the competition is undeniably positive and rich. Many successful musicians are before the general public today who might never have scaled the heights they have reached but for the opportunities the competition has offered them. Yes, the danger remains that winning and the gratification it can bring are valued too highly and respect for the art becomes diminished. But we do not live in a perfect world and so long as the balance remains positive then I hope that what we started back in 1978 can continue to bring the many benefits it is capable of providing.

Transcontinental in Canada

One competition which, while not international, territorially involved country-wide travel, has been the CMC, a nationwide Canadian competition whose acronym ingeniously respected

Canada's bilingual status as identifying either Canadian Music Competition or Concours de Musique de Canada. Its administrative centre was in Montreal with regional rounds held coast to coast over a period of some five weeks. The jury began its work by flying into Vancouver and then headed progressively eastwards, holding rounds successively in Calgary, Edmonton, Saskatoon, Winnipeg, London, Toronto, Montreal, Moncton, Halifax and, finally, St. John's, Newfoundland. The whole experience was as stimulating as it was enjoyable.

The jury, some six of us, was largely recruited in Europe and was basically entirely French speaking. It included Suzanne Roche, Vlado Perlemuter's favourite and arguably most successful student who also taught at the Paris Conservatoire. She used to run an elegant chamber music festival from her home in Paris which I had great pleasure in visiting and where I found a delightful colony of cats mingling freely with the audience. Suzanne Roche was, in many respects, the soul of the party as we journeyed across the vast sweep of the Canadian landscape, encountering a host of interesting and often unexpected experiences entirely new to most of us.

In each centre we would, in the afternoon, hear classes of junior candidates offering a wide variety of instruments, followed, in the evening, by sessions for their seniors. One feature concerning the juniors intrigued us considerably, apart also from the wide variety of standards presented. This concerned the candidates' presentation. In British Columbia, with a substantial percentage of the youngsters coming from oriental families who had crossed the Pacific to settle in Canada, their turnout was meticulous, with shining patent leather shoes, nice white socks and a ready smile. As we crossed the prairies from Alberta to Manitoba, dress became increasingly informal and rural, with cowboy boots and accessories to match. I offer this observation not so much as a social comment but on account of the fact that happily I can report that all the music making we heard was well prepared and committed, whatever variations of platform dress may have been on view.

Our travels were pretty strenuous for the simple reason that often the only available flight between one provincial city and the next was at a stimulatingly early hour. The daily pattern that then followed would see us taking a light lunch, enjoying the afternoon classes with the younger candidates, giving our results, tasting an early evening snack if there was time before moving on to the evening sessions. Finally, the day would end with us delivering our eagerly awaited judgements to parents and competitors alike as late as 11pm before a short night and a very early flight the following morning. An additional stamina test for us was that to reach some of the airports serving towns in the prairie states involved surprisingly long journeys.

Occasionally we were allowed a free day and I remember a highly enjoyable occasion in Winnipeg when we were able to attend a performance of the Royal Canadian Ballet after which we repaired to a distinctly upmarket restaurant for a delicious and relaxed dinner, but one with an unexpected and revealing coda. As we rose from the table, a delightful waitress, who had served us impeccably if silently, came up to me and said, "Excuse me asking, Sir, but what was that language you've all been speaking?" – this, in a fashionable setting and in a country supposedly and officially bi-lingual, but where, in reality, most Canadians cannot and do not speak a word of French.

Once all the regional rounds had been completed, a gap of some two or three weeks followed before all those selected to appear in the finals presented themselves in Montreal. Unfortunately I was not able to return to Canada for the grand conclusion but I am confident that the finals jury will have encountered much difficulty in making their choices between our respective provincial round winners. The most heartening aspect of this whole experience was that the competitors we had been able to select were uniformly of a high standard, often reflecting remarkable precocity.

Munich

A major international competition with which I was privileged to be closely associated for twenty-five years was held every September in Munich under the auspices of Bayerischer Rundfunk but funded and supported by a consortium of all Germany's separate radio stations. In promoting a very wide-ranging and costly annual competition, the Bavarians are supported by a federation of all the other leading German radio stations (ARD) who, acting together, make it possible each year for the spotlight to fall on several different instruments or combinations of instruments. In fact, during the years when I was annually in Munich there were separate juries listening to at least four different categories – even, occasionally, five. For example, in any given year the different disciplines might be pianists or singers (these two generally alternated), a chamber ensemble, say string quartet, a solo string and / or wind player and some less usual choice, such as harpsichord or percussion.

The first year I was invited to the competition in Munich was to join the flute jury. It proved to be something of a landmark occasion. This was because it threw up, for the first time, the need for the competition to have more exacting pre-selection procedures than had hitherto been applied. This arose from our being subjected to a gruelling assault on our stamina such as even Renate Ronnefeld (the competition's benign Director) felt bound to agree should never have been imposed. All the competitors had been obliged, in the first round, to play Jacques Ibert's fine Flute Concerto. Well over one hundred candidates had been admitted and the Ibert concerto lasts slightly over twenty minutes. Since the competition regulations do not allow the jury to stop any competitor save in an emergency, it is possible quickly to compute the hours of sustained listening to which we were subjected throughout nine unremitting long days.

The Ibert concerto has a great deal to commend it – it is brilliant, it is diverting, it is entertaining, it is full of Gallic élan. But even the most compelling work can scarcely withstand over one hundred near continuous performances, let alone permit the application of wise judgement fair to all participants. In the end I should like to think that we eventually arrived at a good decision in that a young Slovenian flautist emerged head and shoulders above the rest and a few months later was to be found sitting as co-principal flute in the Munich Philharmonic Orchestra. But it may have been more by good luck than by good judgement that she did not suffer in the cull of some seventy young flautists who had to be asked to leave Munich at the end of round one. For myself, my most vivid memory is perhaps of coming down to breakfast in the hotel on the tenth morning to find the distinguished Swiss flautist Aurèle Nicolet attacking his boiled egg with the exclamation: "Pas d'Ibert? C'est incroyable!"

Just as the flute competition in 1979 rather dramatically demonstrated the complications of admitting too many candidates, so other later experiences provided fresh challenges and solutions. On a number of years when I found myself chairing specialist juries in some of the less usual categories, we again learned useful lessons. One such occasion was in 2001 when the chosen category was percussion. The practical complications involved can be readily visualised. Each set-up calls for positioning and grouping the many different instruments which every percussionist has to prepare with meticulous care in order to ensure that he or she can meet both the musical and physical athleticism demanded by so much post-war percussion writing. Fortuitously, there is to be found in one of Munich's more industrial suburbs, on the road out to Dachau, Kolberg's impressive and world-famous headquarters. The Kolberg factory and showroom constitutes something of a mecca in the percussion world, and it was there that the ARD organisers found a relatively simple solution to the problem of accommodating the endless range of instrumental requirements arising in any frontline percussion competition. Each day, therefore, the jury would decamp to the Kolberg empire where all these kaleidoscopic demands could be met without apparent difficulty. My memories of those days also remain dramatically vivid for an entirely different reason. One afternoon, as we were relishing the glittering range of instruments nowadays encompassed within the percussion world, cruel events were unfolding in New York and our proceedings were halted in order that we could be shown, on a large screen, the sickening sight of the demolition of the Twin Towers.

Two other years stand out for me, both memorable for revealing outstanding winners, leagues ahead of any other competitors. On my last visit, in 2004, that remarkable young French string quartet, the Quatuor Ebèn, now bestriding the world, instantly found itself in global demand from the moment it decisively won that year's competition. Similarly, my ARD memories fly back to 1984, when I found myself chairing the harpsichord jury on which were sitting many of the world's greatest harpsichordists. For the only time in the ARD's history, the unusually lean crop of candidates coming forward meant we were unable to award a second or even a third prize but we were excited that the competition did attract a first prize winner of quite extraordinary calibre in Władysław Kłosiewicz who, of course, has since delighted audiences the world over.

Yes, the ARD in Munich is a remarkable competition. For many young aspirants it may have represented a hurdle over which they have found themselves unable to vault. But for eminent musicians the world over it will be found proudly recorded in their *curriculi vitae*. When all is said and done it effectively remains the only international competition of indisputable prominence which year by year offers musicians the opportunity to shine internationally, whatever their instrumental persuasion.

Bucharest

Regrettably, not all international competitions observe the ethical standards and rigorous regulations to be found in Munich and elsewhere. One which I was to experience falling short of legitimate expectations was the competition mounted in Bucharest in late summer 1969 as part of the Georges Enescu Festival that year. My visit, undertaken on behalf of the British Council, was in many respects an uneven experience. It followed some disturbing days in Belgrade when the Council's attempts to plant British culture in the Balkans ran into stormy weather in the face of all too clearly mounting Serbian nationalism. I recall in particular one evening when an internationally recognised group of leading Serbian musicians, who gave the impression that they would have been happier handling machine guns rather than violins, launched a tirade of vicious invective against neighbouring Bosnia, which sadly soured an evening intended to harmonise Anglo-Serbian relations. In fact, perhaps the only reassuring element during my visit to Belgrade was the charming hospitality I received from the British Embassy Information Officer at the time, who happened to be Beecham's nephew and who was wont to refer to his uncle as 'old TB'.

Leaving Belgrade in my faithful mini I drove on to Bucharest in a spirit of keen anticipation at the prospect of exploring Romania for the first time. It was to be a visit with not a few unexpected twists and turns. One curious surprise some of us experienced occurred when, during the course of the competition, we were taken on a weekend excursion to visit a remote hilltop monastery noted for its particularly fine icons. Scarcely had we arrived than a procession of black limousines, flanked by police outriders, swept into view. The very important passenger? Our own Edward Heath.

My journey, like the competition to follow, was not short of surprises. The two main hazards on the singularly rough Romanian roads were either large flocks of geese, invariably lurking round a sharp bend, or gaping holes in the road calling for swift circumvention, in one of which, to my astonishment, I came upon a discarded kitchen cooker. Notwithstanding many indications of rural deprivation, I found a general mood of friendly optimism. This was well illustrated by the fact that, in the total absence of any rural transport infrastructure, the briefing I had received advised me to follow the local custom by stopping for travellers requesting lifts in the knowledge that such co-operation was fairly universal and was generally recognised by the gift of a clutch of lei at the end of the journey. Indeed, I swiftly found that all I had to do when topping up at one of the sparsely scattered filling stations was to lean over and grab a fistful of notes resting on the back seat. This degree of natural friendship characterised Ceaușescu's 1969 Romania, which was viewed quite benignly in the west following his action the previous year in offering spontaneous support to Dubček's ill-fated Czech rising and in refusing access to Brezhnev's tanks.

The Enescu Competition offered two categories: piano and song. A particularly happy spirit marked the work of the piano jury characterised by a charming moment when the playing of the very young blonde Pascal Rogé so delighted Nadia Boulanger, a member of the jury, that she spontaneously turned to us and exclaimed, "Mais c'est un petit ange!" Matters were very different for the song jury. Their story should really be told by Lionel Salter, the BBC's then Head of Opera, since I was not a witness to the gruesome sequel which ensued.

The song jury's chairman was the Director of the Bucharest Academy of Music, who bore the brunt of the embarrassment which was to follow. The competition lasted three weeks of which the first was entirely devoted to Round One. There being evidently no pre-selection, it speedily became apparent that a large number of the candidates were hardly likely to progress far. However, every competitor who was recommended to proceed to round two automatically received a *diplôme d'entré* deemed to signal a degree of professional competence at that stage. Among the singing competitors were four Russians and a singularly large lady from Cuba. All five had been recommended for rejection at the end of the first round on the Friday afternoon.

Sitting quietly at home that evening the jury chairman had, until that point, been quite content with the week's work that his jury had accomplished. Good judgement, he felt, had been exercised and they could proceed with confidence to the second round the following Monday. It was not to be. A knock at the door heralded the arrival of two officials, significantly clad in greatcoats, who announced that they had come to verify the results of the first round before publication the following day. "Was it correct, Director, that these five Russian and Cuban candidates would not be receiving *diplômes d'entré*?" The Director assured them that this was correct. The interrogators shifted their ground. "It is correct, is it not, Director, that you have applied for a visa to visit the Juilliard School in New York in November?" "That is correct." "And for your wife to accompany you also?" "Yes," came the reply. "Are you confident that your jury has made wise decisions about these five candidates?" The Director, experienced in the ways of Communism, concluded at this point that it might indeed be desirable to review some of the first round results.

The upshot was that Lionel Salter and other song jury members all received early calls in their hotel rooms advising them that Saturday's intended excursion was unfortunately cancelled and it would be replaced by a short meeting of the jury. After the initial pleasantries the Director explained that it had been suggested to him that some of their decisions might profitably be reconsidered. In Round One competitors had been marked up to a maximum of 10. "Would any colleague like to be a little more generous, since we have room for slightly more candidates than we have selected up to this point? For example, our talented mezzo-soprano from Havana: should she perhaps score 10, or at least 9?" Uneasily, the meeting began to take the point but did not immediately protest too strongly. A little later the Director, ever-alert to international niceties, turned to Lionel, "Professor Salter, there is only one British singer in the competition." Indeed there was; Lionel had described her to me as an undernourished soprano from Birkenhead. The Director pressed the point. "In Round One you only gave her 1. Would you not wish to be a little more generous with your mark?" "Not at all," responded Lionel. "But then she will return to England with no diploma." "So?" "Let us please persuade you to change your mark." "If you insist chairman, then I change my mark from 1 to 0."

Notwithstanding Lionel's principled objection, the jury was persuaded to be substantially more generous to the four Russian singers and the large lady from Havana. All five thereupon received their diplomas, honour was preserved and a form of diplomatic logic prevailed when all five were subsequently discarded after Round Two but were able to return home with the satisfaction of an elegantly embossed certificate in their hands. Perhaps we should not have been unduly surprised or disturbed by this episode, remembering that nationalistic preferment had long been automatic in certain east European competitions. Happily I can also report that the Director duly received a visa allowing him to fly to New York. But – needless to add – his wife did not.

And...

I have many rich and rewarding memories of other competitions. Making no claims for any pianistic skills, I have derived particular pleasure from attending, simply as a bystander, international piano competitions when Renna has herself been serving as a jury member, most notably the Busoni in Bolzano, the Schumann in Zwickau or the Leeds. As a former wind player I also found particular pleasure in the Paris Union Feminim des Artistes Musicales (UFAM) competition, cunningly devised to meet the aspirations of wind and percussion players seeking to excel in chamber music.

A number of other competitions have proved particularly enjoyable and rewarding to judge, notably the one held annually in Geneva. One which was as unusual as it was colourful, took place in Pretoria. In order to increase its appeal throughout the continent, it was endowed with a French title, Concours Pan-Africain. At this competition we were asked to assess two different categories. One, perhaps not too challenging, was for guitar playing; the other, much more idiomatically individual, was for a vast range of African choral groups. These joyous teams, dancing as passionately as they sang, combined to provide a kaleidoscope of infectious happiness which no jury member could resist. I believe that this was one of those rare occasions when we would all genuinely have wished to award a glittering prize to each and every competitor.

Plate 1

PLATE 2

PLATE 3

Plate 4

Plate 5

Plate 6

Plate 7

Plate 8

Plate 9

Plate 10

PLATE 11

PLATE 12

PLATE 13

PLATE 14

PLATE 15

PLATE 16

PLATE 17

PLATE 18

Plate 19

Plate 20

Plate 21

Plate 22

PLATE 23

PLATE 24

Plate 25

Plate 26

Plate 27

Plate 28

Plate 29

Plate 30

PLATE 31

Plate 32

Plate 33

PLATE 34

PLATE 35

Plate 36

Plate 37

RNCM

A New Prospect

One Sunday evening in February 1970 I was quietly at home when the telephone rang. The call was from Sir Charles Groves, at that time Music Director of the Royal Liverpool Philharmonic Orchestra. [Plate 14] Initially I assumed that he might be ringing to talk about the performance of *Fidelio* which he and I were planning to present at Lancaster University later in the year as part of our Beethoven bicentenary celebrations. But no, rather he asked me what I knew about the new music college 'they' were planning to build in Manchester. Unfortunately I knew virtually nothing.

Charles went on to explain that 'they' were a Joint Committee specially formed to represent the cities of Manchester and Salford and the counties of Cheshire and Lancashire. It seemed that this body, officially styled the Constituent Authorities, had been given the task of steering through the creation of what would become, with government funding support, the first new music conservatoire to be built in Britain in the twentieth century. As he warmed to the subject, Charles succeeded in presenting a very intriguing picture about this new project. Before he finished, he also came to one particular point which, it emerged, lay behind his call: could he put forward my name as somebody perhaps interested in the post of Founding Principal of this new conservatoire?

The more I thought about it the more the project seemed to assume increasing significance. But Charles's call had come at a singularly ill-chosen point. I was only in the middle of my second year bringing music to Lancaster University. The timing was, to say the least, unsettling in that it came just when we were moving into overdrive at Lancaster. I was also conscious that some well-meaning friends within the BBC had been looking ahead (rather wildly, I thought) to the time when Sir William Glock might stand down. But to anyone concerned with music and the young, as well as the general future of music in Britain, the concept of a brand new conservatoire seemed as powerful as it was exhilarating. The potential appeared enormous. While in no way diminishing the value and excitement of creating a new music department in a near-new university, the future scope offered by the creation of a major new conservatoire in Manchester, to set alongside its brothers in London and elsewhere, grew on me in increasingly compelling fashion in the succeeding days.

No further developments occurred during the following weeks when my concentration remained firmly on what we were trying to achieve in Lancaster. But, although I was not aware of it, some activity on behalf of the conservatoire project was taking place. In particular, the Joint Committee of the constituent local authorities was concentrating its energies upon securing confirmation that the building of the new conservatoire would be included as one of the designated government-funded enterprises to be started during the fiscal year 1970-1. Encouraged by a positive response in this respect from London, the Constituent Authorities also made swift progress in securing a suitable site in central Manchester. With remarkable speed, land on which had previously stood rows and rows of back-to-back terraced houses was now open ground marked only by the residue of broken bricks and discarded rubble. All that now remained standing on this site were two forlornly isolated pubs: the Nag's Head and the Lloyds Arms. (More about them follows.) Thus a point had been reached when Manchester had taken steps to make available a suitable site once central funding to bear the construction costs was confirmed.

There existed in Manchester two long-established, independent schools of music: one, the Northern School of Music (NSM), occupied a leasehold building nestling under the Mancunian Way; the other, the Royal Manchester College of Music (RMCM), was to be found in Ducie Street near the University. While keen rivalry had long existed between them, some informal discussion about a possible merger had periodically taken place during the '60s, since neither school was in a particularly strong position to sustain independence. It therefore seemed logical to the Joint Committee to undertake discussions with the two schools. These were developed with a renewed sense of purpose once it became clear that the plans for the new conservatoire might constitute a viable proposition.

Whereas each school naturally relished its individual strengths and characteristics, there followed an increasing, if reluctant, realisation that an alliance might prove inevitable if survival was to be assured. In due course, informal understanding between the NSM and the RMCM appears to have emerged, leading to a point where the prospect of investing in a newly built conservatoire came to carry a measure of attraction for both parties. In all this, the political and practical wisdom of the two principals, Ida Carroll at the NSM and Frederic Cox at the RMCM, together with their respective Boards of Governors, provided a timely degree of positive leadership. Each would almost certainly have preferred continued independence had this been a realistic option. But it was not.

Meanwhile, increasing confidence that a building programme could be implemented had encouraged members of the Joint Committee, now sitting under the chairmanship of Kathleen Ollerenshaw[66], to consider in earnest the question of the new conservatoire's leadership and, therefore, in particular, the post of Founding Principal. Various soundings were carried out and appropriate advertisements published. As part of this process, but unknown to me at the time, Simon Towneley[67], a key member of the Joint Committee, paid a visit to Charles Carter, Vice-Chancellor of Lancaster University. The confidential conversation they then shared was to pave the way for a situation in which the University felt it could, in due course, release me with mutual understanding and goodwill.

When the time came, I was interviewed for the post of Principal of the new college by a formidable panel of no fewer than thirteen representatives of the four Constituent Authorities. Mercifully, the proceedings were conducted by Kathleen Ollerenshaw with the skill and wisdom of the seasoned politician she was, thereby ensuring that only a few of the panel members contributed questions. In fact, the interview was remarkably short and perfectly amiable. Predictably, in this context, musical questions were non-existent and concentration was firmly and logically upon where the new College

---

[66] Dame Kathleen Ollerenshaw (1912-2014) served as Chairman of the RNCM Court 1971-1986, was Lord Mayor of Manchester, 1975-76, a noted mathematician and politician, and a dedicated public servant in countless arenas.

[67] Sir Simon Towneley was Lord Lieutenant, Lancashire, 1976-1996. Among many other notable achievements, his contributions to music and the arts have included publishing his authoritative study on Venetian opera in the seventeenth century, lecturing in the History of Music, Worcester College, Oxford, and being founder Chairman of Northern Ballet Theatre. Sir Simon played a key role in the establishment of the RNCM, and was a member of its Court and Council throughout the early years of the College's life.

might progress over the coming years. I only know the names of two other candidates for the position because we shared the same hard cold bench in the same dark cold anteroom in Manchester Town Hall while waiting to be called. In due course, it emerged that this single interview session had sufficed and I was offered the post with effect from 1 September 1971. I left Lancaster with no little sadness, keenly conscious of a job, at best, only half done. [Plate 15]

Construction of the new College was scheduled to commence on 6 April 1971. It could not begin earlier, even though the vacant site was ready, because the relevant regulation dictated that work could only physically start on the first day of the financial year in which the project occupied an approved position. Moreover, as Kathleen Ollerenshaw well knew from experience, unless the site was entirely unencumbered at midnight on 5 April, then the guarantee of government funding would immediately lapse. Some gypsies, who could be potential squatters, were occupying land bordering the site. The wily Ollerenshaw knew that if they were to be allowed to spill over onto the new College site, this would automatically have invalidated the programme which could not then have been restarted until a full 365 days had elapsed. Nowhere has Kathleen's indomitable determination been more decisively illustrated than by the fact that she took it as her own personal responsibility to drive round and round the site in her imposing white Rover saloon as a deterrent to any intending trespassers.

The Joint Committee had taken great pains to select an appropriate firm of architects for the project. Their ultimate choice was reassuring in that it directly reflected a vital musical requirement. Bill Allen, a partner in a Hampstead firm of architects – Bickerdike, Allen & Rich – had been closely involved as the acoustic consultant in the then recent construction of the Gulbenkian Hall in Lisbon. This enabled John Bickerdike, the senior partner, to secure the College contract, with Bill Allen playing a central role advising on acoustics. His influence, for example, led to the use on exposed surfaces of a particular acoustically sensitive brick – to this day, a significant and important decision.

It is to John Bickerdike that we largely owe the bold vision which he brought to the new building, enabling it to offer the visitor a stimulating spatial sweep on entering, together with a compelling vista of ascending concourses, all fronted in glass. Back in the early 1970s this represented a dynamic initiative which still today provides a liberating sense of space. Bickerdike himself was a remarkable man who confronted every difficulty with the unhesitating assumption that it only existed to be overcome. Imposingly tall, he would stride through the building site, his stature symbolising his clear authority and confidence. [Plate 16]

To his wife, who was Persian (indeed, we had not then either lost the Shah or recognised a new Iran), John delegated responsibility for the choice of colours throughout the new College. It was entirely due to her felicitous instincts that, for example, the opera theatre should have emerged with vibrant bottle green seating. Similarly, in the concert hall, her choice of a deep purple motif created a wonderfully rich impression which was substantially retained during the College's strikingly successful programme of expansion in 2014.

Preparing the Way

While building proceeded, I decided to set up a temporary office in my home tucked away in the folds of North Yorkshire. There were several practical arguments behind this decision. Whereas the NSM and RMCM had each generously offered me office accommodation and supporting facilities, I clearly could not effectively work in both, while to choose one rather than the other might have been to send out misleading messages. The other main reason, apart from the pleasure of working in a corner of the country I love, was that I could thereby find time to develop clear thinking about the essence and ethos of the new college without being distracted by quotidian complications. A third consideration was that I would often be away undertaking extended visits abroad – both in Europe and America – to learn and study how widely admired conservatoires, whether in Paris or New York, operate and achieve their acknowledged results.

So, we turned the dining room and my own study into Northern College of Music[68] offices and I appointed two stalwart members of

---

[68] By agreement, the new conservatoire was initially registered as the Northern College of Music, until the necessary approval had been secured from the Palace to transfer the title 'Royal' from the RMCM to the newly merged body.

staff to work here: my first PA, Bryan Fox[69] [Plate 17], a recent graduate of Lancaster University, who had won the first individual prize I had promoted there, and Diana Blaine, a most able secretary. Together we three constituted the total staff of the then NCM until we all came together in Manchester once the new building was complete.

During all these months I also undertook an extensive study of conservatoires abroad. What I learned taught me as much about the pitfalls to avoid as the goals to pursue. In the autumn of 1971, I embarked on an extended visit to the USA, greatly facilitated throughout by the State Department. I was welcomed most warmly in Washington, arriving at a time when celebrating the arts seemed to have become a super-charged activity following the opening a few weeks earlier of the John F. Kennedy Centre. Is it not infinitely to America's credit that the lives of two of its greatest presidents, both of whose careers were cruelly cut short by assassination, should be marked by the emergence of major arts centres, the Kennedy in Washington and the Lincoln in New York?

The first concert I attended in the Kennedy Centre was, however, hardly a flawless occasion. It was given by the Chamber Orchestra of Mexico and the programme promised a performance of Bach's Double Concerto for Two Violins. However, what materialised was hardly more than a concerto for one and a quarter violins. The first soloist was the incomparable Henryk Szeryng, playing with the richness of tone and all the eloquence which always characterised his performances. The second part was undertaken by the Mexican leader of the orchestra, but what emerged was no more than a sadly shriven shadow set alongside Szeryng's mastery. One can but reflect with regret upon the frequency with which artists have been forced to forfeit their national inheritance in order to achieve political security – for, had not Szeryng been obliged to abandon his native Poland while gratefully receiving sanctuary in Mexico? But for this, such a pairing for the Bach concerto would, in all probability, never have occurred.

---

[69] When the College was physically opened, Bryan Fox became its first Accommodation Officer. To this day he remains loyal to the College in semi-retirement both by serving as a wise and experienced part-time Counsellor and by mounting a series of Saturday recitals in Emmanuel Church, Didsbury, offering valuable opportunities for RNCM students to be heard by a wider public.

Hats off, though, to the majestic Szeryng for so wholeheartedly demonstrating his gratitude to the Mexican authorities.

When surveying the origins of leading US conservatoires, one swiftly becomes aware of the many instances where a given individual's passion for fostering music, linked to the acquisition of a personal fortune, has led to the foundation by some visionary philanthropist of a world renowned music school: Curtis, Eastman, Juilliard, Peabody – the roll seems endless. How different to European practice, where many conservatoires are at least consistent to the extent that they perpetuate the names of leading composers. All my American visits were instructive in different ways, although not without one or two compelling surprises. One was the time I spent in Juilliard which happened to coincide with a week in which the School was dedicating all its energies, to a point of near hysteria, towards celebrating an extended visit by Maria Callas. However, while the spotlight remained firmly upon the great diva, I was at least able to undertake some absorbing exploration away from the limelight.

While the quality of work I encountered was ostensibly stimulating, I was frequently disappointed by the recurring level of detached disinterest on the part of the student in anything beyond the immediate concerns of his or her instrument. This came home to me forcibly when I was listening to an enthralling chamber music class conducted by Rudolf Kolisch in the New England Conservatoire in Boston. Did the assembled students realise that they were being guided through Schoenberg's Fourth String Quartet by the very man whose own string quartet had worked so closely with Schoenberg back in pre-war Vienna? For me it was an extraordinary privilege to be afforded, quite unexpectedly, an opportunity to learn personally from Kolisch. What did this unique experience really mean for the students?

My visit to Boston also contained one other memorable experience, no less unexpected but on this occasion immediately personal and entirely non-musical. I was due to meet up with Julian Bream at the conclusion of a recital he was giving in nearby Jordan Hall. I passed the waiting time in a local pub. Perched on a bar stool I ordered a beer in what, for my neighbour, must have been an unwelcome English accent. Turning to me in an aggressively drunken state, he asked if I was one of the sons of bitches whom they had dealt with so effectively in Boston many years before. Guilelessly admitting British nationality, I received a sharp left hook which flattened me there and then. A stiff brandy with Julian half an hour later dispelled any feelings of resentment I might initially have harboured. After all, we British did often get it wrong back in the days of the Tea Party, did we not?

A visit to the remarkable Bloomington campus of Indiana University was no less memorable. I was lucky that it occurred at a time when Dean Bain's[70] inspirational magnetism still personified the vitality characterising the whole campus. One formed the impression that every conceivable form of music-making could be found in Bloomington at any moment. For instance, on the evening I arrived the choice of entertainment ranged from opera to an evening of 'Black Jazz' and a carillon recital. I chose this third option, but at a safe distance from the impressive tall bell tower. Not the least of my special experiences in Bloomington was a wonderful presentation of Bartók's Viola Concerto given by William Primrose, the prince of Scottish string players, whom I had previously heard endowing it with masterful authority during the 1950 Edinburgh Festival.

The State Department also generously enabled me to visit the West Coast. A characteristically concentrated programme took me to a number of campuses forming part of the University of California and included a first visit to the music department at Santa Barbara, where Peter Racine Fricker headed an invigoratingly enterprising team. Some years later I was to enjoy the experience of giving some workshops on new British music in this delightful setting.

On my last day in America, I was scheduled to visit the then all-girls Mills College at Orlando, graced for so many years by Darius Milhaud who, when I arrived, happened to be marking the last weeks of a remarkable twenty-five years' association with the College. Time was running short if I was to catch my international flight home. What would have been fraught with difficulties in Britain, given our stuttering infrastructure, proved no problem at all. I was whisked by helicopter direct from the spacious front lawn of Mills College onto the tarmac at San Francisco airport. It all felt improbably presidential!

Early in 1972 I followed my American visit with a comparable fact-finding tour of European conservatoires. I found it intriguing to note,

---

[70] Wilfred C. Bain, Dean of the Indiana University Music Faculty at Bloomington, 1947-1973, was an irrepressible enthusiast for a wide gamut of music-making from opera to jazz, and his vision and drive inspired the creation of arguably America's most significant and influential centre for musical learning and development.

as my visit progressed country by country, the many differences in the way these important schools were organised. Whatever variations and irregularities emerged, it was reassuring to find that one salient factor remained supremely consistent: the essential heart of practical music teaching must reside in the regular personal lesson between tutor and student. Wherever additional provision such as group classes may embellish this central programme, the core essential remains the one-to-one lesson. As I found in the Paris Conservatoire, this could lead to a notable degree of personal anarchy. However it also served to stimulate competition, much of which was largely endemic and historical, dating back to the days of Cherubini and in no way being attributable to the Conservatoire's delightful director, Raymond Gallois-Montbrun[71], whose hospitality was invariably warm and helpful.

That a measure of consistency emerged in post-war Germany could be attributed to its need to re-establish, state by state, provision for conservatoire music teaching, much of which had all but been demolished by the end of the Third Reich. Some of the Hochschule, such as those in Cologne and Hanover where both cities had effectively been obliterated during the war, were to be found in brand new buildings enjoying the benefits of fresh planning and architecture. Indeed, the Cologne Hochschule, lying close to both the main railway station and the cathedral, is a most stimulating example of a building designed specifically for music, as indeed is that in Hanover.

Meanwhile, other schools, such as those in Frankfurt and Berlin, were housed in older accommodation. In Berlin the Hochschule for Music and Art had been obliged to battle with all the constrictions resulting from Berlin's isolated situation, while it continued to view with fraternal interest the work of its counterpart on the other side of the wall, the Hanns Eisler Hochschule. One other striking older building was that which housed the Hochschule in Munich. This was, in fact, the palatial Third Reich 'temple' where Neville Chamberlain had been induced to sign the fateful Munich "Peace for our time" scrap of paper. It was a building I was to come to know well in later years when it was in regular use for the ARD

---

[71] Born in Saigon in 1918, Raymond Gallois-Montbrun was an interesting French composer whose violin concerto enjoyed particular popularity.

International Music Competition. By then it had acquired a more benevolent aspect. Many of its less desirable earlier features had effectively been eliminated but despite this, one Israeli jury member resolutely refused to use the passenger lift because "Hitler had once stood in it".

In later years I was to come to know the Directors of two Hochschule particularly well, those in Cologne and Frankfurt, with which the RNCM developed various interesting and rewarding links. Such collaboration enjoyed an influential degree of international support, initially through both the British Council and the Goethe Institute. Indeed, I was much indebted to the Goethe Institute for organising what proved to be a most rewarding tour of German schools. Thanks to the generous and extensive way in which the programme had been arranged, I had been able to come away having learned much and with admiration and respect for the fine work then being accomplished throughout the country. I also did so with particularly happy memories of my visit to quite the smallest of the German Hochschule. This engagingly intimate school, offering at the time some particularly interesting courses in chamber music, occupied a delightful woodland setting on the edge of Detmold. In view of the way it contrasted with its larger city-centred counterparts, a visitor could be excused for wondering whether bigger was, in fact, always better.

I had hoped to study some Scandinavian models but this had not proved possible. By contrast, what was possibly the most rewarding individual visit of my entire European tour took me to Budapest and the Franz Liszt Academy. With my love of Bartók's music, I particularly relished the opportunity of attending two performances at the Hungarian National Opera of his theatrical triptych, the riveting one act opera, *Duke Bluebeard's Castle*, and the pantomime ballets, *The Wooden Prince* and *The Miraculous Mandarin*. I was also glad to have the chance to explore the music of a number of rising Hungarian composers such as György Kurtág, already at that time becoming acknowledged in Western musical circles, and Zsolt Durkó, who sadly was not.

The days I spent in the Liszt Academy brought home to me a fresh respect for the benefits and strengths accruing from old and well-established traditions, such as those in which Hungarian music-making so richly abounds. My benevolent guide throughout my visit there was the Academy's head librarian, János Kárpáti, an acknowledged Bartók authority from whom I was privileged to have learned much. I shall also long remember his help in particular when, at my request, he took me to view a small cottage industry noted for its manufacture of particularly fine cimbaloms. To my delight I found myself able, there and then, to purchase a particularly good instrument for the RNCM. Initially it was not clear whether a deal could be struck, but eventually Barclaycard was able to reassure the Hungarians that they could regard the transaction as secure. Some weeks after my return to England a beautifully carved cimbalom, complete with legs and beaters, was safely delivered in Manchester.

Back in Bentham there was much preparatory work to be done. Among the many tasks were a small number which called for once-only action through being peculiar to starting an entirely new institution. For example, the new College needed to acquire its own armorial bearings. To this end I made an approach to the College of Arms. A prompt and positive response followed in the person of Ellis Tomlinson, a leading heraldic expert. We could not have acquired a more helpful or indeed enthusiastic colleague. Letter after letter of wise guidance arrived, all written in Tomlinson's preferred deep magenta ink and distinguished by exquisite calligraphy. It was to be three years before the College was formally granted its armorial bearings but when they were ready for approval the coat of arms comprehensively and boldly symbolised the College's origins and royal title. Above a golden lyre, introduced both as a musical symbol and as an emblem of Apollo, patron of the Muses, shines a white irradiated star representing the Northern Star to emphasise the College's geographical position. A lion, reflecting both the Royal Arms and those of Manchester, is garlanded with various symbolic decorations such as the red roses of Lancashire and the oak leaves of Cheshire. This noble lion duly wears a crown and holds a music score. All in all, the coat of arms proclaims a proud and confident message from the College.

While acquiring a coat of arms we also needed a motto to inscroll below it, did we not? In the end, this was created in a delightfully impromptu and domestic manner. Renna's violin partner, Brigid Ranger, was staying with us together with her husband, John Simpson, then Head of Classics at Malvern College. Once the motto's general message had been established, John went to work to develop it into a suitable Latin axiom. Before long the College's chosen message that "Music enriches all" had emerged as "Fovet musica omnes" (complete with a neat symmetry of two five-letter words framing a six-letter word). At a suitable point this proposal was unanimously endorsed by the Joint Committee whose members were doubtless glad to be relieved of the need for further scholarly pursuit.

Mention of the College's motto prompts me to record here that in 1994 Michael Kennedy compiled a splendidly informative and vibrant account of the College's first twenty-one years. It takes as its title the College's motto 'Music Enriches All'[72]. What I am setting down in this chapter does not, in any way, attempt to provide a methodical and consecutive history of the College's initial years. That record has been wonderfully accomplished by Michael Kennedy and can scarcely be improved upon. As always with Michael's writing, it is immensely readable. My chronicle here offers nothing more than a series of selective personal recollections as these come back to me some forty years on.

While we were vaulting over these small but important once-and-for-all hurdles, steps were also being initiated to resolve the question of the new College's ultimate title. In the nature of such matters, resolution was to be an extended process. However, in due course, on 17 July 1973, an announcement from Buckingham Palace stated that "The Queen has been graciously pleased to command that the title 'Royal' be included in the name of the Northern College of Music, Manchester, in perpetuation of the title enjoyed by the Royal Manchester College of Music with which the Northern School of Music has amalgamated to form the new College." Lasting credit for this is due to Sir Simon Towneley, whose skill in negotiations with the Home Office led to this eminently satisfactory resolution in which Frederic Cox, outgoing Principal of the Royal Manchester College of Music, also played a notable part through his readiness to cede the Royal Charter.

As the summer months of 1972 unfolded, construction in Manchester proceeded boldly [Plate 18], apart from being totally suspended for a period on account of a national building strike. The operation constantly threatened to go over budget and even a modest extension to provide a certain amount of comfort for visiting

---

[72] Michael Kennedy: *Music Enriches All* (Carcanet Press Ltd, 1994).

dignitaries achieved misplaced notoriety within the local press as being an inappropriate indulgence to provide the President with a Royal loo! At the same time the original equipment budget was swiftly seen as being totally inadequate if the new College was to be able to carry out work at the level which we all aspired to achieve. In one particular respect a fundamental challenge had emerged following a survey of all pianos currently in use in the NSM and the RMCM. This had revealed that, a couple of fine but ageing Bechstein concert grands apart, the Colleges's existing stocks of pianos had nearly all exhausted their natural life. This had led me to propose that we should place an order for some forty-eight new pianos with Steinway's headquarters in Hamburg.

At the time, a certain amount of chauvinism was rife in Manchester, where a determined policy to buy British was being actively pursued. What was seen, therefore, by some local authority elected members as being both unreasonably extravagant and unpardonably unpatriotic provoked some apoplectic reaction. This did also lead to an amusing moment when one councillor, who had been outraged by what was being proposed, visited his local music shop, measured all the pianos in stock, found that they were all British-made and were all of the same size, and consequently recommended that this was how the new College's piano requirement should be met. When it emerged that he had only measured actual keyboard width and that all the pianos he had seen had been uprights, the Joint Committee was thankfully able to discount his proposal and secure Manchester city's support for the initial purchase of twenty-four Steinways, with others to follow later.

Nor were the College's patriotic credentials much helped by an earlier decision to commission for the new concert hall an Austrian organ made by the firm of Gregor Hradetzky in Krems, some distance from Vienna. However, this project enjoyed the strong support of Sir Simon Towneley, who steered it forward with great skill and was much helped in turn by the authoritative advocacy of Geraint Jones, a leading organist of the day, who had prepared the organ's specifications. This particular project for a large tracker action instrument represented to the specialist organ world a confident and bold statement by the College regarding its intentions. Symbolically, the Austrian organ and the German pianos aptly illustrated our international intentions for the new College. In both respects bold determination happily brought due rewards:

piano work of a high order became possible at the College while the Hradetzky organ earned worldwide fame, not least on account of the many fine recordings which various leading organists elected to make on it. Its creation also represented the first occasion on which the College mounted an appeal which happily accounted for half its ultimate £40,000 cost.

Such material considerations apart, my principal concerns during this period were naturally directed towards the courses the new College would offer and the people who would bring these to life. I had developed a firm conviction that most existing music courses in Britain were too short and that, as a matter of broad prescription, at least four years' concentrated study and development at conservatoire level would be appropriate to achieve the standards to which we should aspire and to help meet the nation's need in developing musicians of a high order. It proved gratifying to find that within a few years many existing courses in conservatoires up and down the land became extended towards involving four years' initial undergraduate study. Awareness of the collective benefit of such models was also shortly to find expression and forceful endorsement in a report published by the Gulbenkian Foundation under the title *Training Musicians*[73]. I was pleased to find that such thinking also came to enjoy active support among senior members in the existing Manchester colleges, and also among others in key positions whom I was able to consult. Such a measure of agreement also led me to believe that we would be in a position to open new courses of clearly enhanced potential from September 1973 onwards. To assemble a team in such a climate able to pursue these aspirations became the clear priority for the coming months. [Plate 19]

A few individuals or scattered groups giving voice to such aspirations and beliefs can only exert limited influence. It seemed, therefore, desirable to hold a couple of summer staff conferences which I hoped would generate understanding among all colleagues of what we were about and what we were trying to achieve. I resolved to plan for two such conferences, one in summer 1972 designed principally to bring together for the first time the two tutorial teams of the NSM and the RMCM who had hitherto led such

---

[73] Gulbenkian enquiry report published by the Calouste Gulbenkian Foundation in 1978.

different lives with surprisingly little mutual contact, but who would now have responsibility for guiding NSM and RMCM students through the remainder of their respective courses. We would then hold a further conference the following year when the emphasis would be upon the new graduate courses which the RNCM would be introducing in the autumn of 1973 and when many new staff would have the opportunity to participate and become acquainted.

I arranged that we should hold the 1972 conference at Giggleswick School, a decision which threw up its own challenges as some members of staff were quick to emphasise to me when they viewed the somewhat basic ablutionary facilities typical of a boys' public school. As that redoubtable singer, Ena Mitchell, quipped to me: "At least one team could, for the first time, look the other in the eye with naked optimism." I was also much heartened by the feeling of spontaneous camaraderie which prevailed throughout the stimulating and enjoyable days we shared at Giggleswick. I was greatly encouraged by the positive and open-minded spirit evident among colleagues assembling for the first time under the same roof. They now included Terence Greaves [Plate 20] who, to our good fortune, had just been persuaded to join us as Dean of Development after being Director of Studies at the Birmingham Conservatoire. The notes circulated prior to the conference had stressed that there was only a limited amount of single room accommodation available; colleagues had therefore been asked to say if they would be prepared to share. Greaves responded to this invitation by indicating that he would be totally agreeable to sharing provided it could be with either Raquel Welch or Sophia Loren. It was good to find evidence of such uncomplicated frivolity from the outset.

Assembling the Team

The staffing challenges were nothing less than demanding. Extensive negotiations, which had preceded my appointment, had established broad understanding concerning existing staff members in the constituent colleges (the NSM and RMCM). None of their employment arrangements, often sketchily informal, carried any guaranteed element of tenure or continuity. Staff were exclusively engaged on the basis of a given number of hours weekly teaching, often negotiated on a term-by-term basis. Any preparation for retirement which a staff member might have arranged would have owed its existence to his or her own personal initiative. Indeed, it has to be said that at that time few conservatoires, if any, boasted employment provision comparable with normal university practice.

Whereas initially no existing NSM / RMCM staff members could be offered assured employment in the new College, I was particularly concerned in cases where continuity could be visualised to try to ensure a measure of welfare, or if you like soft landing, for those of more advanced years. It was against this background that in October 1971, I embarked upon a series of interviews with all members of academic staff then in the two colleges. I quickly came to appreciate that the majority, lacking any pension provision, viewed the future with an acute sense of anxiety and uncertainty.

It was very evident to me that if we were to create in the new College a unified academic community we needed radically to improve the rewards we could offer our tutorial staff. One of the most important advances we made during long months of negotiation was to reach a point where we could offer significantly more attractive contracts to encourage staff to view Manchester as a natural centre on which to base their careers and lives. This would be achieved by offering either full-time appointments or, in cases where tutors could not enter into a full-time commitment, pro-rata arrangements and other related hourly provision.

Behind these improvements lay the important consideration that, from the outset, we were resolved to provide two hours every week of individual tuition on each student's principal instrument. In parallel, we could then implement a range of supporting study with an emphasis upon seminars such as had hitherto been seen as too exotic for normal application within the conservatoire world. Here again we would, to some degree, be mirroring university teaching, while also concentrating upon intensive group work to endow all students with a ready aural awareness.

Once scope to offer such improved contracts to our tutorial staff had been secured, I could then proceed to make a number of significant appointments on a basis which would provide a prospect for a rewarding career firmly rooted in Manchester. It was therefore appropriate that we should first identify those existing members of the constituent colleges whose abilities qualified them to form part of a strong tutorial nucleus within the new College.

In preparing to assemble a new tutorial team, it seemed clearly desirable to move towards the dual benefit of strengthening the work of existing staff through the stimulus of fresh colleagues arriving to develop new goals and practices. First steps in this direction were greatly assisted by the ready agreement of three colleagues to steer the overarching arrangement I was proposing. It was to our infinite good fortune that Ida Carroll [Plate 21], formerly NSM Principal, generously agreed to be our Dean of Management, thereby helping to establish a well-balanced academic community while ensuring smooth completion of the final NSM courses. For me her appointment carried a personal message which I naturally relished. There was I, who had first learned Walter Carroll's music as I fumbled my way on the piano in the Oribi dining room, now privileged to be able to invite his daughter to assume one of the three central roles of Dean in the new College. That Dr. John Wray [Plate 22] similarly agreed to serve our best interests while overseeing continuity of existing RMCM courses also gave me personal pleasure in that in his youth John had taught at Haileybury and was still warmly remembered there. Not only was he a fine musician but a man of clear and affable dignity. For some reason he never seemed to relish answering his own telephone but regularly assigned this task to his manservant at home who would intone with grave authority, "Dr. Wray's residence".

Renna and I also had good reason to delight in the arrival of Terence Greaves who had made a characteristically light-hearted contribution to our Giggleswick conference. As our Dean of Development his central responsibility was, as you might assume, to oversee the introduction of the new courses which the College would be offering from September 1973. We had seen much of him during our days working in Birmingham and had long come to respect his fine natural musicianship, his versatility and his irreverent good humour, all of which were to serve the College extraordinarily well right from the beginning through to a later phase, when he became the College's Dean of Undergraduate Studies.

I determined at an early stage that it was important, in the interests of both coordinated progress and internal competition, to create, discipline by discipline, six separate, identifiable Schools of Study [Plate 23]: keyboard studies, strings, wind and percussion, vocal studies, academic studies and composition. Every tutor and student would automatically belong to one of the resulting departmental teams which would then benefit from a sense of natural group identity. Each School of Study physically occupied a separate designated area within the College, complete with its own individual secretary and office provision.

The process of appointing heads of schools, to which I then was able to bend my energies, proved a wholly enjoyable and stimulating process. The first appointment I could secure was that of Clifton Helliwell, to the post of Head of Keyboard Studies. [See Plate 7] I had come to know and respect Clifton as a gifted and versatile accompanist during my time at the BBC where his collaboration with many a fine artist must have led him to hesitate seriously about life in a conservatoire. But Clifton was also dedicated to teaching and for a number of years had enriched the work of the RMCM in his own inimitable way. He and his wife, Jessica, lived in a charming Cheshire village, Lower Peover, where they had developed a particularly beautiful garden of which one outstanding feature was a number of paving stones marked by dinosaur imprints. These were trophies which Clifton had acquired in Egypt while serving with distinction in the North African campaign, where his rank had helped him open the necessary doors to the importation of these dinosaur imprinted tablets. He used to delight in telling me of the time when he and Jessica had decided to move to a smaller property and had been receiving would-be purchasers at Lower Peover. On one occasion a possible buyer was accompanied, as Jessica put it, by a peroxide blonde Cockney lady who, when the dinosaur imprints had been pointed out to her, exclaimed with exquisite naivety: "Cor, you wouldn't fink they'd come so near the 'ouse!"

The next head of school I was able to entice to Manchester was Cecil Aronowitz[74][Plate 24], a South African violist recognised the world-over. For five too short years before his premature death, Cecil threw himself wholeheartedly into the work of the College. I shall long remember the invigorating atmosphere surrounding the recital he and his wife Nicola generously gave to launch the College's Student Travel Scholarship scheme, a fund which was to prove invaluable to many students as the years rolled by. It was with Cecil's ready support that I was also able to appoint to the College a clutch of his colleagues from the Melos, at that time unquestionably the country's leading large chamber ensemble. These very special new colleagues included the cellist Terence Weil, whom I appointed as the College's first Director of Chamber Music, Adrian Beers, the pre-eminent bass

---

[74] Succeeded on his premature death by the cellist Eleanor Warren and, in due course, the double bassist Rodney Slatford.

player, the noted oboist Peter Graeme, and the inimitable William Waterhouse[75], who brought his infectious natural enthusiasm to the work of the College, not only as an admired bassoonist but also as a born archivist who was to delight in developing the College's collection of many historic instruments and other treasures.

To take charge of composition it gave me great delight to tempt my former colleague in Lancaster, Anthony Gilbert [Plate 25], to join us in Manchester. He was an inspiring and sensitively perceptive tutor. The fruits of his work swiftly became apparent in the early years of the College, as gifted composers such as Simon Holt [Plate 26] and Martin Butler made their way and rewarded Tony for the inspiring teaching he so selflessly provided.

An initially reluctant head of school whom I was ultimately able to persuade to join us was Alexander Young [Plate 28], that most gifted of lyric tenors, best known in the world at large for his enchanting Schubert recitals and as the man who created the title-role of Tom Rakewell in Stravinsky's *The Rake's Progress*. I was convinced from the outset that Basil (as he was known) Young would be an ideal Head of School of Vocal Studies if he could ultimately be persuaded to transfer his priority concerns to us. Eventually the breakthrough moment came when I visited him during a time he was artist-in-residence at the Aldeburgh Festival. Together with his charming wife Jane, we had set out on a long country drive in his sturdy green Rover at the conclusion of which he finally concurred with the heartfelt words, "Yes, damn it, I suppose you are right and that the time is probably coming when I should sing a little less."

Another indisputably distinguished head of school appointment I was able to make, although it was unavoidably delayed for some months, was that of Philip Jones[76][Plate 27], pioneer trumpeter whose eponymous brass ensemble was by then famous the world over. Philip, as Head of School of Wind and Percussion, was a tonic to us all and set a marvellously rigorous example to all colleagues, as

---

[75] William Waterhouse's *New Langwill Index: A Dictionary of Musical Wind-instrument Makers and Inventors,* was published in 1993 after ten years of research developing Lyndesay G. Langwill's personal bequest to William Waterhouse of his correspondence and books.

[76] Succeeded, in 1977, by Timothy Reynish whose irrepressible and infectious leadership of the College's School of Wind and Percussion was to bring it unchallenged global renown.

he was to do subsequently when Trinity College of Music, London, astutely appointed him Principal. Philip's services to music before his too early death were legion. Not only did he significantly improve brass playing in general but he also radically altered attitudes and approaches towards brass playing. He was supported in the College by three notable lieutenants serving as senior tutors within the three key elements in his school: Sydney Coulston, for many years the first horn in the BBC Northern Orchestra; Sidney Fell, the noted clarinettist; and an old friend from BBC days, Gilbert Webster, who developed at the College a widely admired percussion studio.

No challenge was too great for Gilbert even if his acquisition ambitions sometimes threatened to engulf the entire equipment budget. At any moment we might, for example, be setting out to acquire a two-octave chromatic set of boobams or a sophisticated set of cow bells. Gilbert had resolved to acquire the bells only from authentic Alpine sources which he visited during his summer holiday in 1974. Returning triumphantly, but shaking his head in mock sorrow when I asked him about the cost, he replied, "Sorry, boss" (as he always called me), "try as I might, I couldn't find any at less than…" and here he paused mischievously, "… 3,000 feet!"

A call at the percussion studio was invariably much enjoyed by any guest I might be taking round the College. Gilbert always received them with infinite charm and would, for example, delight in demonstrating his or a student's skill on the cimbalom I had bought in Budapest. He also established a wonderful tradition, which his successor, Ian Wright, maintained, of requiring all percussion students to compose for their instruments. One particular outcome which Gilbert especially cherished came about when Mark Glentworth, preparing his final exams, spontaneously happened to produce a minor masterpiece, a beguiling vibraphone solo to which he gave the title *Blues for Gilbert*. It is still widely played today and constitutes, long after Gilbert's death, an enduring personal tribute.

The next steps were then to appoint key tutors to support this powerful spread of experienced leadership. For example, within the School of Academic Studies[77], I derived particular satisfaction from being able to take early steps to ensure that the new courses

---

[77] Initially headed by John Wray and subsequently by Percy Welton when the RNCM developed its general academic as well as its degree courses.

should include a strong element of historical work. It was particularly exhilarating to be able to appoint at one fell blow a clutch of wide-ranging historians whose teaching could underpin and therefore illumine the performances given by their charges. Joining us within a single year were such fine scholars as Peter Syrus, celebrating the riches of the Renaissance world; David Ledbetter, as a pre-eminent Bach scholar and harpsichordist; David Young, steeped in Haydn and his contemporaries; Colin Beeson, whose Doctorate from Reading University bespoke a deep love of all that Beethoven represented; Geoffrey Norris, a Rachmaninov expert who unfortunately was tempted too soon into the world of musical journalism, but whose expertise was more than covered by Geoffrey Jackson from the RMCM; and especially Douglas Jarman, whose remarkable research and globally recognised authority on the music of Alban Berg remains unchallenged. Together, they covered the whole panoply of Western music since the Middle Ages, providing for our students fresh awareness and understanding of all that lay behind the notes they were performing.

Turning to the all-important question of developing the student's aural awareness, I was anxious from the outset that we should succeed as far as possible in emulating the wonderful record of the Paris Conservatoire in training acutely sensitive ears in all its students. To this end I asked the incomparable Nadia Boulanger if she could identify for me an ideal person to help us replace traditional English keyboard harmony teaching with the French solfège system of ear training. Nadia's response was characteristic: "Of course, Pierre Boulez would be the best but he, I feel, will not come to Manchester! To be serious, the best man for you is hiding in the opera pit in Cologne. He is a Frenchman who will bring you just what you want." This man was Michel Brandt who developed in the College a specialist aural training team which included Simon Parkin, the composer, and Karen Humphreys who, to this day, brings the RNCM the considerable benefit of heading its Junior Department.

However strong might become the new College's teaching faculty, and however gifted might be the students it was called upon to guide, good work in these spheres would patently be put at risk if the administration of the College was not comparably strong and resourceful. The pivotal appointment, which one was all too conscious of a need to make as strongly as possible, was that of the first Secretary to the College. I personally needed to know that in this key position would be a colleague upon whom I and all the musicians could rely with complete faith and confidence. I did not believe it would be possible to make an entirely secure appointment in this case without taking steps to move beyond the traditional screen of the interview room. I was concerned, as far as possible, to plumb both the person and the personality lying behind any likely candidate's façade.

Accordingly, once the necessary searches had been carried out and a shortlist had been assembled, I was concerned to find a better way of identifying and understanding individual temperaments and partialities within this group. All had demonstrated positive interest in working for a new music conservatoire but I needed to devise an opportunity to relax the formality inevitably associated with an interview situation. To this end, I booked a private dining room in the Midland Hotel to which I invited the seven selected candidates (all male, as it happened) for a gentleman's club-type dinner in relaxed circumstances where individual enthusiasms could emerge and character impressions could be better formed.

This arrangement proved invaluable in that during the course of an increasingly genial evening, it became crystal clear to me that one candidate stood out far beyond all the others. In the event, truth to tell, I did not really need the following day's formal interviews in order to make the decision which I confidently reached in favour of Air Commodore, Mansel Vaughan [Plate 29], who joined the College as Secretary from September 1972 and who was to render us immeasurable service for the next ten years. He, in turn, and with my full agreement, recruited a strong senior secretariat by appointing two erstwhile Royal Air Force colleagues, Squadron Leader Buckley and Wing Commander Palmer. This convivial triumvirate, bringing with it all the disciplined dedication of senior military officers, endowed the College from the outset with an administrative machinery of outstanding quality and resilience, well equipped to deal with the many complications we were to experience during those years of the faltering Heath government, local authority unrest and a general degree of national depression. The Vaughan / Buckley / Palmer troika was to see the College through to the more confident years which followed, their dedication being delightfully exemplified by the generous way in which each in turn observed the RAF mess tradition of donating, on retirement, an inscribed piece of silverware.

Another key support area calling for early and vigorous action was that of the library. It was immediately apparent that such library material as we might inherit from either the NSM or the RMCM would, at best, be nominal and largely limited to a haphazard collection of sheet music in varying degrees of disintegration. Moreover, the brief given to the new College's architects had also failed to provide adequately for the needs of a new conservatoire in the technological age that had now dawned. The only provision in the architects' drawings was just one far too small room. It was necessary to ensure adequate space with scope to expand. The priority was clearly to identify and appoint as chief librarian a paragon able to create, almost from scratch, a library fit to meet all these challenges.

To the College's great good fortune we were able to identify such a gem in the person of Anthony Hodges [Plate 30], whom we found lurking in the depths of Liverpool public libraries. Tony, with his insatiable enthusiasm, was to prove a godsend to the whole College community for the next twenty-five years during which he ensured that the library would provide a rich harvest for all its users, whether in pursuit of books, performing material, recordings and indeed all other technological aids. Many of the early steps we took, once we had solved the accommodation problem, were down to his enterprise. Soon we were bidding effectively at a sale of the Barbirolli estate. To our gratification, it was not long before the College was also being generously endowed with treasures such as Dame Eva Turner's operatic vocal scores, Jascha Horenstein's conductor's scores and, most precious of all in one respect, Alan Rawsthorne's surviving manuscripts[78]. It was symptomatic of Anthony Hodges's innate sense of initiative that shortly after Rawsthorne's manuscripts had been received, he founded and established the Rawsthorne Society which flourishes to this day and constitutes a living testament to his enterprise.

It was both logical and necessary that we should, in parallel, also take early steps to establish within the College a recording department whose facilities and services were to prove invaluable

---

[78] The Rawsthorne bequest not only embraced all his surviving manuscripts but also included an arresting death mask fashioned by the sculptor, Roy Noakes.

from the start. To this end I was fortunately able to recruit as our first recording manager an immensely gifted former BBC colleague, John Bower [Plate 31], who, until I enticed him to Manchester, had been Chief Engineer for the BBC Transcription Service. In turn, and very swiftly, recording provision within the College was expanded to include everything from a 'dead room' to direct linking between opera theatre, concert hall, recital room and the recording studios. The value to the students of such arrangements cannot be exaggerated. A young executant's ability to use recording either to check on progress or to demonstrate ability had become indispensable in the highly competitive prevailing conditions. John Bower also developed an enthusiastic team of assistants headed by John Egan, who remains with the College to this day and who carried on John's good work after the latter lived quietly in retirement in Bournemouth.

One further fairly monumental challenge remained: that of providing good catering provision. Successive cost-cutting briefings from the Joint Committee had limited plans for the College's kitchens to a scale barely capable of meeting primary school expectations. Eventually, after strenuous argument, we succeeded in convincing all concerned that, if the College was to be in use from early morning to late evening and was to satisfy the needs of hundreds of visitors when concerts or operas were being presented, then an adequate catering operation would be essential. Once this argument had eventually been won, there remained a further series of challenges in which we were initially far less successful: how to find a catering director who could satisfy the resulting range of requirements and who could assemble a harmonious and willing staff. I have to record that we made many mistakes along this road; early appointees either wished to recreate The Ritz at a blow or might have found it hard to keep a job at Joe's Transport Café. Having set our face against resorting to contract caterers, we were mercifully spared further indignities by the timely arrival of Martin Angel, who swiftly and surely developed a range of in-house catering to meet our communities' needs, while providing visitors with welcoming bar and restaurant options. Today the College's success as an arts centre owes much to the warm welcome it offers its patrons while not overlooking the students.

Whereas there had been need for urgent action to improve upon the limited original specifications in such areas as the library, no comparable criticism can in any way be levied against the broad sweeping vision which so informed and inspired the plans which the architect, John Bickerdike, had prepared. From the imaginatively conceived roof garden, generously endowed by Robert and Kathleen Ollerenshaw in memory of their daughter [Plates 32 & 33], to the breath-taking sweep offered by the main entrance and the glass-fronted concourse, the immediate sensation is one of light and air and bold breadth. This splendid sense of space is then fully sustained by the beautifully designed opera theatre and the lofty concert hall (magnificently enlarged and refurbished in 2014 by the inclusion of new balconies). The College cannot exaggerate the extent of its debt to the Founding Fathers for the resolution with which they supported and implemented Bickerdike's confident vision.

In particular the opera theatre, modelled, we were told, upon the then recently opened City Theatre in Dortmund, provided the College, and its opera department in particular, with a facility which remains to this day much admired by all who have occasion to enjoy performances in it. The creation of this jewel called, in turn, for much skill in assembling a team of theatre staff to run it to best possible use, with its wide 66-foot deep stage, its spacious opera pit capable of being raised or lowered at the press of a button, its substantial scene-building docks, its extensive lighting provision and all the other technical facilities – to say nothing of the auditorium itself, with its steeply tiered seating allowing perfect sightlines from every seat in the house.

Our first Theatre Director, David Keetch, moved on quickly, to be followed by Richard Griffiths, a long-standing and immensely resourceful friend of the College now living in France, who was ultimately succeeded by Matt English, a true man of the theatre, who was to guide its destinies with skill and devotion for many years. At his side, we were fortunate to appoint from BBC Television a lighting controller of unusual artistic sensitivity and versatility, Philip Edwards, who was to be found at the heart of every opera production in the theatre for the next forty years, and by whose death in 2014 the College lost one of its finest and most dedicated servants.

Making a Start

As the summer months rolled forward, and as the stark uncompromising outline of the new building began to dominate the surrounding area, we all grew progressively more excited as the point neared when real activity could begin and the first of our carefully prepared plans could be put into practice. As completion approached, we were increasingly permitted a degree of selective occupation. The first such occasion occurred on 15 November 1972 when it was agreed that we could arrange for an invited audience to occupy the concert hall for the first time.

To celebrate this opportunity, I was delighted that Michael Vyner, the adventurous director of the London Sinfonietta, had readily agreed to bring the orchestra to Manchester to give the inaugural concert in the new hall. The BBC decided to record what was then fast becoming quite a glamorous occasion although, in the continuing absence of some supporting facilities, they were effectively obliged to treat our nascent concert hall as an 'Outside Broadcast' site. I was determined that, from the outset, we should make a strong and clear statement both by bringing to Manchester London's premiere orchestra devoted to the performance of contemporary music, and to reinforce and complement that statement by choosing a programme demonstrating Manchester's prominent role in creating fine new music then travelling the world at large. This we achieved by devoting the whole programme to what had become known as the Manchester School. In simple terms, this meant a concert of works by three remarkable composers who had studied together under Richard Hall at the RMCM during the 1950s – all of them by 1972 outstanding ambassadors for new British music: Harrison Birtwistle, Peter Maxwell Davies and Alexander Goehr.

Since this was to be the first occasion on which the new College would present itself in its new surroundings, it was entirely appropriate that many of the invited audience should reflect the role that the constituent authorities had so resolutely played in bringing the College into existence. Thus we welcomed row upon row of dignitaries representing Cheshire, Lancashire, Manchester and Salford, all resplendent in their chains of office. So, too, did we delight in the presence of so many other people who, for so long, had played various key roles in bringing the College into being. Presiding, with evident pride and characteristic vigour, was Dr. (soon to be Dame) Kathleen Ollerenshaw, to whom more than to any other single person did we owe the fact that the College was now a reality.

The concert itself passed off quite splendidly. Both the BBC and the College could record a milestone of some significance. The occasion also had its amusing moments: as he took charge of the operation, Mansel ('Manny') Vaughan issued a note guiding members of the orchestra on where "to stow their kit" on arrival – shades of the old RAF symphony orchestra, whose members, such as Dennis Brain and Norman Del Mar, would never have thought twice about being instructed to "stow their kit". At one point, a member of the audience, but not one wearing any municipal regalia, shouted "Rubbish!" Musical history is, of course, littered with instances when premieres, such as that of *The Rite of Spring*, were greeted with vociferous dissent; we could perhaps conclude that our friend's interruption symbolised a point when we could say we had arrived. Certainly I derived enormous reassurance from Sir Denis Forman, the head of Granada Television, who quietly said to me after the concert, "Well, you really have set the place alight: long may it burn".

This concert, together with a number of acoustic exercises we immediately undertook involving a much larger orchestra and chorus, revealed that a sharp edge to the concert hall's acoustic needed to be somewhat softened. To this end, a series of hessian-covered baffles were strategically added to the side and rear walls, while the general character of the hall was strikingly transformed by the installation of a vividly arresting weaving, commissioned from Elda Abramson, to whom we had been introduced by my first secretary, Susan Foster[79], herself an accomplished weaver. This very large tapestry, in a deep rich red and flecked with orange (and appropriately for a concert hall entitled 'Firebird'), not only helped to bring balm to our ears but also provided colourful relief from the uniform grey brick. Indeed, so stark had been the initial impression that the new building was swiftly dubbed, especially by the students, 'Colditz'. Strenuous efforts were then put in hand to secure funding to provide discreet decoration and embellishment to soften its general character.

The early weeks in 1973 saw us conducting our first auditions in preparation for the new courses we would be launching in September. It proved to be a distinctly sobering experience. We only found eighty-seven applicants, among them a mere three cellists, who met the standards we were determined to establish from the outset. This represented barely half the number of available

---

[79] A nationally accredited weaver, Susan Foster later left the College in order to establish her own studio in Kendal, where a reminder of her life's work survives in the form of a wall plaque marking the site of her studio at the foot of Windermere Road.

vacancies. What all this brought home to us with some force and urgency was that, inevitably perhaps, the rest of the world still remained unaware that a new college was opening its doors. If anything, it galvanised us there and then to do everything in our power to make our mark at large.

Fortunately, I was able to attend all these first auditions. Whereas many applicants were disappointing, we were able occasionally to enjoy the excitement of discovering an exceptional talent. One such experience was the moment when Peter Manning, a 17-year-old violin student at Chetham's, appeared. He quickly became the leader of our symphony orchestra playing with real distinction, most memorably on tour in Scandinavia when excelling in Strauss's *Ein Heldenleben* with its notoriously testing solos. Peter's subsequent achievements have fully borne out that striking early promise, as his illustrious career reveals: leading two ensembles bearing Benjamin Britten's name (quartet and orchestra) and now serving as Concert Master and Leader of the Royal Opera House Orchestra in Covent Garden, while also busy passing on to fortunate students the fruits of his rewarding career.

Whether from curiosity or because we had begun more effectively to advertise ourselves, visitors came in increasing numbers during the spring and summer months of 1973. We had long visualised the College becoming a distinctive Arts Centre for Manchester, and to this end we immediately promoted a number of concerts such as a short series devoted to the music of Schubert, given by Thomas Hemsley, John Shirley-Quirk and the Allegri String Quartet. Happily, before long, the opera theatre would be enlivened by visits from such leading companies as Opera North, Scottish Opera, the Royal Shakespeare Company, Northern Ballet Theatre and Ballet Rambert, while the concert hall would become the home of the Manchester Chamber Concerts Society with frequent visits from the BBC Northern Symphony Orchestra (now Philharmonic), the Hallé and Manchester Camerata.

In all this the College's image was wonderfully served by the engagement of Keith Murgatroyd as our design consultant. Keith had been largely responsible for the design of the new *Book of Common Prayer*, widely admired within the Church of England and beyond. He swiftly established for the College in clear and strongly distinctive ways what is, in today's commercial jargon, glibly called a brand image. His skill led to the College receiving an RSA Design Centre award.

For this we attended a ceremony in London when four beneficiaries received their accolades in alphabetical order, starting with Bovis, the house builders, and ending with the RNCM. Presenting the awards, the Duke of Edinburgh initially seemed somewhat perplexed, as he turned to us and murmured, "Well, I suppose, come to think of it, you can have design in music – can't you?"

Excitement mounted as we approached midsummer and the formal opening of the College, conducted by The Duchess of Kent, on 28 June. [Plate 34] In brilliant sunshine, the young Duchess personified the spirit of the new College into which she there and then, and for the next thirty and more years, entered with wholehearted enthusiasm and unstinting support. Indeed, the College was to be immeasurably enriched by the continuing interest which, as President (the Queen graciously becoming its Patron), the Duchess took in each and every aspect of our development, the encouragement she invariably offered and the way in which she so often enthused about the College in various situations far and wide. [Plate 35]

While our Founding Fathers had wrought near miracles in preparing for the creation of the new College, there remained one area for which it had not been possible to lay earlier plans. This concerned the vital matter of student accommodation, likely to assume ever-increasing importance as the College's reach and numbers enlarged. Our need to provide adequate arrangements, particularly to accommodate freshers and students from overseas, and ideally in the form of a self-contained student residence, was clearly now both urgent and fundamental.

Seemingly out of the blue, a possible solution presented itself for which enduring thanks are due to Ida Carroll and a former member of her Board of Governors, one W. P. Lockley, then a member of the Methodist General Conference. He had chanced to mention to Ida that, reflecting reduced recruitment to the priesthood, the Methodists would be selling one of their three residential colleges in England. The one in London would certainly be retained, but either Bristol or Manchester would have to be sold. Alerted to this situation, we waited with a measure of anxious impatience to learn where the axe would fall. Before the decision became public, Lockley discreetly let us know that Bristol would be retained and, therefore, that Hartley Victoria Methodist College, near Alexandra Park in South Manchester, would be placed on the market. We expressed immediate interest and were particularly gratified that our constituent authorities indicated spontaneous readiness to support a reasonably priced purchase.

Two serious obstacles soon presented themselves. It appeared that the Trusthouse Forte hotel chain was expressing keen interest in acquiring the college in order to develop this site in view of its convenient location near the main route from the city centre to Manchester airport. Fortuitously, however, it quickly emerged that the Methodist authorities had, with great prescience, taken the precaution of specifying that, after any sale, the college had to be maintained for educational purposes. To our great relief this provision immediately removed a hurdle which otherwise would have rendered the proposition totally beyond our means.

At the same time, it appeared that Manchester University was also interested in making a bid. Our instinct was to explore the possibility of reaching some understanding with the University. There followed a very agreeable luncheon with Manchester's then Vice-Chancellor, Arthur Armitage, whose memory is still warmly held and marked by such legacies as the Armitage playing fields on Moseley Road. A convenient solution emerged when it transpired that the University was facing strong demands for additional facilities from its Student Union, while we were in a position to make available a former building of the RMCM in Devas Street, ideally situated for University Student Union use. It seemed that an arrangement offering mutual satisfaction was therefore available and that, in consequence, the University would not be making a bid for the Methodist college.

The way being clear, we could now sit down with the Methodist authorities to negotiate a mutually acceptable price. To our considerable excitement we soon became the proud possessors of the college for the sum of £304,000, a modest figure scarcely credible even in those days. Renamed Hartley Hall, it brought us at a stroke a range of fine buildings accommodating some 170 students together with good dining and kitchen facilities, a large lecture hall, a number of recreation rooms and a delightful chapel, complete with a good small organ. Thus we became, to the best of our belief, the only music conservatoire in the world with its own chapel. These invaluable facilities enabled us to use Hartley Hall for a wide range of events such as celebrations and fundraising dinners, to say nothing of an annual carol service in the chapel, for which we adopted the King's College, Cambridge model. The college's grounds also extended to some six acres providing a football/cricket field, a tennis court, a croquet lawn, flower and vegetable gardens and numerous outhouses. The whole college was dominated by a prominent clocktower with its traditional bell-toll. [Plate 36]

It was immediately apparent that an entirely new central heating system would have to be installed and that further modernisation was needed. To our good fortune we also inherited the former warden of the hall, Dr. Percy Scott, whose goodwill in helping with the transition rendered the whole process marvellously smooth and harmonious. He was always available to help at any hour, except if Manchester United were playing at home on a Saturday afternoon. There soon developed a settled student community able to benefit from the various facilities Hartley Hall offered, while enjoying what for many was a first alternative to home life. In addition, its facilities enabled us to accommodate sporting enterprises such as a College cricket team and an annual inter-conservatoire football tournament during the mid-year recess. Hartley Hall also provided a suite for use by our President, The Duchess of Kent, when she was in residence, in addition to guest flats for visiting tutors and accommodation for student groups from other conservatoires. Before long, it also found itself in demand as a vacation conference centre.

The purchase of Hartley Hall represented one physical aspect of the College's growth. Another was the process of acquiring land bordering upon the main new building in order to meet an increasing need to extend our facilities. Some delay proved unavoidable on account of the fact that the immediately adjacent plot from which housing had already been cleared boasted two surviving pubs. One, the Nag's Head, was swiftly condemned and demolished after we had stimulated police interest in some of its more nefarious activities. The other, the Lloyds' Arms, had a different history. Its owners, Bass, were initially somewhat reluctant to sell, but a deal was eventually sealed during an afternoon's racing at Haydock Park with a local representative of Bass, who was both a music and a racing enthusiast. Until we were ready to develop the land, we put the erstwhile pub to a number of interesting uses. Predictably perhaps, one was as an overspill practice amenity for brass players. The other, however, emerged when our enterprising catering department created a sandwich-making arm to meet a developing demand, initially so successful that it even extended to providing sandwiches for the annual snooker tournament at the Crucible Theatre in Sheffield.

As we laid our plans for the first full academic year, we tried hard to stimulate interest in our work from around the city and beyond. For example, we instituted a number of public talks by notable personalities whose presence we hoped would be of general interest to students and public alike. Thus, Sir Christopher Bonington gave a particularly engaging account of how, nearly but not quite, to reach the top of Everest, whilst Joyce Grenfell brought her own inimitable brand of humour to an overflowing concert hall. Meanwhile, students ready to peer beyond the parameters of their particular instrument were offered a series of talks by visiting historians tracing the development of music and arts patronage from its monarchical and ecclesiastical origins to the present day.

One particular visit, in October 1973, will live long in the memory. In 1848, the last year of his life, Chopin gave final recitals in Edinburgh, Manchester, London and Paris. To mark the 125th anniversary of his death, the Chopin Society of Warsaw resolved to make handsome awards in each of these four cities. Whereas I understand that Edinburgh simply received a rather beautiful plaque, we were generously treated to the gift of an imposing statue in bronze by the eminent sculptress, Ludwika Nitschowa, Poland's counterpart to Barbara Hepworth. The statue, standing some six feet tall on a marble plinth, portrays Chopin appropriately wrapped and shrouded against wintry conditions.

To prepare for the unveiling ceremony in October, we arranged, in consultation with our friends in Warsaw, that this magnificent creation would be put on a ship sailing from Gdansk to Liverpool All went well initially, but it then transpired that HM Customs in Liverpool required the deposit of a £5,000 security bond before the statue could be released to us. Eventually, goodwill and common sense prevailed, and the statue, complete with plinth, was delivered to the College and placed on the concert hall concourse. Rumours swiftly began to circulate that the spirit of the statue was prone to walk the corridors at night.

As guest of honour to conduct the unveiling, I had earlier written to the Polish Ambassador in London. But no response was immediately forthcoming, and I well remember reaching the point that if no letter arrived within the next day or two an alternative arrangement would have to be made. To celebrate the gift of the statue, we had also organised an all-Chopin concert to precede the unveiling. Thankfully, when I walked into the office the next morning, Susan Foster, with a broad smile, was able to hand me a letter of acceptance from the Polish Embassy. The concert and the whole ceremony passed off perfectly. Later, during dinner, I allowed myself to confess to our guest that we had rather resigned ourselves to the likelihood that he might not be able to accept our invitation, since we had discovered that on our chosen evening England would be hosting a 'friendly' football match against Poland. "Ah," responded his Excellency, "it was precisely because of this match that I decided I should come to Manchester. You see, whenever I attend the Polish national team, they lose. Only when I am not there do they win."

One other visit, a few months later, was not without its complications. Edward Heath had, by now, been released from life in No. 10, and we decided that it would be interesting to invite him to deliver a talk about the ping-pong politics in China, in which he, like Nixon, had been engaged. The reply from Heath's office was less than immediately helpful: surely we wished him to talk on music, did we not? As courteously as possible, I tried to emphasise our wish to benefit from his authority on Anglo-Sino relations. Eventually, a compromise was reached, reflecting Heath's earlier devotion to the organ. He would accept an invitation to spend an extended hour alone in the concert hall, enjoying our much-admired Hradetzky organ. This would then be followed by a well-advertised book-signing, itself being preceded by a few introductory remarks from Heath. Mercifully, he seemed to have enjoyed his organ hour in that when he emerged the distinctly frosty atmosphere which had prevailed on arrival now gave way to an altogether more relaxed mood, helped not a little by the fact that the book-signing had also yielded fruitful results.

A particularly rewarding visit we all much enjoyed was when the Duke of Edinburgh, as President of the World Wildlife Fund, came to deliver a public lecture about its work. His Royal Highness had let it be known that he had never previously visited a music conservatoire and would like to know more about how we functioned. Naturally we were delighted by his expressed interest and responded by arranging for an informal reception to precede his lecture. This proved to be a most agreeable occasion at which senior staff did their best to satisfy the Duke's curiosity. As we dispersed, we all found ourselves sharing unstinted admiration for the remarkable way in which our guest had so quickly and comprehensively formed a clear understanding of what we were about, a perception unmistakably sharpened by the astutely penetrating nature of the questions he asked.

As the years rolled on, we were to enjoy many other memorable visits, for example when, in the course of a degree congregation [Plate 37], a distinguished guest might express thanks on behalf of fellow honorands. Some of these occasions remain vividly in the mind, such as when Sir John Drummond exploded with timely wrath on account of the way in which successive governments appeared content to allow state support for culture to become increasingly pared down. But perhaps the most moving occasion of all was when Lord Boyle, Vice-Chancellor of Leeds University, presented a visionary expression of his concern for the future of state education. As Edward Boyle, he had been an imposing and substantial figure on the front benches in Alec Douglas-Home's administration, when he had more than once inspired the Commons by his vision for education in Britain. Now, years later, a frail figure wracked by the all too evident signs of the advanced cancer from which he was suffering, he once again spoke of his belief in the culture of education. The hush that fell upon the hall when he finished speaking constituted the most eloquent testimony that could have been offered to any politician.

Out and About

My memories of the College during the succeeding twenty-one years, until I retired in 1996, remain a jumble of widely contrasting recollections. By turn colourful, joyous, astonishing or unnerving, and much more besides, I shall not attempt here to offer them in anything like methodical fashion. [Plate 38] As I have recorded in a previous chapter, anyone seeking a sequential chronicle of the College's early years should turn to Michael Kennedy's comprehensively informative record[80]. Some of my particular memories relate to external influences upon the development of the College – none more so than the Education Reform Act of 1989. This dictated a fundamental change to the way in which we ran the College by decreeing that a single Board of Governors should

---

[80] Michael Kennedy: *Music Enriches All* (Carcanet Press Ltd, 1994)

replace the bicameral governance of Court and Council which we had hitherto enjoyed. Thereby we lost the invaluable services of two who had done more than any others to steer us to progress and near prosperity – Dame Kathleen Ollerenshaw and Sir Charles Groves.

Another potentially critical point was reached when we were threatened by serious political interference early in Margaret Thatcher's administration. Without warning, her first education henchman, Sir Keith Joseph, let it be known that he was minded to accord to the Royal Academy of Music a *primus inter pares* status, with preferred funding to match. He contended that he saw this as a way of stimulating standards and helping to develop in Britain individual musicians of international calibre. Had his intentions been realised, the effect would have been to reduce all other conservatoires in the country to secondary status. Mercifully, sufficient outrage was voiced to deter him from implementing this proposal, but for a time something approaching conservatoire civil war had existed.

One other politically provoked situation prompted a youthful prank which eventually produced amusement throughout our College community. It came about during the Falklands War, at a time when I was undertaking an extended tour in Canada. The fertile imagination of a small group of junior staff and students brought about the publication of a notice which I was alleged to have issued and which announced that the College had received a joint approach from the Ministry of Defence and the Department of Education and Science, calling upon us to provide a volunteer Forces Entertainments Group to go to the Falklands and "assist in maintaining morale". The notice stressed that it was a call for volunteers but warned that, if insufficient numbers came forward, conscription might follow. It further stated that the College contingent would be under the command of Air Commodore Vaughan, the College Secretary, and called upon all to demonstrate their patriotism by volunteering immediately. I am told that this provoked interestingly contrasted responses within the College and that no small degree of confusion swirled around until the originators of this ingenious spoof ultimately revealed their authorship.

As each School of Study grew in strength and achievement, so the College, young as it still was, could begin to boast of gifted talent emerging to enrich our concert halls and opera houses. If my stray recollections may appear to concentrate particularly on opera, this is not for a moment to suggest that I was in any way less concerned for the welfare of our instrumentalists. It is simply a reflection of the fact that opera, by its nature, encompasses talent from all musical and artistic disciplines and can, therefore, be reasonably said to represent the institution's most collective achievement. Over the years we certainly produced as many fine instrumentalists as singers, to say nothing of significant groups of composers, conductors and scholars.

Among our pianists I would unhesitatingly list four, although this is not for a moment to discount several others. First, joining in mid-study from the RMCM, was Peter Donohoe, and I recall a particularly interesting discussion which Peter and I shared at one point. He was to enjoy something of an *année célèbre* in that he was entered for two of the world's most prominent international competitions, the Leeds, followed by the Tchaikovsky in Moscow. While Peter had been selected as one of the six finalists for Leeds, he ultimately only secured sixth place. This, he came to tell me, had prompted him seriously to consider withdrawing from Moscow, in that he felt that, having failed to win in Leeds, he could not expect to be victorious in Moscow. I do not claim to have been instrumental in dissuading him from these conclusions but, as all the world knows, he competed in Moscow and duly emerged as joint winner.

Closely following upon Peter came Stephen Hough, a finalist in the first BBC Young Musician of the Year competition in 1978 and today a strong favourite throughout the land, with repeated and thoroughly well-merited successes at the BBC Proms and elsewhere. Stephen has also emerged as an interesting composer. Another piano prizewinner of some significance was Ian Fountain who, in 1989, enjoyed the distinction of winning the Rubinstein Competition in Tel Aviv. A man of many interests, not least cricket – he and I would chance to meet at Lord's more than once – Ian has not enjoyed as much prominence as might have been his due. Finally, another Steven, in this case Osborne. A passionate Scot, he has brought as much lustre to his homeland as has his counterpart in the tennis world, Andy Murray. I shall long remember attending, with Renna, his tutor, his first truly triumphant occasion when in 1991 he won the Clara Haskil Competition in Switzerland, playing Mozart's C minor Piano Concerto with fine stylish authority. Apart from many other pianists, our keyboard world has also produced a number of organists who have enriched our cathedrals such as Matthew Owens, first in Edinburgh and now in Wells, or Graham Barber, leading the music department in Leeds University when not also making many fine recordings.

The College's School of Strings, under the successive leadership of Cecil Aronowitz, Eleanor Warren and Rodney Slatford, produced a commensurate clutch of fine string players. I have already written about Peter Manning. To his name I would add that of Michael d'Arcy, an Irishman and an outstanding player, to whom is due the greatest credit for the sweep of fine string playing emerging from his native land and resulting from his dedicated work as both leader and teacher. The College's cello school, under the inspiring leadership of Ralph Kirshbaum, has produced many a fine cellist including Gregor Horsch, who came to us from Germany, won the coveted Pierre Fournier Award in 1988 and is now principal cello in the Concertgebouw orchestra in Amsterdam. By contrast, I also think of another accomplished cellist, Hannah Roberts, whose musical playing is matched by the extent to which, as a teacher, she is now responsible for the emergence of many gifted young cellists.

Nor is there any shortage of exceptional College-trained viola players, such as Yuko Inoue, who found her way to Manchester at the age of 17 from Japan on her own initiative and without a word of English to her name, but determined to study with one of our tutors, her compatriot Nobuko Imai. Many fine double bass players passed through the College during these years, but one in particular comes strikingly to mind in that he represents what some might call a contradiction in terms, being a virtuoso soloist double bassist: Leon Bosch, who came to us from Cape Town and to whose credit now lie a number of very fine recordings to set alongside a distinguished concert record, for example in his capacity as principal double bass in the Academy of St. Martin-in-the-Fields. Neither should we overlook the extent to which young guitarists from the College, such as Craig Ogden, have made their way in this burgeoning but highly competitive world.

Under the inspiring leadership of Timothy Reynish, succeeding Philip Jones, many a fine wind player and percussionist has emerged to bring colour and vitality to orchestras up and down the land. In particular, the College's pioneering work in the field of the wind band has led to successful recordings and BBC Prom appearances, while bringing the RNCM new recognition, not least in America where the wind band occupies such a central role. Perhaps I may, however, permit myself to name just one wind player and one percussionist. The wind player who has inspired a new respect for the saxophone as both a solo instrument and in chamber music is Rob Buckland. The percussionist is Adrian Spillett who first sprang to notice when winning the BBC Young Musician of the Year competition in 1998 and whose percussion ensemble, 4-MALITY, is now in wide demand.

Soon after its formation, the College also evolved a policy of creating fellowships for young conductors whereby, effectively as junior members of staff, they were enabled to learn their craft in concentrated and intensive ways, ranging from directing off-stage bands and accompanying film scores to directing large scale choral and orchestral concerts. Notably successful among them has been Sian Edwards, who entered the College as a horn player, delighted Michael Tippett when conducting his Fourth Symphony and subsequently when, as the first female conductor to appear at the Royal Opera House, she conducted his opera, *The Knot Garden* (1969).

Benefitting from the inspiration and guidance of Anthony Gilbert, and visiting composers such as Harrison Birtwistle, Peter Maxwell Davies and Petr Eben, the College soon began to produce a number of interesting and highly original composers. Two who emerged during the earlier part of the College's history were Martin Butler and Simon Holt. Both remain prominently before the public today, each with a folio of arresting and significant works, thereby demonstrating that Manchester remains a good place in which creative gifts can flourish.

Whatever may be the artistic achievements of which Manchester, or indeed Britain for that matter, can legitimately boast, a danger of relapsing into a measure of contented parochialism may always lurk. To guard against such tendencies I was determined from the outset that we should seek to develop purposeful associations with fellow conservatoires abroad, to learn from their examples and for our students to benefit from international interaction. Happily, we were able quite quickly to establish early links with a number of outward-looking and well-established conservatoires.

Our first transatlantic association was with the Curtis Institute in Philadelphia, who sent us an engaging string quartet bringing us new works by a number of American composers. The Curtis Institute's new Director, recently appointed in succession to Rudolf Serkin, was John de Lancie. Prior to joining Curtis, de Lancie had been principal oboe in the Philadelphia Orchestra, where he had enjoyed something approaching a thirty year association with its conductor, Eugene Ormandy. John had once told me that, at Ormandy's invitation, Edward Heath was coming to conduct the orchestra in Elgar's *Cockaigne Overture* in a concert otherwise devoted to a Bruckner Symphony conducted by Ormandy. When, later, I asked how the visit had gone, John replied "Well, you know, we were quite enjoying it until your Mr. Heath started to give us a lecture on English constitutional history!"

Many years previously, John, despite already being principal oboe in the Pittsburgh Symphony Orchestra, had been conscripted as a young GI, in which capacity he spent the first weeks after the war in a force occupying southern Bavaria. Part of their duties involved house to house visits in the course of which John one day found himself standing on the lawn of a large house in Garmisch which happened to be occupied by none other than Richard Strauss. He told me that, at one point during this wholly unexpected encounter with the great man, he was emboldened by the senior composer's quiet courtesy to ask Strauss if he had written an oboe concerto. No, he had not, came the reply. But only a few months later he did, in fact, write his widely admired concerto, of which John was to become a fine exponent, although denied the opportunity to give its first performance.

Over the years we established a number of particularly rewarding links with European conservatoires. One of the first, with the Prague Academy, was similarly initiated by an exchange of string quartets. In Manchester we had just reached the point of forming the first student quartet which really excited our hopes for the future. Searching for a title, we decided to use the name of Adolf Brodsky, first leader of the Hallé Orchestra and subsequently second Principal of the RMCM. Unwittingly, this caused some unexpected alarm since the Czechs, upon receiving from us confirmation that we would be sending them the Brodsky Quartet, responded with a discreet but emphatic plea emphasising that they had not expected to be receiving a Russian quartet! Happily, we were able to reassure them by listing the very English names of the members of the quartet, while explaining the source from which the Brodsky title had been derived.

Another early association, which was to continue well beyond my retirement, was that which the College established with the Frankfurt Hochschule für Musik, whose Rektor, Hans Dieter Resch was, together with his wife, Beate, to become good personal friends with Renna and myself. The annual exchanges which ensued generally took the form of a student foursome accompanied by a tutor. Perhaps the most bizarre group Frankfurt ever sent us took the form of a quartet of double bass players, each member being marginally taller than the next. They were accompanied by the organist of Munich Cathedral, Edgar Krapp, whose masterful playing and courteous bearing swiftly silenced any student tendencies towards schoolboy homonymic frivolity.

Many of our international associations were to take much larger forms than being simply concerned with soloists or small groups. For example, the RNCM Chamber Orchestra was to develop a rewarding tradition of annual tours of Southern France, under its French conductor, Michel Brandt. Predictably, these tours proved enjoyably life-enhancing for the orchestra's young members and also, we liked to think, our French audiences. A typical tour would be launched in the Salle Varèse in Lyon, where we also established a mutually rewarding association with the École Supérieur under that immensely gifted French composer, Gilbert Amy. Similarly, a visit to Italy by the RNCM Symphony Orchestra was to become a no less rewarding feature of each year's calendar. This Tuscan visit, based on the dynamic summer school at Montepulciano, also owed much to the local encouragement of an eminent composer, in this case, Hans Werner Henze. [Plate 39]

The RNCM Symphony Orchestra's very first overseas experience had also been closely linked to the start of the College's operatic enterprises. It involved tours of Denmark and Sweden with programmes featuring such substantial orchestral masterpieces as Mahler's *Das Lied von der Erde* and Strauss's *Ein Heldenleben*. Many of our most interesting early operatic initiatives would similarly involve undertakings away from Manchester, whether elsewhere in Britain or abroad, in addition to those which we presented in our own opera theatre. It is on these and some of the young artists and incipient stars that the remainder of this chapter will dwell.

Our initial operatic impetus derived from the fact that we had been endowed with an absolutely splendid theatre, large in terms of stage and pit depth, wonderfully equipped and, above all, with acoustics to delight singer, orchestra and audience alike. We would have been sadly failing not only in our obligations but in our advantageous opportunities had we not, from the outset, laid special emphasis upon opera, logically treating it as representing the sum of all the College's parts. [Plate 40]

I had originally hoped that it might be possible to open the theatre with a new commission, and with this in view had extended an invitation to Alan Rawsthorne. Sadly he died before the project could progress and, with time pressing, our all-Lancastrian solution was to feature Gordon Crosse's *Purgatory* [Plate 41] in a double bill with Walton's *The Bear*, in which John Rawnsley was characteristically compelling in the title role. Our first full-length production followed just three months later, in May 1973, when Joseph Ward's wonderfully characterised production of Britten's *A Midsummer Night's Dream* was aided not a little by Juanita Waterson's ravishingly original costumes [Plates 42 & 43], and sung and played with great verve to hearteningly enthusiastic audiences. To the young and inexperienced cast and orchestra in this production, Sir Charles Groves brought his customary calm assurance and authority.

An important additional service which RNCM Opera was in a uniquely favourable position to provide would be to offer well-established conductors their first opportunity to work in opera. This policy, which was also to see such conductors as Richard Hickox (*Aida*), Sir Neville Marriner (*La Bohème*) and Sian Edwards (*The Consul*) conducting their first operas at the College, was initiated by our inviting Elgar Howarth to conduct the next full-length production, presented in December 1973 – Stravinsky's *The Rake's Progress*. We were fortunate to have a strong and well-balanced cast for this production in which Nigel Robson was an engaging Tom Rakewell, Glenville Hargreaves an appropriately sinister Nick Shadow, Miriam Bowen a touchingly innocent Ann Trulove, and Paul Arden Griffiths a beguiling auctioneer, while Jennifer Heslop flounced outrageously as Baba the Turk. Anthony Besch skilfully recreated Hogarth's world with a particularly compelling mad scene at the end. The production did not altogether run smoothly in rehearsal, for which Besch's demands were, as we might have expected, considerable. But matters improved noticeably when we strengthened the team by the addition of an assistant producer for which role a young undergraduate singer applied enthusiastically. Who was this, thereby receiving his initiation in opera production, but Graham Vick, destined to bestride the world's great houses as part of a generation of new, young opera producers in much demand.

We had deliberately chosen the Stravinsky in order that, together with the Britten, Crosse and Walton works, we could present a unified repertoire of four twentieth-century operas when we promoted a short London season of these works at Sadler's Wells in December 1973. Many thought, and not a few voiced the view, that it was foolhardy for a College in Manchester to hire a prominent theatre such as Sadler's Wells, let alone then present so challenging a programme. But staff and students alike responded with wonderful determination, confidence and, above all, artistic standards. As a consequence, we returned to Manchester having won many new friends and shoals of favourable reviews. Yes, we may have been lucky in some respects, such as fortuitously choosing a time when there was limited competition in London. But perhaps we deserved a little bit of luck as well. Nor did we protest too loudly when we were told by some commentators and critics that our cheeky cuckoo had made what they saw as a timely invasion of the long-established London conservatoire nest.

Encouraged not only by our Sadler's Wells experience, but especially by the refreshingly bold and persuasive attitude of Paul Birkelund, Principal of the Royal Danish Academy in Copenhagen, we prepared to undertake our first overseas opera season. This we presented at the invitation of the Danish Ministry of Culture, with a welcome amount of local sponsorship, both at the Royal Opera in Copenhagen and, in the following week, at an arts centre in Aalborg. For this tour we took two double bills which were in themselves interchangeable, by reviving *Purgatory* and *The Bear* and adding Falla's *Master Peter's Puppet Show* and Ravel's *L'heure espagnole*. It transpired that, with the exception of Ravel's delightful masterpiece, none of these works had previously been seen in Denmark.

The value to a young student company of double bills will be self-evident. Returning to Manchester we therefore added a new pairing of Vaughan Williams's *Riders to the Sea* and *Stars and Shadows* by Brian Hughes. This work, parodying an audition session for the revival of a musical, represented the College's first commission of a new opera. For his libretto, Brian ingeniously and appropriately turned to Vaughan Williams's widow, Ursula, herself widely acknowledged as a gifted writer.

To this new double bill we then added a production of *La Bohème*, conducted by Sir Neville Marriner who would, I believe, be ready to agree that Puccini's masterpiece is not the easiest first opera for a conductor, however experienced, to undertake. In this production

Joseph Ward once again demonstrated his imaginative theatrical flair by ingeniously deploying the revolve to allow Act I to glide smoothly into Act II. It has to be admitted that in this second season at Sadler's Wells we did not succeed in making the same impact as on the first occasion, four years previously, although our reviews broadly suggested that we had, at the very least, consolidated our earlier advantage.

In the following year, we were to set ourselves what was certainly our most ambitious challenge to date: Wagner's *Das Rheingold*. For a young cast and orchestra, it represents a test of stamina quite like no other. Thankfully, when all was concluded, it was generally agreed that David Jordan's sensitive conducting had ensured that no tender voices had been harmed, while all had received a life-enhancing experience. Euan Smith, a member of the Royal Shakespeare Company's production staff in Stratford, had ingeniously met all Wagner's taxing theatrical demands. Our well-matched Rhinemaidens soared about on trapezes counterbalanced backstage by unseen acrobats, while the descent down to Nibelheim and the ultimate ascent into Valhalla were no less graphically presented. In a fine cast too numerous to mention in detail, Philip Joll offered a majestically sustained Wotan while Robert Dean's sinister Alberich was well-matched by Robert Buning's delightfully cringing Mime.

From Wagner we turned our attention in two very different directions: to Poulenc's *The Carmelites* and Handel's *Orlando*. Timothy Tyrrel's production of Poulenc's wonderful monastic study presented a guillotine of Grand Guignol proportions as each time the shining blade flashed to earth the crowd's macabre pleasure was dramatically accentuated by a decapitated head being hurled into the air to the hysterical delight of the whole crowd. Most productions of *The Carmelites* avoid such direct representation, these moments being conducted off-stage. Thankfully I can report that for the rest of our production, a suitable measure of reclusive serenity prevailed, particularly on account of the calming influence of Vanessa Williamson's Mère Marie.

Our production of Handel's *Orlando* by Brian Trowell, stylishly conducted by Richard Vardigans, was destined to enjoy an interesting life. After its initial presentation in our theatre in December 1978, it was revived at the invitation of Sir William Glock for the 1979 Bath Festival and then, in the following November, travelled to the Maison de La Culture in Grenoble. An amusing moment occurred in the press conference we were invited to hold on our arrival. It became evident from one question in particular that some of those present had not previously encountered a countertenor. After Robin Martin Oliver, in the title role, had sung a short excerpt to illustrate the music, a member of the press raised a question in a manner distinctly lacking in discretion and marked by derogatory anatomical implications. This immediately spurred Anne Dawson, Robin's wife and also a member of the cast, to rise with defiant French to the defence of her husband's manhood.

It was sometimes suggested among composers that when you encountered a colleague whom you had not met for a while, an opening gambit could usefully be to ask, "How's your opera coming along?" I entertained the hope that if, from time to time, RNCM Opera were to commission new work, it could in this way nurture potentially important additions to the repertoire. Following shorter works by Brian Hughes (*Stars and Shadows*) and Alison Cox (*The Time Killing*), I invited the leading Welsh composer, Alun Hoddinott, to undertake our first full-length commission. Our invitation was spontaneously welcomed with energetic enthusiasm, and within a matter of weeks Alun was telephoning to tell me that he had invited Myfanwy Piper to prepare a libretto based on Thomas Hardy's historically evocative novel, *The Trumpet Major*. From start to finish the whole experience proved infinitely rewarding, while accruing incidental benefits included the fact that John Piper, as Myfanwy's husband, also spent many interesting days with us. It is my belief that this opera must rank prominently within Hoddinott's prolific output, and it is my hope that Welsh National Opera, if no one else, will wish to keep it alive.

By now the range of operas we undertook was widened to include such varied stylistic challenges as those presented by both Paisiello and Rossini in their respective versions of *The Barber of Seville*. Exploration of operatic repertoire, new and old, also broadened during this period to include Dvořák's Slavonic elegance in *The Jacobin*, and Bartók in his macabre masterpiece, *Duke Bluebeard's Castle*, in which Stephen Richardson opened each dreaded door with commanding authority.

However inventive our choice of works might become, we always returned to the genius of Mozart and at this point we were about to present what I believe to this day was the most consummately perfect production of Mozart's *The Magic Flute* that any student company could have hoped to present. Not for the first time, our opera school was enjoying a fine stream of young singers of exceptional quality. Never was this more convincingly apparent than in our production of *Die Zauberflöte* sung in German, featuring Joan Rodgers as Pamina, elegantly partnered by Barry Banks as Tamino and supported by such fine singers as Ian Platt (Papageno), Linda Kitchen (Papagena), Nicholas Buxton (Monostatos), Stephen Richardson (Sarastro) and Evelyn Nicholson (Queen of the Night). To cap it all the Queen of the Night's three attendant ladies were none other than Jane Eaglen, Elizabeth Gaskell and Yvonne Howard. I list this cast in full simply to illustrate how fortunate we were, thanks to gifted tutors and students alike, to be able to mount at one and the same time so uniformly strong a cast. We knew, on that night in April 1982, that when Joan Rodgers's Pamina delivered an "Ach, ich fühl's" of extraordinary tenderness, an indelible star had indubitably arisen. Joan was also to be the first RNCM student to win the Kathleen Ferrier Award, although many others such as Anne Dawson and Stephen Gadd were soon to follow. With stylish work in the pit under the guidance of Noel Davies, on loan to us from English National Opera, and a production achieving a perfect balance between hilarity and solemnity by Joseph Ward, this was one of our opera nights none could easily forget.

Die Zauberflöte was followed by another highly successful Mozart opera. This time the choice fell on *Idomeneo* for which our distinguished guest conductor was Wilfried Boettcher while the producer, bringing with him additional Mozartian authenticity, was Peter Ebert. The set was a meticulous recreation of a Cretan temple.

Whereas I should like to feel able to claim that RNCM opera never relaxed its determination to achieve the most attainable professional results, we had not, until now, entered into co-production with an established professional company. This landmark was reached by means of a co-production with Welsh National Opera of Verdi's *Ernani*. It was conducted by the late Sir Edward Downes who, more than any other British conductor, could realize Verdi's intentions. His encyclopaedic knowledge of Verdi's operas may have been in some small way attributable to his poor eyesight, but it was incontestably incomparable.

Our second co-production was to follow a few years later, in 1987, when we collaborated with Opera North in Massenet's *Manon*. This was, as far as I can recall, the first occasion on which opera-goers had been able to admire the stylish work of Richard Jones, then emerging as a young producer of exceptional gifts. Idiomatically conducted by David Lloyd Jones, *Manon*, delightfully sung by Sally Harrison, also featured a new star destined to dominate the world's opera stages, the baritone Simon Keenlyside as Lescaut, Manon's cousin.

During the mid-'80s we undertook three consecutive new productions of operas by Benjamin Britten. The first, which we presented in November 1983 specifically to mark the seventieth anniversary of Britten's birth, was a production by David Penn of *Gloriana*, with Deborah Stuart-Roberts, a dignified Queen Elizabeth and John Connell an intensely moving Blind Ballad Singer. *Gloriana* may have experienced a less than satisfactory launch when it first appeared at Covent Garden as a Coronation celebration, but I like to feel that our production did something to restore the opera's reputation. It certainly succeeded sufficiently for the Aldeburgh Festival to ask if the production could be revived there, but this did not prove practicable.

We next presented a well-received new production of *The Rape of Lucretia* before turning, in 1985, to what many, myself included, regard as Britten's supreme masterpiece, *Billy Budd*. This production boasted an outstandingly sinister Claggart in Clive Bailey and a supremely sensitive Captain Vere in Geraint Dodd, together with Mark Tinkler, unfailingly moving as Billy. A particular moment will probably remain in the minds of many who were in the theatre one evening when the production had to be halted on account of a fire alarm at the pivotal point when Billy, in chains, was being tried for his life. It was an astonishing tribute to all concerned that, one hour later when the performance was resumed, this scene was replayed with all the passion and intensity which had been cruelly cut short the first time. I have often written about Joseph Ward's remarkable productions, but none was more outstanding than his *Billy Budd*, a significant feature of which was that the crew never left the ship and one was always conscious of their oppressive presence.

In the late 1980s RNCM Opera also presented two new Verdi productions. The first, *Rigoletto*, also enjoyed the advantage of three strong principals: Bruno Caproni in the title role, Sally Harrison as Gilda and Geraint Dodd as the Duke. This was followed by a new production of *Don Carlo*, produced by Stefan Janski, who was destined to play a vital role in the continuing development of RNCM Opera and who remained the College's Director of Opera until 2015.

His production courageously confronted and conquered the enormous challenges which this great work presents, particularly in its spectacular crowd scenes. The dynamic conductor was Ole Schmidt, whom we had, by now, appointed as the RNCM's Principal Guest Conductor. Loud were the criticisms voiced in the operatic press, particularly by those who told us that a student production of *Don Carlo* would be a monumental miscalculation, harmful to young participants. But I am delighted to be able to record that those who came to see our *Don Carlo* did not endorse this pessimistic prognosis but were uniformly favourable. What the reviews generously recorded was that we were fully justified in deciding upon a production of *Don Carlo* precisely because we were fortunate enough to be able to call upon a cast in which all the principal singers were well-matched and capable of producing a balanced and convincing result. Their names will be largely familiar to opera followers since the cast featured Sara Fulgoni as Eboli, David Ellis as Rodrigo, Edith Pritchard as the Queen, Pavlo Hunka as King Philip and Andrew Slater as the Grand Inquisitor, with Peter Ruane in the title role.

Peter Ruane was also to feature prominently in another new production that year, this time of Janáček's *House of the Dead*. In my belief, this of all Janáček's operas, being a conversational piece, is enhanced if sung in the original Czech, thereby coming closer to the composer's original intentions. As may be imagined, it took a great deal of individual graft and goodwill to achieve the point where all the cast could present plausible Czech. A helpful way of achieving this took the form of each and every participant being given a cassette with his or her lines in spoken Czech, thus enabling them, if only in parrot-fashion, to reach a reasonably convincing standard. A slightly amusing sequel occurred on the night when the Czech composer, Petr Eben, was visiting us. After the performance, I took Eben backstage and introduced him to Peter Ruane, who had sung the prominent part of Luca Kuzmič. Eben instinctively paid Ruane the compliment of addressing him in Czech, only for Ruane, suitably perplexed, to collapse into a vernacular more readily understood in Manchester.

At this time, another incontrovertibly shining star, Amanda Roocroft, rose in our operatic firmament. In the title role of Handel's *Alcina*, stylishly conducted by Richard Vardigans, her stellar gifts and compellingly beautiful voice immediately excited all the scouts representing professional opera companies. The same had been no less true when, a few months earlier, she had sung the role of Fiordiligi in a revival of Mozart's *Così fan tutte*. It was immediately clear to all, but especially so after *Alcina*, that opera houses the world over would be forming a queue at Mandy's door, and so, indeed, it has been.

Two other monumentally ambitious opera productions marked my final years at the RNCM. But before I turn to these I must briefly mention a few others, such as those in which Sara Fulgoni followed her vividly dramatic Eboli in *Don Carlo* with a ravishingly sung Cinderella in Massenet's *Cendrillion*, an impressively authoritative account of Schoenberg's *Erwartung* and a touchingly sensitive Suzuki, supporting Rosalind Sutherland's Butterfly. Much pleasure was also derived from two further Britten productions: *The Turn of the Screw*, splendidly conducted by Timothy Reynish, and *The Rape of Lucretia*, this time with Christine Rice in the title role.

After we had managed to present Janáček in Czech, we were confident, when we turned to Tchaikovsky's *Maid of Orleans*, that we could present a production in convincing Russian. The experience of singing in Slavonic languages during their student years can but be beneficial to young singers when they find themselves working anywhere with limited rehearsal time in foreign language productions. I believe that Jane Irwin, who was our very convincing Joan of Arc, would unhesitatingly agree with this view. Conducted with great flair by Paul McGrath, this was another Stefan Janski production which excelled in the way it marshalled the crowd scenes and used the inviting spaces of our opera theatre's large stage.

From a personal standpoint, I cannot but regard the production, again by Joseph Ward, of Vaughan Williams's *The Pilgrim's Progress*, as representing the crowning glory of RNCM Opera over its first twenty-three years. When we resolved to present this epic masterpiece, it had been neglected by all professional companies for far too long. What we offered was, moreover, the first full version without a single cut. A double CD, which I believe is still available, amply demonstrates the rich beauty of this great work. Our Pilgrim, possessed of both enormous stamina and a singularly beautiful baritone voice, was Richard Whitehouse.

Without indulging in misplaced sentimentality, I hope that some may feel a measure of sympathetic understanding if I allow myself to suggest that this far-reaching production, with its enormous

PLATE 38

PLATE 39

PLATE 40

PLATE 41

PLATE 42

PLATE 43

PLATE 44

PLATE 45

PLATE 46

Plate 47

physical, vocal and orchestral demands, can be said to have epitomised the College's own journey through its first twenty-three years, and not only in operatic terms. If, then, the College is the Pilgrim, perhaps friends and observers may be indulgent enough to regard the progress that we made during those years as having been interesting and well-enough founded to provide a strong platform for the future.

Bombed Out

Saturday 15 June 1996 will live long in the annals of Manchester as the day on which the heart of the city would be ripped apart in evil and devastating fashion. That morning, the IRA exploded a large bomb in the Arndale Centre, causing untold injury and damage, to say nothing of the chaos which inevitably ensued. It also so happened that this was to be my last weekend in the College and, on the Sunday, an occasion for a celebration generously organised and mounted by my colleagues, the memory of which, to this day, leaves me inordinately grateful and humbled.

Within the College the day had begun inauspiciously. A window cleaner working on the imposing high glass entrance doors had fallen from his ladder, seriously injuring himself on the stone floor below. An ambulance was immediately called but an age passed without response while a policeman cradled the suffering cleaner where he lay. It eventually transpired that no ambulances were available on account of the whole city being gridlocked as a consequence of the Arndale Centre explosion.

This unspeakable event not only led to mounting confusion, but complicated the travel arrangements of many friends arriving in Manchester to rehearse for, or participate in, events planned to take place at almost hourly intervals during Sunday. Among them were the College's President, The Duchess of Kent, who had, with characteristic generosity, volunteered to sing with the Chorus, and who then, without hesitation, headed off to the Arndale Centre to offer succour to casualties of the explosion. Others found that no taxis were available at Piccadilly Station to bring them to the College with the city centre now in a state of complete crisis emergency.

Remarkably enough, everything within the College still preceded as planned. Alfred Brendel gave a monumental performance of Beethoven's A major Sonata op. 101. Joan Rodgers sang Benjamin

Britten's *Les Illuminations* with all her ineffable charm. Ralph Kirshbaum played Tchaikovsky's *Rococo Variations*, Stephen Hough and Ronan O'Hora delighted us in piano duets, and various College ensembles ranging from string quartets to brass quintets, from string orchestra to wind band, contributed a wonderful variety of celebratory sounds.

Then in the evening came the supreme delight of RNCM Soloists, Opera Chorus and Orchestra, under Noel Davis and Sir Edward Downes, presenting the closing scenes from both *Der Rosenkavalier* and *Die Meistersinger*. Thus, the final curtain came down in a way which provided a wonderful climax as the Mastersingers triumphantly celebrated on that legendary meadow overlooking Nuremberg. In both these operatic masterpieces, the range of solo roles on stage represented an impressive cavalcade of fine singers who had passed through the College during the preceding twenty years.

Could any conservatoire Principal have been offered a more generous or richly imaginative send-off provided by wonderful friends and colleagues past and present? To all who participated I shall forever remain deeply grateful. The whole experience was, in short, totally overwhelming.

Here and There

Chetham's

In 1969, shortly after I had left the BBC to join Lancaster University, I was approached to head an enquiry into the future of Chetham's School. The brief was nothing less than to assess the feasibility of Chetham's becoming a specialist music school.

Chetham's had changed little over the centuries from the foundation which Humphrey Chetham had established back in 1653 when the school was, in his own words, endowed to provide an education for "the sons of honest, industrious and painful parents." It continued to occupy some of the oldest surviving buildings in central Manchester and, nestling close to the cathedral, had developed a music strand by providing both a home and an education for the choristers of Manchester Cathedral. The same weather-worn red stone buildings also continued to house the unique historic library which Humphrey Chetham had bequeathed to the nation, along with the hospital he had also founded.

The possibility of extending the school's interest in music was essentially the brainchild of the school's governors. In particular, the decision to explore the potential for Chetham's to become a specialist music school was due to Ewart Boddington of the brewing dynasty who became chairman of the governors in 1969 and who had first approached me about the projected enquiry. Yehudi Menuhin's action when, in 1963, he established his own small specialist school in Surrey doubtless played its part in stimulating ambitions for Chetham's to emulate this example.

Ewart and others had assembled a strong and wise committee which I was invited to chair in what proved to be a swift and purposeful exercise. The members included the redoubtable Ida Carroll, then Principal of the Northern School of Music, and Sir David Willcocks, Director of the Royal College of Music, together with representatives of Manchester Cathedral, the Department of Education and other wise heads. In all this, an underlying concern may well have been a realisation that Chetham's – long established, steeped in tradition, but vulnerably small – might find survival hard in the developing climate. The prevailing and more positive belief, riding on a measure of contagious enthusiasm, was that the time might well be ripe to establish a multi-disciplined music school, significantly larger and more broadly based in instrumental terms than the Menuhin School. While Chetham's had, until then, bravely maintained many traditions associated with its origins, the new educational age tended to view some of its practices with impatience.

As our enquiry developed, it became evident that a specialist music school could only be effectively established if a number of fundamental changes were made. These, regretfully, had to start with the school's leadership, where the post of head still carried the anachronistic title of House Governor, dutifully occupied at the time by Harry Vickers. With regret, we concluded that a fresh dynamism was sorely needed. Responsibility for music in the school then largely rested with a gifted luthier, an ancient craft which lay comfortably within the school's traditions but which was unlikely to provide much by way of inspiration for burgeoning young performing talent. It followed that our recommendations logically centred upon the need for the school to appoint a new headmaster and a new director of music, if it was to present credible specialist credentials. With great courage the governors accepted our radical recommendations. The relevant appointments were made and the new Chetham's prepared to take wing.

As this new era was launched, with the admission of girls not only changing the face of Chetham's but also outnumbering boys, the course was confidently set for what were to be forty and more years of remarkable achievements. Almost from the outset individual pupils began to make their mark in national competitions and by their accomplishments on a range of well-publicised platforms. To the school's lasting credit, these musical successes were also matched by a comparable academic record. Indeed, for a school where more than half of each day was devoted to music in a heavily committed way, its success in gaining year by year strong Oxbridge admissions was in itself remarkable, thereby underscoring the conviction that dedicated study of music enhances, rather than undermines, progress in other academic pursuits.

Many of the school's alumni carry names now recognised worldwide in music circles. Composers, conductors, instrumentalists, singers and teachers: in all these spheres former Chetham's pupils have excelled and enriched the world they inhabit. While some of those who took the decision to establish Chetham's as a music specialist school may have harboured serious concerns regarding the very feasibility of the undertaking, they, the early staff and all concerned, disguised such reservations well. The rewards they received for pursuing the courage of their convictions have been richly represented in all that stands to the school's credit today.

It would, however, be idle and irresponsible to gloss over the fact that information has more recently emerged to scar and disproportionately disfigure and debase the school's reputation. Some of the more serious shortcomings may be traced back to mistakes occurring in the early years through failure to recognise difficulties which resulted all too easily from the school's proximity to Victoria Station and other less salubrious elements in inner Manchester. In the pupils' interests, discipline needed to be more rigorous than all too often was the case if youngsters were to be protected from extraneous problem areas and allowed unfettered scope to build upon their undoubted motivation and skills. Benefitting from the resolute leadership of the former Head, Claire Moreland, the school recovered with strength and determination from such difficult experiences. It is now in an undoubtedly good position and seems set fair to maintain its considerable record of outstanding individual and collective achievement. It continues to win friends worldwide and indeed to set proud examples to those further afield. Moreover, following upon an invigorating programme of building and general expansion, the school is well-placed to extend its facilities in a range of significant and rewarding ways conducive to helping its gifted young charges realise their full potential.

The history of the new Chetham's has been marked by many significant advances and also a number of particularly happy and rewarding occasions. One such occurred a few years ago when Her Majesty the Queen opened the new girls' boarding house. The formal opening was followed by a short concert. This consisted of just three short pieces played by the excellent school orchestra, of which the final item was Strauss's *Hunting Polka*. It may be remembered that this piece breaks off midway to allow for an isolated rifle shot, this shot then being repeated at the end. A young member of the school orchestra playing the triangle was also deputed pointedly to raise his arm in such a way that it was clear to all that he was aiming at the ceiling and that Her Majesty could be assured that no assassination attempt was in progress. All passed off well and in the appointed moment's silence the pistol shot rang out. Warming to his task, the young man repeated the process at the end of the work, again ostentatiously taking aim at the ceiling. Thereupon we all trooped out of the hall. To do so we had to move round the side of the orchestra and passed the young pistol-shooting triangle player. As he did so, The Duke of Edinburgh put his hand on the shoulder of the young man and remarked in his own inimitable way, "You're not much of a shot; missed the wife twice!"

El Sistema – an early glimpse

Back in 1978 I received, via the British Council, an unexpected but interesting enquiry. It appeared that steps were afoot in Venezuela to develop a national youth orchestra, prompted in part by a desire to emulate our own National Youth Orchestra and models in America. Might it be possible, the British Council was asked, for somebody from England to provide some advice?

The upshot was that I received a visit in Manchester from a young Venezuelan violinist, by name Igor Lanz – not a naturally Venezuelan name you might think, but a more passionate patriot one could not wish to encounter. He was also, as I was to discover, a very able violinist. He explained that he came to see me at the behest of one José Antonio Abreu, a name unknown to me or many then but one which has since become legendary as El Sistema has conquered the world. It was Abreu (originally a harpsichordist, I was told, although I never heard him play) whose inspiration and passionate resolve was to form a national youth orchestra in Venezuela.

In response to an invitation from Abreu I agreed to spend some time in Caracas, and other centres from Maracay to Maracaibo, in order to assess whether I might be able to offer any help. It proved to be a very rewarding visit during which I met various key people including the Minister for Dessarollo, a title which I was told translated best as Minister for the (Intelligence) Development. He was one Dr. Machado, a small man with beady black eyes but with a driving sense of compelling commitment. His passionate belief was that any child, once offered the opportunity, could achieve anything to which he put his mind.

There being a clear need to create a strong body of strings as the foundation for any new youth orchestra, I arranged for a small group of distinguished European string specialists to take up residencies in Venezuela. Their central task was to train the Venezuelan teachers. To reinforce and spread the benefits of their practical influence, we then arranged to film and record their model lessons for distribution throughout this large and scattered country.

I was fortunate enough to be able to persuade the legendary Polish violinist Bronislav Gimpel (brother of the no less prominent pianist, Jacob) to head our little group and to commit himself for a full three months to what he came to see as a torch he was particularly passionate to carry. Supporting him were a husband and wife violin and cello team from Britain, Richard Deakin and Emma Ferrand, complete with their first born, Ben, then barely out of his swaddling clothes. I also persuaded John Bower, formerly Chief Recording Engineer for the BBC Transcription Service, to join the team. John was responsible for recording the model lessons given by our string envoys, and these were then distributed throughout Venezuela and, in particular, to some of the farthest reaches of the country.

By the time that I made my next visit to Caracas, Dr. Machado's influence had begun to exert a strong practical effect by securing government approval for the purchase of inexpensive instruments from Czechoslovakia. These were distributed nationally – for example, to settlements of Pemono Indians living on the banks of the Orinoco. I recall a wonderful cartoon appearing in a Caracas newspaper which depicted an excited throng of 11-year-olds rifling through the latest crate to arrive from Prague and leaping about with whoops of joy to celebrate their acquisition of shiny (if rather too red) violins, but brandishing them in the manner of machine guns.

This energetic determination towards developing a national youth orchestra was quite astonishing. Venezuela at the time was a very young country. I forget the exact statistic but over half the population was still aged under 30. In the slum hovels that covered the hill slopes around Caracas radios, televisions and a ceaseless blaring racket was the all-consuming and dominant feature. Noisy it may have been but it was also symptomatic of the sheer drive and endless energy which so characterised this young nation.

I paid only one further visit to Caracas in my advisory capacity. Regretfully it had become clear to me that to keep pace with this phenomenally enthusiastic new drive towards bringing the joys of music-making to countless young people would necessitate a much more extensive commitment than I could realistically contemplate. But the culmination for me of that early period was one I shall never forget.

On the inspiration of those such as Abreu and Lanz, who were guiding the early stages of this exciting development, a bevy of smiling 11-year-olds were brought to Caracas and lined up to entertain the President. These youngsters had been taught, entirely by rote, in simple arrangements of pieces such as the Venezuelan national anthem, Haydn's *Toy Symphony* and Beethoven's *Hymn of Joy*. They played with solemn but infectious dedication, and the reward was to see tears of emotion rolling down the fat cheeks of the portly President, Luis Herrera. If, until that point, anyone still needed to be convinced that El Sistema was a golden concept, then that conviction was both vividly and touchingly evident when one observed this large and burly politician so visibly moved by the enthusiasm and achievements of his smiling young protégés.

Since that time El Sistema has taken flight worldwide. Abreu's inspiration has now reached the point where Prom audiences in the Royal Albert Hall metaphorically rock to El Sistema, to its inspiring conductor Gustavo Dudamel and to the point where in many European countries the Venezuelan El Sistema is seen as a model to inspire and rejuvenate older cultures. I wish I could claim to have foreseen such a phenomenal explosion of exhilarating talent when my dedicated little string group from Europe began their pioneering work all those years ago. I must confess that I did not for a moment glimpse the peaks that these young Venezuelans would so swiftly scale. Thanks to Abreu's inspiration this has surely become one of music's most remarkable revelations in our time.

The British Council

In 1973 I was not a little surprised but wholly delighted to be invited to become Chairman of the British Council's Music Advisory Committee in succession to the Earl of Harewood. As a member of the committee I had been able, during the preceding years, to learn much from my predecessor's wise and judicious guidance as the Council's music activity abroad expanded exponentially. So the scene was set fair for further development during the next seven years. This was a period when the Foreign Office and the Council's paymaster, the Treasury, were generally in positive support of the

British Council. In this propitious situation we were able to enjoy a phase where a combination of ambition and encouragement could breed positive and rewarding results. Sadly, however, this was not to continue into the '80s. Fresh constraints and a general downgrading of the role of the British Council sadly became all too apparent, despite the Council's strenuous defence, determinedly led by the Chairman, Charles Troughton[81]. Indeed, these were years during which the Treasury seemed less and less convinced of the value attaching to the British message abroad, something also to be seen in the way its support for the BBC World Service was similarly scaled down.

The British Council's music department during these good years was headed with much wisdom and a keen sense for opportunity by Barrie Iliffe, who had succeeded the remarkable John Cruft as Music Director. It was a recurring pleasure to work on project after project with Barrie, whose music knowledge was breathtakingly compendious. Aside from music, Barrie entertained a constant enthusiasm for narrow-boating. He and his wife, Caroline, kept a much cherished boat at Camden Lock. If he was not to be found in the British Council's old offices in Davies Street, then it was likely that the Iliffes might be discovered exploring one of Britain's many delightful waterways.

On one occasion they had, when doing so, encountered an unexpected experience. If I remember correctly, they had cruised up to the Midlands to spend the Christmas holiday with Caroline's family (in Sutton Coldfield, I believe). They were, however, to experience a chequered return when, over New Year, their trusty boat's engine suddenly expired. As luck would have it, their canal route had brought them to a point directly under the multi-motorway intersection north of Birmingham, popularly known as 'Spaghetti Junction', when this misfortune occurred. The outcome was that they were obliged to remain marooned in this ill-chosen location until help was to hand after the holiday period. Against all expectation, Barrie told us, their enforced stay was extraordinarily peaceful in that the noise of all the traffic pounding above scarcely penetrated to their silent seclusion on the canal below.

---

[81] One of a number of old Haileyburians occupying prominent roles in arts and education at this time.

Barrie was well served by his senior staff. They included the deputy Music Director, Ian Keith, whom I was fortunate enough to be able to recruit some years later as the imperturbable and infallible lead officer in our European Music Year office. He, like all of us, also delighted in the invariably relaxed good humour of our colleague, Avril Wood, Sir Henry's daughter, who frequently took a whimsical view of life and who delighted in describing the British Council's task as being that of providing "all forms of assistance short of actual help". A young recruit at the time was Hazel Wilson[82], who had first sharpened her spurs in Romania and was to become a vital member of the British Council music team.

Among many fresh enterprises we were especially gratified to find that we could forge ahead in the field of gramophone recording. The British Council had, in earlier days, issued a record of Holst's *Planets*, conducted by Sir Adrian Boult, which had proved not only a great artistic success but had actually made money for the Council[83]. Why should we not add to the still too limited catalogue of British music on record, we asked ourselves? That question was soon answered in the affirmative by a decision that the British Council should sponsor a carefully prepared sequence of recordings.

An initial choice alighted on Michael Tippett's opera, *The Midsummer Marriage*, and an outstanding recording, conducted by Colin Davis, appeared in due course. One potentially awkward problem had threatened progress during the planning stage. Colin was determined to cast Alberto Remedios in the leading tenor role of Mark. The recording company voiced some concerns regarding what they felt might be Remedios's limited capacity to absorb an extended and complicated contemporary role. These concerns were highlighted by indulging in a comparison with Richard Lewis's peerless performance in the opera's original cast. Anxieties were only assuaged when Colin Davis personally undertook to rehearse Remedios on a weekly basis; this, I understand, he duly did for much of the six months which it took Remedios to master the role.

While the British Council's primary purpose abroad remained

---

[82] Hazel also, in due course, married the leading British composer, Paul Patterson.
[83] This historic recording was reissued by EMI as recently as September 2013.

that of spreading and teaching the English language, support for British culture also blossomed during these good years. Precisely where particular initiatives were launched depended to some extent upon the 'indicators', by which were defined those areas around the globe where both the Foreign Office and the Treasury were agreed that investment seemed potentially justified. Such locations could be found worldwide and ranged, for example, from culturally concentrated European countries to remoter regions in Africa. Indeed, one of the most amusing meetings our advisory committee ever held was when we were entertained by Denis Matthews with an uproariously illustrated description of pianos in isolated East African towns, whither he had been despatched to present the marvels of Beethoven to audiences varying from expat sugar planters to dutifully bewildered local residents.

My work on behalf of the British Council's Music Committee entailed periodic invitations to participate in various events abroad promoting British culture. One such, which was to have improbable consequences, was held in Brussels in 1974. It included a special focus on avant-garde developments in British music, notably in the field of electronics. To present a challenging exposition, we had invited the composer Tim Souster, whose premature death in 1994 remains a painful loss to British music. The event was highly successful and a gratifyingly large audience, enjoying the reception which followed, seemed to have responded to what they had heard.

Tim and I were sufficiently stimulated by the Council's hospitality that when we emerged for a leisurely saunter in the night air, we did so with a giddy degree of exhilaration. By chance, we had each recently seen and been rather taken by a new ballet choreographed by Robert Cohan for his London Contemporary Dance Theatre, his *Waterless Method of Swimming Instruction*. Despite its clumsy title, it offered a delightful portrayal in dance of passengers onboard an ocean liner disporting themselves around an empty swimming bath. When, in the course of our late-night stroll, Tim and I reached the Grand-Place, we began, for no good reason, to offer puzzled bystanders our own interpretation of waterless swimming. Before long the Belgian police, dispensing with any breathalyser tests, bundled us unceremoniously into a car and drove us without explanation to the outskirts of Brussels, thereupon ejecting us with a gruff instruction in Flemish which we took to mean, "Now you can walk back and sober up!"

One region where particular efforts were made to promote English language and British art in general was Tito's Yugoslavia, then increasingly seen in political terms as a bridge between east and west. The result was that during the '70s much resolute emphasis was laid on sowing seeds in both Croatia and Slovenia. With a view to reinforcing this initiative, I undertook more than one interesting and rewarding visit to what we now know as these proud independent nations but which were then all in a state of uncertain constraint under Tito's all-embracing dictatorship. For example, individual events were promoted in various parts of Croatia such as a televised music competition in Rovinj in a delightful setting on the Istrian coast near Pula, where is still to be found a near-perfect small replica of the Coliseum in Rome. Most fruitfully rewarding of all was work carried out in the Croatian capital, Zagreb, where the university's English Department was of outstanding quality and commitment. In parallel, an important contemporary music festival, the Zagreb Biennale, under the direction of Josip Stojanović, proudly presented itself to the world as Croatia's counterpart to Darmstadt or Donaueschingen. It was here that a great deal of the most interesting new music of the time first entered the Balkans.

One example of Stojanović's enterprise led to an improbable sequel. Here again, Michael Tippett figures. John Ogdon had been invited to give a performance in the Biennale of Michael's piano concerto, playing with the Ljubljana Philharmonic. What John's agent, the august Emmie Tillett, had failed to recognise was that Ljubljana's orchestra naturally resided in its home town, the Slovenian capital, and that only the final rehearsal would take place in Zagreb. One evening, Renna and I were enjoying late drinks in the lounge of Zagreb's Excelsior Hotel when, struggling through the revolving main door, emerged Ogdon's sturdy frame, battling with some substantial luggage. Surprised to see him, since he had only been expected some days later, it transpired that John was now only a few hours away from a first rehearsal due to take place in distant Ljubljana at 10am the next morning. A call I made to Stojanović only elicited the curt reply that he was hardly responsible if English concert agents possessed insufficient geographical awareness. "You must find the solution."

The result was that, a few hours later, we were to be seen celebrating a beautiful early dawn by piling into the Ford Cortina in which Renna and I had driven to Zagreb. In a spirit of some exhilaration we sped up the 'autoput', the Serbo-Croatian term for a highway riddled with rather fewer potholes than were then to be found on ordinary roads. Unfortunately, after an hour or so, a large clatter announced that our exhaust pipe had come adrift. A few minutes later passers-by were treated to the unlikely sight of John's legs protruding from under our Cortina where he had squirmed, determined to rectify the problem by somehow securing the displaced exhaust pipe. Not surprisingly, friends in England never quite believed this story, since an image of John Ogdon as a roadside mechanic seemed too improbable to be credible. But so it was. Those who know Croatia may not be altogether surprised to be told that when, unavoidably besmeared, we eventually arrived at the rehearsal hall in Ljubljana, it was to discover that the rehearsal had been postponed until the afternoon.

The Arts Council

In 1976 I was invited to become a member of the Arts Council of Great Britain, ACGB as it was then styled. I soon discovered that the Council was, in essence, still the creature which Arnold Goodman had so tellingly shaped some ten years previously. At its heart a deep-seated respect for the main art forms dictated the priorities guiding the Council in its work. Within its gracious London headquarters at 105 Piccadilly I found a remarkable team of men and women dedicated to fulfilling those beliefs.

That I was able to form this appreciation rather more quickly than might otherwise have been the case was directly due to the fact that, soon after I had joined the Council, I was invited to participate in a four-man team asked to assess the morale and effectiveness of the Council's staff. I was very much a junior participant in this review, the others being Lord Jeremy Hutchinson, one of the most successful defence counsels of the day, Sir Howard Newby, Controller BBC Third Programme and a widely read novelist and Sir Angus Stirling, destined to become Chairman of the Royal Opera House and subsequently of the National Trust. Our work was conducted in a spirit of relaxed discretion, and swiftly established two essential factors: that the key staff within the Arts Council represented a wholly committed and dedicated body, but that it was one which to some degree felt that its endeavours were insufficiently appreciated. Our consequent recommendation was basically that here was an excellent team but one which would do even better if its morale was boosted by a conviction that its work was suitably valued.

Very soon after this exercise had been completed, I was invited to become Chairman of the Council's Music Panel. I served in this capacity until I stood down in 1984 and much relished being able to admire at close quarters the work of two very different, and also very gifted, music directors. The first was John Cruft, an oboist of no small distinction who had previously been Director of the British Council's Drama and Music Department. John also generously dedicated his wisdom and experience to a wide range of music organisations, most notably the Royal Society of Musicians. Interviews with John were seldom unnecessarily extended, a situation he achieved in a skilful and decisive manner by the simple method of always leaving the windows of his corner office wide open in all weathers, come summer or winter. The consequence, needless to add, was that visitors not possessing John's sturdy constitution seldom lingered longer than could be helped.

John was succeeded by Basil Deane, who had previously been Professor of Music in the University of Manchester where, as close neighbours, he and I had become good friends and colleagues. We were periodically amused by the way in which the musical press would refer to our dual Mancunian 'power-base'. Once he had moved to London, Basil and I were able to develop a highly effective working partnership at the Arts Council. During this period the music department's growth even dictated a move out of Piccadilly and into separate offices in Long Acre. This was partly on account of the fact that dance was yet to become a self-standing department within the Arts Council's structure and remained under the aegis of the Music Department. In this connection, it was a happy coincidence that our principal dance officer, Jane Nicholas, was also the daughter of the prominent viola player, Bernard Shore.

No less stimulating in an entirely different way was the work of the Arts Council's Touring Committee, of which I was also fortunate enough to be Chairman for a few years. The Touring Director was Jack Phipps, an irrepressible enthusiast in all that he undertook, with limitless energy and a tireless determination to ensure that any Arts Council touring project should be a resounding success. As with Basil Deane, partnership with Jack was marked by a contagious delight in the task in hand. During our collaboration we were, for example, able to bring into being English Touring Opera, and I shall long remember a dash to Plymouth for the Company's first night in the Theatre Royal. It, in turn, had owed its refurbishment to another committee of the Arts Council on which some of us were lucky enough to sit, the Housing the Arts committee. These were fortunately years when money for capital development flowed fairly easily. This enabled us to help with the restoration of a number of important theatres up and down the land where that investment still pays off today, such as the Buxton Opera House, the Theatre Royal in Bath and the Everyman Theatre in Cheltenham.

At this time ACGB, as its full title indicated, also maintained a responsibility for supporting the arts in both Scotland and Wales, although naturally much of this work was already devolved to each country's respective Arts Council. Their representatives would join us at our meetings in London and elsewhere, and always brought a stimulating breath of challenging fresh air with them. This was colourfully true, for example, of Mathew Prichard, Agatha's Christie's grandson, who represented Welsh interests with verve and determination.

So, too, if in a quieter mould, did Sir Gerald Elliot, a patriotic Scot with an unequivocal dedication to the arts. At one point we were able, entirely in a spirit of fraternal frivolity I stress, to suggest that Gerald could playfully be accused of starting the Falklands War. This originated as a consequence of an advertisement which Elliot's firm, Christian Salvesen Ltd, had, in all innocence, circulated in Argentina to invite interest from scrap metal dealers in acquiring a disused whaling station in South Georgia. When, after a buyer had been secured, a small cargo ship duly arrived to collect the spoils, it transpired that on board were not only the expected merchants but also a small troop of Argentinian soldiers sent, under cover of this transaction, to take possession of the island and hoist the Argentinian flag over South Georgia.

During my eight years on the Arts Council it was a real pleasure to serve under three extraordinarily able Chairmen: Lord Gibson, Sir Kenneth Robinson and Sir William Rees-Mogg. Robinson's tenure from 1977 to 1982 represented, in my view, a particularly fruitful period for the Arts Council, during which time he guided it with quiet affability but also a degree of measured determination which many of us found wholly admirable. Robinson had a strong love of music. A lasting benefit he brought about continues to this day in the shape of the highly successful Young Concert Artists Trust, which has done so much to further the careers of young musicians and which Robinson co-founded. [Plate 44]

My time with the Arts Council concluded with a celebratory dinner at the Box Tree restaurant in Ilkley, when we launched the Arts Council's 'manifesto' for the future, *The Glory of the Garden*. Its central message, which could hardly have been more strongly delivered, was that the nation's support for its arts and artists should be more evenly distributed up and down the land. It is not a little depressing that, thirty years later, statistics indicate that investment in the arts continues to be evermore weighted towards activities in and around London, with deleterious consequences elsewhere.

European Music Year

In 1980 the Council of Europe, with a respect for history and a flair for celebration beyond the imagination of its prosaic and overweight counterpart in Brussels, declared that 1985 should be designated European Music Year. To a not inconsiderable extent this was the brainchild of the Council's Secretary General, Franz Karasek[84], a dedicated Austrian music enthusiast.

In turn Karasek drew his initial inspiration from the fact that 1985 marked the tercentenaries of the births of Bach, Handel and Scarlatti, to say nothing of the quatercentenary of Schütz's birth in 1585. With considerable skill he assembled a tripartite international team led by Walter Scheel[85] who, with Massimo Bogianckino[86] and Rolf Liebermann[87], headed the preparations for a Europe-wide music celebration honouring these anniversaries. Supporting this august trio was a further group forming with them the project's Executive Committee in whose work I had the tremendously enjoyable pleasure of participating.

Rolf Liebermann was a marvellous raconteur, as when he regaled us over dinner with a delicious story set in post-war Vienna. In

---

[84] Franz Karasek, Secretary General, Council of Europe, 1979-1984.
[85] Walter Scheel, born 1919, formerly President of the Federal Republic of Germany, 1974-79.
[86] Massimo Bogianckino, 1922-2009, author of a highly regarded study on Domenico Scarlatti's harpsichord music and Intendant of the Paris Opera, 1983-85.
[87] Rolf Liebermann, 1910-1999, Intendant of the Paris Opera, 1972-78.

advance of a meeting which Otto von Habsburg was due to chair, one of his staff came to present apologies for unavoidable absence on the part of a key committee member. "You see, Your Highness, his duties really oblige him to attend this evening's Austria / Hungary football match." "Of course, I understand," responded Otto von Habsburg, but added, after a moment's thought, "and who are we playing?"

The membership of this committee reflected a carefully selected cross-section of European states. Two of the smallest were the Vatican, the voluble enthusiasm of whose lay representative knew no bounds, and Liechtenstein. This delightful little enclave was represented by Josef Frommelt, who headed the Vaduz School of Music. I was curious to learn more about Frommelt's school and began by asking him about his student numbers, knowing that the total population of Liechtenstein was only some 30,000. Quite casually, he indicated that the school numbered some 1,500. Since, on a quick calculation, this represented roughly five per cent of that little nation's entire population, I could not help expressing some surprise, until Frommelt proudly explained that, under a local regulation, all music teaching in Liechtenstein, whether to kindergarten toddlers or dedicated adults, had to be taught in the Vaduz School of Music.

As the work of this EMY committee progressed, principally in Strasbourg, we were enormously strengthened by our far-seeing and imperturbable Committee Secretary, Thomas Alexandersson[88]. Meanwhile, at home, to its infinite credit, Her Majesty's Government immediately and unhesitatingly subscribed to the EMY concept. A British Committee for EMY was formally established, with the enthusiastic interest as its Chairman of His Royal Highness, The Duke of Kent, who kindly invited me to serve as Vice-Chairman.

Holding the majority of its meetings in the spacious drawing room in the Arts Council's Headquarters at 105 Piccadilly, our committee also enjoyed the good fortune of occupying comfortable sponsored offices just off the Strand. We were lucky enough to secure, as Secretary to this committee, the services of Ian Keith. Whenever difficulties arose, Ian invariably solved them with calm

---

[88] Thomas Alexandersson, Secretary to EMY International Executive Committee, Swedish civil servant and diplomat.

and wisdom, qualities which had long marked his career as the British Council's Deputy Director of Music. In turn, Ian was ably assisted by Christine Headley, with whom I found much in common since it transpired that she was an avid cricket enthusiast and statistician who, if my memory serves me correctly, subsequently became the first woman to be elected to committee office by the Kent County Cricket Club.

Walter Scheel's international committee quickly developed a very simple brief: that of encouraging authorities throughout Europe, by capitalising upon the coincidence of EMY's three prominent composer anniversaries, to stimulate widespread music festivities across the continent. In the event, this encouragement to make music everywhere swiftly took wing in countless delightful ways, nowhere more prominently than in France whose national project, *Fêtes de la Musique*, emerged in the form of a ministerial decree that every town or village should celebrate midsummer's day with some form of music manifestation. To the satisfaction of the French representative on the Executive Committee, Alain Surrans, French towns and villages up and down the land seized on this idea with contagious enthusiasm and, as events transpired, thereby gave birth to a tradition of public midsummer music-making festivities still vigorously maintained to this day.

By contrast, Britain largely reacted to this French initiative with studied caution and reserve. We may indulge our various national forms of celebration, whether with sword dances in Scotland or by handkerchief-waving Morris-men with bells on their legs in England, but we largely limit our open air and street festivities to occasions for royal celebration – unless, of course, we have just won a war!

Most of the work of the EMY Executive Committee was carried out in Strasbourg where the Council has its headquarters. This, needless to say, was scarcely a hardship, since modern Strasbourg offers countless delights, not least gastronomic. Returning there after an absence of some thirty-five years since my student days in this fine old city was, for me, something of a sentimental journey. But there was little time for misplaced retrospection; there was much work to do and many meetings to attend in the years leading up to 1985 itself.

Travel to Strasbourg from Britain in the early '80s could be more problematic than might have been expected, given Strasbourg's acquired status as an international capital centre. Direct flights from

Heathrow were largely limited to a service provided on old Fokker 65 planes, whose reliability was not beyond question. On one occasion the plane was unexpectedly diverted to Lille. Not only was this inconvenient but equanimity aboard our flight was also disturbed by the barely restrained invectives offered to fellow passengers by the incorrigible Ian Paisley[89] who, for whatever reason, was on this occasion a singularly reluctant and unhappy passenger. I was also mildly amused to discover the length to which an otherwise privileged politician would go to save paying parking dues at Heathrow. The cunning wheeze which one particular English MP delighted in revealing to me was to drive his car to Hounslow West underground station, outside which was a pub where the barrier giving access to its car park was raised by the insertion of a 50 pence piece. The appropriate airport terminal could then be reached simply at the cost of a couple of stops on the Piccadilly line.

In fact, since I was more frequently travelling to Strasbourg from Manchester, I found it infinitely preferable to fly to Paris Orly, nip across to the Gare de l'Est and then take what was widely regarded as a flagship of the French railways' TGV service, boasting a particularly luxurious wood-panelled dining car with menu to match.

Most of our Strasbourg meetings were conducted in the elaborate and beautifully situated European Parliament building. They generally proceeded swiftly and fruitfully, with multilingual translators to hand, and with all the sophisticated technical support which the European Parliament itself enjoys on its monthly jaunt from Brussels to Strasbourg.

Before one of these meetings we were warned of an imminent demonstration due to take place outside the building. Although we had been asked not to provide an audience for the demonstrators by too obviously observing them from our windows, it was hard to resist the temptation to do so in view of the elegant restraint with which the proceedings were conducted. The event that then unfolded offered a classic example of the supreme skill and sophistication with which France can sometimes conduct its civil disturbances.

It appeared that French farmworkers were intent upon highlighting whatever was the current grievance. To do so they

---

[89] Reverend Ian Paisley, 1926-2014, fire-brand politician in Northern Ireland.

had assembled a convoy of agricultural vehicles, including wire cages normally reserved for carrying loads of hay but now filled, Trojan horse-like, with protesting farm workers armed with picks and shovels. Once the lead tractor had brought the convoy to a halt on the avenue fronting the Parliament building, all dismounted and proceeded with quiet deliberation to remove the large square wooden blocks forming the surface of the grand approach road. These blocks were then carefully and tidily stacked on the pavement. This whole process was conducted in impressive silence. The French riot police, with their forbiddingly long shields, simply watched impassively. When the process was complete and the road had been denuded of all its paved surface, the assembled strikers remounted their vehicles and drove quietly away. At this point an army of municipal workers, assembled in readiness, calmly proceeded to reinstate the wooden blocks and thereby allow the highway to regain its usual smooth surface. All was now restored to normality, but the concern of French agriculture had been heard and dissatisfaction had been voiced with stylish distinction.

Meanwhile, back at home, our own Committee for EMY was hard at work. In true British fashion we set about forming a clutch of sub-committees. Some, inevitably, proved more fruitful than others. One which made quite dramatic advances was that formed to have concern for early music. With great skill it enlisted the support of Green College, Oxford, to establish as part of EMY, and as a direct tribute to its 'founding composers', an intensive European course in Baroque playing. This led very swiftly to the creation of what was to become the European Union Baroque Orchestra (EUBO). Working under internationally recognised leaders in the field, such as Ton Koopman, Roy Goodman and the Kuijken brothers[90], it sustained pioneering work at a high level of authentic Baroque interpretation. As a direct outcome of EMY, EUBO became one of the EU's clutch of regularly funded arts organisations continuing to this day to enjoy, along with such as the European Opera Centre and the European Youth Orchestra, regular funding support from Brussels. For many years EUBO would hold a formal annual dinner

---

[90] Three Belgian musicians, Sigiswald, Barthold and Wieland, collectively acknowledged internationally for their authentic mastery as conductor, violinist, cellist, recorder and gamba player.

in the Banqueting House. These were always occasions for genuine celebration, although not always without controversy, as when one evening Edward Heath, as the guest speaker, felt it necessary to round on the organisers for not doing enough to further interest in the music of John Stanley. Perhaps Heath, the organist, had a point, since one too infrequently hears any of Stanley's six organ concertos.

Coincidentally, another British enterprise launched during the year stemmed from the decision my wife, Renna Kellaway, took to found an annual festival and summer school, Lake District Summer Music (LDSM), which began life in Ambleside in 1985. It continues robustly to this day providing the Lake District with a fortnight's galaxy of internationally eminent music-makers who, at the same time, also teach in LDSM's Academy at Brathay Hall on the banks of Lake Windermere.

EMY was indubitably strengthened by the influential international leadership it enjoyed, especially from Walter Scheel but also from many important participants such as The Duke of Kent, who gave liberally of their time and energies. The driving authority of men like Bogianckino and Liebermann also ensured that the Executive Committee and its work never stood still. Scheel himself was a quite remarkable chairman who, when relaxed over dinner, was not only entertaining but revealed himself still possessed of a fine baritone voice in which he would offer us a private glimpse of his artistry as a folksinger. Recordings of his singing can still be unearthed by connoisseurs and he once told me – I felt with some satisfaction – that the royalties he received from his recordings had exceeded the salary which came his way as German President. His capacity for work astounded us all as, for example, when he indicated at the conclusion of a lunch in Strasbourg that he would not be able to remain with us for the afternoon session. He explained that he had to make a speech in New York later that evening, a swift transition then made possible by using a Concorde flight to New York from Paris.

Not all our meetings took place in Strasbourg; periodically, we were hosted by the Ministry of Culture in Paris. On one occasion we had reached the point where we had good grounds to celebrate the fact that our work in anticipation of 1985 itself was now nearly complete. A special lunch had been organised in a restaurant a short distance from the Ministry, to which we all repaired on foot. The guests that day included not only The Duke of Kent but also Prince Klaus, the husband of Queen Beatrix of the Netherlands. As we made our way back to the Ministry we passed a particularly fine looking boulangerie. On an impulse Prince Klaus exclaimed, "My wife is so fond of French baguettes, I must take some back to her this evening." Thereupon all security dissolved in disorder as the Prince sped away from his minders in order to carry out this special purchase which was to give so much domestic pleasure. [Plate 45]

Northern Ballet

In 1986 I was invited to become Chairman of Northern Ballet Theatre, as it was then called, although the 'theatre' reference was subsequently dropped. I did so in succession to Sir Simon Towneley who had cared for the young company's interests with much personal dedication from soon after its inception. I was to continue in this capacity until my heart attack obliged me to stand down in 1989. They were three years filled with many challenges, delights and unexpected developments.

I was soon to discover that the young company was then in a somewhat frail and uncertain condition, sorely in need of additional support and defined ambition. I formed the impression that its continuing annual support from the Arts Council owed less to conviction regarding the company's quality and rather more to the convenient way in which its ability to tour northern theatres reinforced the Arts Council's 'Spheres of Influence' policy at the time.

It was not long before we were presented with a significant and unexpected challenge. This arrived in the form of an aggressive approach from Sir Ian Hunter, the globally influential impresario, acting in his capacity as Chairman of English National Ballet. Its Board had resolved to propose what it termed a merger with Northern Ballet. This, it speedily became evident, would, were it to be implemented, constitute not so much a merger as a takeover. The English National Ballet case was that together, the two companies would bestride the nation geographically and provide enhanced competition to the Royal Ballet. My whole instinct, viewing the respective sizes and power houses of the two companies, was, however, that Northern Ballet would run the risk of losing not only its independence but also the essential characteristics which distinguished its work from that of English National Ballet.

The arrival of this challenge presented me, as the new Chairman, with an early opportunity to call the whole company together for an initial meeting to consider English National Ballet's approach. I was very pleased by the form which this occasion took, since it proved to be both delightfully informal and produced an immediate feeling of a bond between all those taking part. My traditional view of a meeting with participants politely seated round tables immediately disappeared when I arrived at the Zion Centre, the company's Manchester base. The company members were individually scattered around the studio – on the floor, against the wall, or performing discreet exercises at the barre but never still and with each individual ceaselessly twitching and moving. Unfamiliar as I initially found the relaxed and informal atmosphere, it did not stand in the way of reaching an immediate and clear response. "No," the company chorused in impressive and spontaneous unison. "We could not work with them as they are too different from us and far too big. Let us please sink or swim on our own merits."

In consequence, and after taking soundings from the Arts Council, I had no hesitation in rejecting the English National Ballet proposal. It subsequently transpired that they had, in part, been proceeding on the mistaken assumption that Northern Ballet was on its last legs and that their proposed merger would have provided an ultimate lifeline to save it from going under.

If anything, however, this experience highlighted the urgent need for the company to acquire a new sense of direction and initiative. It had been run by its long-serving Artistic Director, Robert de Warren, upon distinctly traditional continental lines but those appropriate for a large company with a big *corps de ballet* and hardly practical for a small English company able to work effectively within precise and manageable proportions. The company's less than healthy situation was unhappily demonstrated when we promoted a gala week of *Coppélia* in Manchester starring, as the company's guest, Rudolf Nureyev. But the Nureyev who reached us was wracked with evidently diminished physical ability owing to the fact that he was by then suffering from AIDS. The whole affair consequently became a pale, sad and embarrassing reflection of what it should have been. The need for the company to undertake radical change could not have been more evident.

We found the solution to this challenge in two forms which happily coincided, both in terms of opportunity and significance. We managed to secure an agreement with the BBC to make a ballet film tracing the life and work of the artist L. S. Lowry whose death, ten years earlier, was at the time very much in the nation's mind, even if his work had then still to acquire the universal acceptance which soon followed. Both as choreographer of an extensive new biographical ballet, and to dance the role of Lowry himself, we engaged that remarkable and invigorating actor / dancer, Christopher Gable. The result proved to be an immediate and inspirational salvation for the company. Its balance sheet benefitted enormously from the proceeds of this collaboration with the BBC, while our Lowry ballet, which enjoyed the title *A Simple Man*, won universal accolades.

By then, Robert de Warren had moved on to an appointment in Monte Carlo and we were able in unfettered ways to appoint Christopher Gable as the company's new Artistic Director and permanent choreographer. The result was to be several years of very fruitful development.

The company grew in strength and numbers, with a newfound confidence and, above all, character. This derived from our decision, as a matter of central artistic policy, to concentrate upon what we termed 'narrative ballet' – a ballet which clearly told its story in graphic detail and with a concentration on subtlety of characterisation. One of our earliest successes in developing this genre was Christopher Gable's new *Don Quixote*, which more than one critic credited with adding new light and point to literary subtleties inherent in Cervantes's masterpiece.

A somewhat reshaped and refreshed Board for Northern Ballet both relished and further encouraged these developments. This owed an enormous amount to the dynamic dedication brought to it by our new Vice Chairman, Jeremy Fry, of the chocolate dynasty. Jeremy, who had been an RAF pilot, subsequently became an inventive entrepreneur who not only produced a remarkable four-wheel drive wheelchair but even guided James Dyson in his early career. Jeremy had all his life been a saviour of the arts, as indeed he had been of the Theatre Royal, Bath, which he personally bought in 1979. Thereupon, as its Chairman, and with substantial support from the Arts Council, he had the Theatre renovated to the beautiful masterpiece we know today. After I moved on Jeremy, as the Company's new Chairman, led Northern Ballet with growing distinction in the 1990s, during which period it also moved its base from Manchester to Leeds, where it today enjoys significantly enhanced civic and local support.

We also derived no little encouragement from the tremendously enthusiastic support given to us by our Patron, Princess Margaret. She publicly proclaimed herself a fan of the company. A recurring source of some embarrassment to me as Chairman was that occasionally she would declare, but only at very short notice, her intention to attend a performance at which I had not intended to be present. Indeed, I have memories of breathlessly reaching the Empire Theatre in Liverpool just a few short minutes before Her Royal Highness's own cavalcade arrived.

Princess Margaret's infectious enthusiasm even extended to one epic occasion when the company was playing at the Wimbledon Theatre, to which Her Royal Highness decided to bring her nephew Prince Edward. The evening got off to a stuttering start on account of a bomb scare which necessitated a delayed start until the Royal party was able to arrive. To compensate for this and also, as I was able to observe, to satisfy Prince Edward's evident delight in matters theatrical, the Royal party and consequently the whole company, to say nothing of the Theatre's management and attendant security, were all obliged to stay until the small hours to indulge this clear interest and enthusiasm.

One other theatre night which will live long in my memory was the occasion when Northern Ballet played a week in Jeremy Fry's old Theatre Royal, Bath, and Princess Margaret attended on the last night. When all was over the company was generously invited to repair *en masse* to the Fry estate at Freshford, some six miles south of Bath, for a night of delightful revelry, during which a wonderful feeling of mutual pleasure prevailed throughout. When, after due attention had been paid to the sumptuous refreshments and dancing began, Princess Margaret turned to me and said, "Well, I shall have the first dance with you and after that I shall dance with people who CAN dance!"

European Opera Centre

During my later years at the RNCM it became clear that emerging students were confronted with increasingly challenging considerations in launching their professional careers. This was particularly true of European opera singers who were faced with especially hazardous problems in making their way within the opera world. Their difficulties had been highlighted for me by an old colleague, Franz Müller-Heuser, Chairman of the German Music Council and himself a former professional singer.

He pointed out that at that time two thirds of the non-German principal singers enjoying secure contracts in the eighty or so German opera houses were American. This clearly highlighted the need for an effective mechanism to strengthen the capabilities of young European post-graduate singers, not least in respect of the theatre skills also required of them. These were well-taught in many USA schools but were less well-served in many parts of Europe.

As a consequence, I became more and more convinced of the need for a scheme whereby young singers might receive early professional experience in opera on a sustained basis and with the benefit of a supportive management. This belief then developed into the idea of a Europe-wide professional 'nursery' for those keen to pursue a career in opera, notably singers but also repetiteurs and those interested in theatre production.

Casting around for allies who might share this concern, I was delighted to find that they were many and that some were well-placed to help establish such a body. With encouraging rapidity we were able to form a small group of those who shared my idea, based partly on a consortium of leading opera houses. Thus it was that in April 1995 a strong team was beating on the doors of the European Commission and the European Parliament, an initiative which proved seminal in securing funding to establish the European Opera Centre. In our approach to the Commission we were enormously assisted, indeed invaluably guided, by Sir Christopher Audland, a former deputy Secretary-General and Director of Energy in Brussels, whose belief in the EOC concept never wavered.

The consortium of opera houses to which I have referred was initially three strong, while other sympathetic theatres periodically also lent support. These three were the Royal Opera House in London, the Royal Danish Opera in Copenhagen, and the Opéra de Lyon. The authoritative team representing this dedicated group included Sir Jeremy Isaacs of the Royal Opera House, Elaine Padmore for the Royal Danish Opera and Jean-Pierre Brossmann, initially intendant at the Opéra de Lyon and subsequently at the Châtelet Theatre in Paris.

An important early enthusiast for the scheme was Kent Nagano, at that time both Music Director of the Hallé Orchestra and of the Opéra de Lyon, who remained energetically committed to the EOC as its enthusiastic and active President. He in turn was most ably assisted by Laurent Pillot, Head of the EOC's Singer Development and Artistic Programme. Such high powered enthusiasm and conviction was to be enormously welcomed. But it also needed to be coordinated and directed to maximum benefit.

I believed I knew in Kenneth Baird the ideal man to take on this very considerable task. Kenneth had had extensive experience both at the Aldeburgh Festival and with English National Opera at the Coliseum, before becoming Music Director of the Arts Council of Great Britain (as it was styled before devolution took its toll). The moment when I became convinced that the EOC could be created and made into something of both permanence and significance was when Kenneth, at a private dinner in Covent Garden, finally indicated that he was ready to forsake the Arts Council and become the EOC's Managing Director, a post he still holds at the time of writing.

Battling to secure a foothold in Brussels was never likely to be easy. Nor was it. But here Sir Christopher Audland's authority, experience and wisdom were invaluable. Without him I doubt that the critical doors would ever have opened. But from the outset he showed enormous skill in securing us access to influential Commissioners at the time. They included Leon Brittan, Neil Kinnock and the then Secretary-General, David Williamson. As Lord Williamson of Horton, he remains a member of the EOC's Council of Honour along with authoritative friends from Belgium, Italy, the Netherlands, Spain and Sweden.

Thanks to the City of Manchester, which allowed the EOC generous use of its Brussels office, the EOC was able to lobby on a fairly regular and widespread basis. This led with encouraging rapidity to a point where the first formal submissions for European Union Funding could be launched. A number of meetings later and we had our first vote of ECUs, as the forerunner currency to the Euro was then called.

To this day the EOC has continued to receive funding each year from the EU and to prove itself fully worthy, I believe, of receiving such support. Inevitably, the grants have never been easily secured or as high as one could have wished. Without these awards the EOC might well have remained a figment of the imagination, whereas it has now been sustained for eighteen years since it first announced itself with concert performances of Tosca with the Hallé Orchestra and Kent Nagano in Manchester in 1997.

Needless to add, an immense amount of fieldwork had to be undertaken before we could reach this point and before Opera Europe, the EOC's touring title, could announce itself to the world. Our first steps were to hold auditions in key centres in Europe, principally those of the EOC member opera houses. Auditions initially took place in London, Copenhagen, Lyon and selected centres in Germany, Italy and Spain. Those were immensely exciting days during which we listened to countless young aspirants who surged forward in response to our advertisements.

A not untypical example of them in fact became our first Tosca, Lada Biriucov, who found us in Lyon at the end of a very long day when we had actually finished auditioning and were packing up. At this point a staff member came to tell us that a young soprano had just arrived from Moldova. "We have told her it is too late but she is here with only 30 ECUs and is desperate that you should hear her". Her belief in herself which had brought her all the way from the Black Sea to the Rhone Valley proved, as nothing else could have done, that it was right that an organisation like the EOC should be created.

Our first full production was of Mozart's Lucio Silla, for which we were fortunate enough to secure the services of that great singer Brigitte Fassbaender as our producer. I had always contended that if more singers were to work as opera producers there would be fewer occasions when singers found themselves asked to perform an unreasonable range of physical antics. But Brigitte had her own ideas and it was not long before a young Turkish tenor in the title role, Bülent Bezdüz, was required to undertake contortions shorn of any imperial dignity.

The way in which we developed our initial production of Lucio Silla was also indicative of the way in which Opera Europe worked. We first undertook four preview performances at the Buxton Opera House in Derbyshire. These were followed by two London performances presented at the Shaftesbury Theatre. Partly in order to celebrate the UK's Presidency of the European Union in the first half of 1998, we toured Britain quite widely, visiting Oxford, Llandudno, Edinburgh, Norwich, Canterbury and Northampton. A short Irish tour followed taking in Dublin, Cork and Belfast. Our presentations in Britain then concluded with appearances at both the Brighton Festival and the Bath Festival. Finally, the Company gave what were believed to have been the first presentations of Lucio Silla ever seen in Denmark by undertaking a week's residency at the Royal Opera in Copenhagen.

Our repertoire grew quite quickly. One early choice in particular was instrumental in spreading the reputation of the young Opera Europe more widely. This was a production of Benjamin Britten's The Rape of Lucretia, specially prepared for easy touring to multiple destinations and in potentially complicated conditions. A particularly well reviewed launch in Southport was immediately followed by a tour of Hungary, in the course of which we gave performances both in Budapest and in Hungary's delightful university city, Szeged. Some weeks later this production took to the road again with a short Baltic tour starting in Riga, where we were the guests of Latvian National Opera, and culminating in a visit to St. Petersburg, where we enjoyed the privilege of playing in the historic Hermitage Theatre.

As the tour unfolded I occasionally allowed myself to imagine how Britten might have reacted had he known, back in the 1940s when the opera first saw the light of day, that over fifty years later a young multinational company would be taking it to such interesting destinations. Even when the opera was delighting Alderburgh Festival audiences with the incomparable Janet Baker in the title role, an appearance in St. Petersburg might have seemed somewhat unlikely to the anonymous author of a rather mischievous limerick circulating in Aldeburgh at the time:

> Our Lucretia this year was dear Janet,
> Though Kathleen Ferrier began it,
> But the scene of the rape
> is glossed over at Snape,
> They've a couch but no one to man it.

Another deliberately lightfooted touring production swiftly followed – on this occasion of Rossini's La Scala di Seta. Our silken ladder could hardly have been more delicate or diaphanous, but it served its purpose in elegant fashion when, following a home run at Tatton Park in Cheshire, Opera Europe made its Swiss debut near Sion. This alfresco production enjoyed the great advantage of using part of a fine old castle, itself enhanced by the surrounding Alpine setting. To our delight, this led to an invitation to present the production in the EU Pavilion at EXPO 2000 in Hanover.

The EOC has also specialised in reviving a number of rarities by prominent opera composers. A particularly happy choice might be said to have brought the company nearer to its operating base within Liverpool's Hope University. This was Donizetti's Emilia di Liverpool, our production of which then took wing to north European opera houses as far apart as Bremen and Gdansk.

In addition to full productions, EOC's quest for unusual operas also extended to making a number of concert recordings in collaboration with the Royal Liverpool Philharmonic Orchestra and its conductor Vasily Petrenko. In this way the EOC has been able to extend the availability on record of unfamiliar operas. These have included seldom performed examples by the Russian composer Veniamin Fleishman as well as works by Liszt, Mendelssohn, Offenbach, Rameau, Shostakovich and Wolf-Ferrari.

Not content with theatre productions, the EOC has also been concerned to carry out a widespread educational role through the use of film. It was first able to do this through a striking, and in many respects unique, project mounted in collaboration with the BBC. This was to present an animated film of Janáček's The Cunning Little Vixen. The animation was brilliantly brought to life by Geoff Dunbar's skilful team of animateurs working under the guidance of Rodney Wilson. It was first broadcast by the BBC in an English language version in 2003.

So great was the interest in it, and in the particular objective of making this film available for use in schools and colleges throughout Europe, that we were encouraged to issue recordings in a number of European languages. Logically this process began with a version in the opera's native Czech, which in due course led to this film receiving the 2004 TV International Festival Gold Award in Prague. As a result, the EOC's The Cunning Little Vixen is now available in Czech, English, French, German, Polish and, in Spain, both Castilian and Catalan. The idiomatic value attaching to this exhilarating linguistic expansion has been significantly strengthened by engaging largely separate casts for each recording. The technical process is for each cast to lip-sync on the film, with the vocal line backed by the soundtrack made by Kent Nagano and the Berlin Symphony Orchestra. The combination of a charming fairy story, brilliantly brought to life by animation and then lent idiomatic conviction by each new cast, provides an enchanting invitation for young and old alike to enjoy opera.

Has the EOC all been worthwhile? Yes, unquestionably – in my favourably-inclined view. Can it long continue? I hope so. In this way the EOC can maintain a facility for young people alongside other comparable initiatives such as the European Union Baroque Orchestra, the European Union Youth Orchestra and the Gustav Mahler Orchestra all provide. Too often our national leaders tend to ignore the enduring value to our civilisation of music in all its forms. If the EOC can reinforce this message while providing critical career opportunities in opera, then I believe that this alone will justify its creation and continuation.

And, in brief:

CHELTENHAM

One part of my life on which I continue to look back with the most enormous pleasure is represented by the thirty-three years during which I had the enjoyable privilege of being associated with the Cheltenham Music Festival. An account of those years could well occupy another book, so packed were they with a colourful range of exciting and sometimes improbable events. To anyone who might care to read accurate and authentic accounts of the Cheltenham Music Festival since its remarkable inception in the dying days of the Second World War, I would commend *The Cheltenham Festival: a History of the First Twenty-five Years*, written by Frank Howes, a former Festival Chairman and published by OUP in 1970. This was followed by a more ambitious and extended survey by Graham Lockwood, also a former Festival Chairman, *Cheltenham Music Festival at 65: a Perspective on its Theme and Variations*, published in 2009.

Initially, it was while I was in Birmingham for the BBC, and therefore because broadcasts from the Cheltenham Festival fell within the purview of the BBC's Midland Region, that I came to form a sincere admiration and no small affection for the remarkable people who, while Britain was still at war, had been courageous enough to launch a festival whose central mission, much encouraged by Sir John Barbirolli, was the performance of music by living British composers. My association with Cheltenham was also prompted within a few weeks of my arrival in Birmingham by a call from William Glock who, it transpired, had been approached by the Festival Committee in Cheltenham wondering if the BBC could provide additional guidance and support in planning its programmes.

The consequence was that I was asked to respond to that request and so began six years in which I helped, as a voluntary adviser, to steer the Festival towards fulfilment of the bold and imaginative goals it had set itself. Necessarily I was obliged largely to make this contribution from my desk in the BBC, initially in Birmingham and subsequently in London, when the demands became so great that once the outline for the 1967 Festival had been prepared, I felt obliged to withdraw. However, by this time, the committee working under the guidance of Cheltenham's Entertainments Manager, George Wilkinson, was well-practised in implementing the suggestions and recommendations I was making with the result that such processes as commissioning new works from a multitude of composers each year came to be swiftly and effectively accomplished. The fruitful outcome was that during the six years in question the Cheltenham Festival was able to present well over a hundred new works, many of considerable significance. These are listed in detail in the Appendix 3.

After I had retired from the BBC in 1968 (without any association with the Festival in that year), I was approached in early 1969 by the Festival to become its programme director and, being largely free of other responsibilities, felt able to accept this invitation with spontaneous delight. During the twenty-six Festivals which I directed from 1969 to 1994, I was able to arrange for the performance of no fewer than 316[91] new works, the majority of them commissioned from British composers. They ranged from the first productions of new operas such as Judith Weir's *A Night at the Chinese Opera* and Michael Berkeley's[92] *Baa Baa Black Sheep* to a number of important opera revivals. These included recognition of Holst's position as Cheltenham's own son by presenting as a double-bill *Savitri* and *The Wandering Scholar*, and by turning to Lennox Berkeley, as the Festival's well-loved President, for his opera *Ruth*, staged in a simple but intensely moving sack-cloth and sandals production in Tewkesbury Abbey.

Aside from opera, we were fortunately able, particularly on

---

[91] Also listed in Appendix 3.
[92] It was my very great pleasure to recommend that Michael Berkeley should succeed me as Artistic Director from 1995. He proceeded to direct ten memorable Festivals, each richly filled and firmly dedicated to reinforcing the Festival's central mission supporting new music.

account of a gratifyingly large amount of generous sponsorship and continuing loyal support from the BBC, to present a significant range of large orchestral works together with many smaller but no less important or significant works. If there is one year which I recall with particular satisfaction, it would perhaps be 1983 when, in addition to widespread celebration of Lennox Berkeley's eightieth birthday, we also succeeded, within the seventeen days of that year's Festival, in marking the centenary of Webern's birth by presenting every single one of his published works.

If I may allow myself one additional short paragraph, it must be to express sincere thanks to key colleagues who shared in the pleasures which those years yielded: to successive Festival Presidents – Sir Arthur Bliss, Sir Lennox Berkeley, Peter Racine Fricker, Melvyn Bragg, Sir Michael Tippett and Sir Peter Maxwell Davies; to successive Chairmen – Frank Howes, George Budge, Ronald Henson, Charles Fisher and Sir Peter Marychurch; also to our indestructible Treasurer, the late Keith Nutland; and, above all, to two long-serving and immensely accomplished full-time music administrators on whose broad shoulders the whole well-being of the Festival at all times indisputably rested, and who, thankfully, I can to this day still call good friends – Kim Sargeant and Jeremy Tyndall.

Covent Garden

My deep love of opera was granted a near miraculous fresh dimension when I was invited to join the Board of the Royal Opera House in 1989. The first meeting I was due to attend, which virtually coincided with the fall of the Berlin Wall, should properly have been my last, had not the resident nurse at the Royal Opera House quickly identified the chest constriction I was experiencing and, there and then, sent me in an ambulance to St. Thomas's Hospital for urgent heart surgery under Professor Cranston. To him I shall always gratefully owe the twenty-seven years which I have since been permitted to enjoy.

My responsibilities on the Board were chiefly in relation to musical matters. They entailed, for example, the enormous pleasure of collaboration with that great musician, then the House's chief conductor, Bernard Haitink, when he and I would allow ourselves the periodic indulgence of a leisurely lunch in the Savoy's spacious dining room as we sat looking out over the Thames. During this period the Board enjoyed the leadership of two remarkable Chairmen: Lord (John) Sainsbury and Sir Angus Stirling. On it sat a bevy of prominent bankers and industrialists, which prompted one facetious observer to suggest that of the Board's members perhaps only myself, and possibly Bamber Gascoigne, of *University Challenge* fame, would be likely, at any one point, to have a reasonable idea as to what we might individually be worth. Incidentally, much of Bamber's time was occupied, to the great benefit of all Royal Opera House Patrons, in ensuring that all who came to savour its delights should enjoy quality hospitality.

So many other colleagues, such as Lord (Robert) Armstrong, the late Sir Denis Forman, Sir James Spooner, who chaired the Opera Board, and Tessa, Baroness Blackstone, who chaired the Ballet Board, made contributions of incalculable value to the House. So too did Vivienne Duffield, whose achievements in securing monumental funding for the Royal Opera House were, at that time, nothing short of heroic. I can only complete these reflections by expressing untold admiration for the tenacious way in which Sir Jeremy Isaacs, General Director during this period, defied the mounting difficulties confronting the House and continually displayed exceptional qualities of invigorating leadership. This country's artistic life will always owe much to Jeremy for all that he has done to strengthen the arts: as broadcaster (never forgetting his years at the helm of the nascent Channel 4), as a resolute protagonist for the Royal Opera House and, above all, as a fearless crusader for culture.

Codetta

Arriving at the last pages of my memoir, my foremost feeling is one of relief at finally coming to the end of what has been both a challenging and rewarding road. This impression of an extended journey also prompts me to call to mind one of Somerset Maugham's splendid yarns, although one which I can only now remember in outline. A highly successful New York lawyer reviews his life on reaching middle age. Continuing in his lucrative practice now holds no attractions for him, and he resolves to turn to what has for him always been a subject of passionate interest – the culture and history of Ancient Greece. In pursuit of this end he devotes much of his considerable wealth to buying a Greek island on which he then, for the next twenty years, devotes his life to researching and writing up his island's story. Sadly, he dies just before his life's work is finished and so, Maugham concludes, never knows the awful disillusionment of a long task ultimately accomplished.

Apart from this factor of a long haul, any connection between my story and that of Maugham's lawyer is, at best, remote. Although I have now reached a good age, I have not yet died and, in reaching the end of this memoir, I have not, until now, experienced any sentiments of acute disenchantment. At the same time, anyone reading it in search of a story about some youngster striving to overcome the cruel disadvantages of a deprived childhood will be sadly disappointed.

On the contrary, I gladly and gratefully acknowledge that I have experienced a singularly fortunate life. With generously supportive parents, a wonderful wife and a delightfully rewarding family, I have enjoyed many blessings. While I do no more than lay claim to being a very minor composer, I also freely acknowledge that much good fortune has come my way. For example, at various pivotal points it has been my privilege to have been handed three distinctive and very considerable challenges: to develop and direct the BBC's first all-day music channel, to open a brand new music department in a brand new university, and to be invited to found the first purpose-built music conservatoire in Britain in the twentieth century. This sequence constituted a troika of outstanding opportunities such as no mere mortal could legitimately hope to receive. Recording some of the people and places I have had the good fortune to encounter over the last eighty or so years, has, in its own way, been curiously satisfying. I can only hope that in evoking these memories, I may have been able to reflect some of the interest and pleasure I have been so richly privileged to enjoy.

Appendices

APPENDIX 1

Manduell the Composer: an appreciation
Anthony Gilbert

Sir John Manduell CBE first sprang to my attention at a Society for the Promotion of New Music workshop in the Arts Council Drawing Room, late in 1959. Manduell was in charge, and was introduced to the audience by Howard Hartog, then Chair of the SPNM, as "a modest composer". This caused raised eyebrows, though it was quite obvious, once Manduell began to speak, that the adjective applied not to his status but to his personality. Certainly the insights and help he gave to the participants, and to anyone else involved, showed authority and incisively positive understanding, tempered by gentle courtesy and charm. Nor did he waste words.

At this point in his distinguished career he was a BBC music producer. With William Glock as Controller of Music, the BBC were then recruiting the best young music graduates as part of a project, to be realised in 1964, involving the creation of the BBC Music Programme on the wavelengths of the Third Programme, to broadcast a weekly 71 hours of classical (including serious contemporary) music. Quite soon, among other composers, Alexander Goehr and Tim Souster were to form part of the new team of producers which also included David Drew, Stephen Plaistow and Misha Donat, with Hans Keller as their guiding light.

But the route to composition had not been a direct one. John Manduell was in fact born in Johannesburg in 1928, coming to Britain ten years later. He did study music as a boy, but when it came to phase one of his higher education he opted for modern languages, first at the University of Strasbourg and then at Jesus College, Cambridge. The composing bug did not bite until after his return to South Africa, to Durban in fact, and indeed had met the gifted young pianist Renna Kellaway, who was to become his wife. It was Renna's mother who drew his attention to the Performing Right Society scholarship, advertised in a South African journal, involving the submission of a portfolio of works. The successful applicant would have his or her fees paid for the duration of a course of study, as well as being awarded a generous living allowance. Few South African composers had received the award; John Joubert was one such. John Manduell was the next, on the basis of three works written before receiving formal tuition: an *Overture to Activity* for orchestra, a piano work for Renna Kellaway and a *Scena* for orchestra to words by Shelley. On arriving at the Royal Academy of Music in London in September 1954 he initially studied Composition with William Alwyn, exactly the right tutor to provide the necessary grounding and to instil a readiness to take creative risks. On Alwyn's resignation in 1955, the 27-year-old Manduell chose Lennox Berkeley as his next and final tutor, and an altogether different but equally rewarding period of study ensued, intuition-based, with enriching connections to Berkeley's own ongoing work. The French connection was also enriched, by Berkeley's having been a student of Nadia Boulanger. In parallel, Manduell studied conducting with Maurice Miles.

During all this period he was also employed on a very part-time basis by the Performing Right Society, to vet returns and identify works still in copyright, something which these days would be done by computer not composer. But the BBC were already interested, hence his smooth passage, in 1956, into the post of Music Producer in London. Thereafter progress was rapid: the late David Cox, Head of BBC World Service Music, with whom he had worked on attachment for a period, described him to me as hugely gifted and knowledgeable in the field of broadcasting. Within five years he had become BBC's Head of Music for the Midlands and East Anglia and then in three more years was appointed Chief Planner for the BBC Music Programme, a post he held until 1968.

During these twelve years very little composition was done, and only a handful of works from his Academy years survive, all notable, and nearly all still performed. The String Trio of 1956 was written while studying with Berkeley and carries subtle echoes of his tutor's influence, not to mention that of his tutor's tutor, Boulanger. A clear and creative understanding of the value of silence is resonant among these echoes. In the following year came *Chansons de la Renaissance* for soprano or tenor and piano, perhaps the first work of Manduell's true maturity; and then in 1962 the work which made us all sit up: *Gradi* for 3 wind and 2 strings, dedicated to the memory of his friend, the composer Mátyás Seiber, whose sudden death two years before had shocked the whole contemporary music world. These are works

I shall describe in more detail in a few paragraphs' time.

But whereas in those same twelve years the BBC and a growing family had occupied almost all of John Manduell's energies, suddenly in 1968 these huge and unique resources were to be shared in multiple directions. This was the point at which he entered the academic world, first as Director of Music at the University of Lancaster (receiving the title of Professor in 1971), and then as Founding Principal of the Northern (later Royal Northern) College of Music, a post he held until his retirement in 1996. In 1969 he was appointed Programme Director of the Cheltenham Festival, (which immediately became the Cheltenham International Music Festival), and began too to serve on boards, committees and panels as varied as those of the British Council which involved much travelling abroad, the Arts Council, UNESCO, Covent Garden, the Prix Italia, the BBC and many other notable organisations. Particularly through the British Council, he was responsible for developing vibrantly fruitful cultural exchanges between Britain and a number of Eastern European countries then still part of the communist bloc.

But our concern must be with the tremendous positive impact John Manduell's presence made on Manchester's musical life. Just two examples may suffice. One simply needs to multiply them by twenty-five years, then by the number of instances in each of those years. So, the first was the inaugural concert at the then NCM's new Concert Hall in 1972, in which the London Sinfonietta were invited to present works by composers of the so-called first Manchester School. The effect on the audience, on the press and on various notables and authorities, was unprecedented and electrifying, separating once, but thank goodness not for all, those opposed to the new and those thirsting for it. One heard groans of "what have we brought here?" almost, but not quite, smothered by cries of "thank goodness, at last!" Then there was opera. Manduell took charge of this from the start. As Head of the School of Composition and Performance, he immediately introduced contemporary British opera into the student repertoire: multiple performances in the splendid new Opera Theatre to which, due to non-deterrent ticket prices, everyone came. The contemporary opera programme over those twenty-five years included several by Britten, two by Vaughan Williams, one by Gordon Crosse, one by Walton, one by Hoddinott (specially commissioned), and also one by Alison Cox, then still a student. We heard Weill, Schoenberg and Janáček too. These productions received a tremendous reception, several awards and opportunities for repeat performances in Cheltenham, London and abroad. An offshoot was the enormously successful Music Theatre Project, funded by the RVW Trust, entirely devoted to contemporary work including much by Manchester composers.

And where was the 'modest composer' in all of this? Not being an obsessive, as he himself admits, the work emerged only when opportunity presented itself. *Gradi*, for instance, was written during a break involving a holiday by sea from Liverpool to, and in, Madeira. Another inhibiting factor was confrontation with works by some of the world's leading composers, on panels such as that for the Paris 'Rostrum', which selected the best broadcast works from all over the world. Manduell admits having his own confidence undermined by such experiences. But come 1968, pressures eased temporarily, so creativity bloomed over the ensuing four years. One virtue of having heavy duties as filters for one's composing energies is that only the best ideas get through, and some of these had been waiting to be uncorked for years, wonderfully maturing the while. Although he actively encouraged performances of works by other Manchester-based composers, for which I myself have good reason to be grateful, modesty tended to prevent his own being heard in Manchester. Indeed it was part of Manduell's self-imposed policy not to gain compositional benefit from his powerful position, but at least his work was heard in other musical centres, in Britain and abroad. Productivity returned to John, by then Sir John Manduell, CBE, once he retired in 1996, and there has been a steady stream of significant works from his pen ever since. For Sir John, the ideal solution to this conflict would be to "allow composers two lives".

This writer has a fierce objection to adjectives being allowed to precede the word 'composer'; nevertheless, I believe in the importance of, if not categorising, at least attempting to define the nature of a composer's work. For the Manduell output, this is comparatively easy at first sight, but less so on closer acquaintance. I say this to contradict any preconception that the work may be stylised, like that of so many past Heads of English music colleges, however distinguished. Most Manduell works seem to be written for the standard concert environment, yet they either treat that environment somewhat unconventionally, or work at least as well in a non-standard set-up – typically, the foyer of the Bridgewater Hall, jolly tea-parties upstairs notwithstanding.

Similarly, over the half-century or so this output covers, there is consistency but never predictability. The idiom is consistently highly personal, drawing unequally upon British and French melodic and harmonic procedures, but in each work it has a wholly different embodiment without losing its subtle identity. The differences depend on texture and rhythm, and indeed upon which of the melodic or harmonic procedures from its two source-cultures the music draws. This does not create inconsistency, merely variety and range of expression. Structurally the music is fairly unorthodox, but completely logical. Manduell composes by musical instinct and not by method or system, but it is an instinct conditioned by rationality and supported by sound technical foundations. Two principal chamber works will serve as examples.

Gradi (1963) is a threshold work, both technically and idiomatically. As well as being a memorial to Mátyás Seiber, it is also a subtle tribute, embodying Seiber's non-dogmatic approach to serialism, to texture and to structure. No attempt is made to disguise the tonal implications of the twelve-tone material; indeed these are celebrated in the opening subject-and-answer phrases on flute and clarinet. The harmonies are spicily, rather than spikily, dissonant, and the rhythms crisply cellular. Seiber's own quintet, *Permutazioni a Cinque* for wind, is brought firmly to mind by the opening figure, which derives directly from that work's own opening and ending, albeit transposed. *Gradi*, however, has no bass instrument proper – indeed although the horn is given a few notes in the bass range, the texture has an extraordinarily aerated, un-anchored quality, enhanced by a constant crossing-over of parts, a technique Seiber too explores in *Permutazioni*. The oboe and clarinet work as a pair, as do the violin and viola, with the horn acting initially, when it does appear, as a stabilising influence between the pairs, only later admitting its natural allegiance to the woodwind. As with *Permutazioni* the form is wholly unconventional, but perfectly clear and logical: Prelude, followed without interruption by six arching *gradi* or steps, each beginning on a higher degree of a scale, climaxing on the fourth and leading to an Interlude, an inverted transformation of the Prelude, then six more arching steps and finally a long, summatory Postlude ending with the biggest climax of all. Barring is all in multiples of 7: x2 for the *Gradi*, x4 for the Prelude and Interlude and x8 for the Postlude. The composer in fact attributes the overall structural modelling to Boris Blacher's *Orkester Ornament*.

Did Manduell cross the threshold on which this incisive work stands? In one sense he certainly has, in that major works such as the String Quartet of 1970, the Double Concerto of 1985 and *Vistas* for orchestra of 1997 followed its lead in developing a highly personal, if non-iconoclastic idiom. In another sense possibly not, in that new works followed too slowly for their creator's composerly reputation to establish itself firmly at the time. We all know about the short memory of most British promoters but also, it must be said, composers need feedback. Their work needs to be heard by them in the places and by the live audiences it was intended for, and not just by joggers with MP3s. To state the obvious, feedback feeds, and even the most creative imagination needs nourishment. Without it, it cannot in its turn nourish and enrich the surrounding culture.

Seven years, then, separated *Gradi* and the String Quartet in its first presentation, as a work of two complementary movements. The first of these is dense, taut and passionate in its warmth and earthy energy; the second is slightly longer and ethereal, its expressivity depending on poise, tautness and timing. An unconventional form again, one might think – on paper incomplete, yet to the ear and mind prepared to set aside preconceptions of classical form, both emotionally and intellectually fulfilling.

The structural detail of the first movement seems designed quite deliberately not to work, with its spasmodic, disconnected and very varied messages, some strict and one free; yet it does work, compellingly. There are three possible reasons. Any composer knows that if you are going to do something unorthodox, do it unequivocally. Manduell certainly observes this dictum. But also, being a composer who from the outset and particularly from his time with Berkeley has learnt to rely on a pretty flawless instinct, he judges all his eccentricities perfectly, making the whole completely comprehensible to the hearer's instinct too. A third reason could be that despite its explosive contrasts and disjunction, the movement's overall shape is founded on classical sonata form anyway. The apparent lack of connection between movements 1 and 2 is prepared for in the same way, and our expectations are fulfilled by its utterly different sound-world without there being the slightest hint of predictability. But analysis shows that overall, or should I say underlying all, there is nothing at all illogical or disconnected in all this varied material anyway. Movement 1 is a mosaic made from no more than three strongly-defined, self-interrupting ideas, each evolving in its own way, whilst movement 2 takes as its initial, and ultimately all-pervading harmony a transposed version of the final chord of movement 1.

When the third movement came along, late in 2006, some hearers failed to pick up the point that disconnectedness can in its own way be a unifying factor. Think of Messiaen or Dali. But now the Dali-esque thoracic drawer, which had seemed firmly closed, has been drawn open to reveal a range of new but related mysteries. There was bound to be a new dimension, since this movement's dedicatee, Christopher Rowland, RNCM's Director of Chamber Music and former leader of the Sartori, Lancaster University's Quartet-in-Residence, whom Sir John had known and admired for thirty-five years, was now terminally ill. So just as the first movement has a half-hidden classical formal principle, the third now is a partially-revealed, light-touch recapitulation, in reverse order, of all that went before – a retrospective echo, one might say, of many years of fruitful collaboration. Once more its commencement links, now pitch-to-pitch, with the end of its predecessor, and by the mid-point we are already gently in touch with subtly-transformed echoes of the main linear procedures in movement 1. Sir John says that this is all unconscious, intuitive logic, which merely supports my earlier assertion that the creative instinct, if well programmed, can perform greater wonders than conscientious pre-planning.

This quartet had been the first product of a long and fruitful friendship with Alun Hoddinott, for whose Cardiff Festival the work was commissioned. Second came a group of five cameos for solo clarinet, *Prayers from the Ark*, based on French poems in a translation by Rumer Godden; the poems could be read as part of any performance. These beautifully characteristic miniatures were first performed by Jack Brymer in the 1978 Cardiff Festival.

The chamber music, then, represents one intriguingly unorthodox side of Sir John the composer. Another such peeps out brightly from the orchestral music, not least from the Double Concerto of 1985, the third product of the Hoddinott friendship, again commissioned for the Cardiff Festival.

This is a 20-minute concerto for two Chinese instruments and orchestra. Manduell had been introduced to Chinese traditional instruments by the work's dedicatee, Professor Basil Deane, formerly of Manchester University and by 1984 Director of the Hong Kong Academy of Performing Arts. The instruments chosen are the *di-zi* or *ti-tzu*, a bamboo flute whose oboe-like sound is the result of a membrane-covered hole next to the player's lips, and the *er-hu*, a two-string fiddle with small, box-like body, played resting vertically on the thigh. The balance problem created by these relatively quiet instruments was solved by reducing the orchestra to strings, timpani and a goodly array of percussion shared between just three players.

A slow introduction brings in the di-zi, slow, expressive and slightly rhetorical; faster music then introduces the er-hu's long, flowing lines, soon to be overlaid by di-zi comments. These generate a friendly conflict between the two, with orchestral mediation which eventually becomes a little frenzied. A calming passage links to a double cadenza in which the soloists' differences are resolved before a rousing, unified ending. The second, central movement is the focal-point of the work. Slow-to-moderate in tempi, it is characterised by a richness of orchestral texture enhanced by the range of percussion instruments involved. Tempi change freely, some being linked through the device of metric modulation, whereby a subsidiary metre at the end of one section becomes the main one in the next. The soloists compete as a pair with this richness episodically, borrowing for their purpose passages of string harmonics and ultimately a range of percussion textures – the closest the work comes to evoking an eastern sound-world. This slightly unbalanced conflict is left unresolved in delicate suspense, only to be equalised in the finale by a coming-together of the soloists to confront the orchestra in a lively game, disrupted by dramatic percussion episodes creating an even stronger unity of purpose between the soloists. The ending is an explosively exuberant coming-together: now 'the twain' have truly met, albeit on largely Western idiomatic terms.

However, the relatively small number of di-zi and er-hu players in the Western world, along with a certain lack of double concertos for oboe and cor anglais, prompted the possibility of creating a variant of this Double Concerto, with di-zi replaced by oboe and cor anglais substituting for er-hu. This obviously reduces the contrast that exists between the two Chinese instruments, but reinforces the overall sense of linear direction and consistency. It is fair to say, though, that despite overall structural and motivic detail remaining almost unchanged, this substitution has created what is in effect a new work. The gentle, lyrical delicacy of the original has flowered into increased warmth and expressivity, with the character of the focal central movement now spreading outwards, creating, if possible, more continuity and unification. So despite the orchestration remaining the same, and the interesting oriental slant not having been lost, in this 2012 form the Double Concerto is not a mere adjustment, but a re-creation. It is superbly recorded on Métier msv 77201.

Vistas for orchestra followed twelve years later, in 1997, the year after Sir John's retirement as Principal of the RNCM. This was a Hallé commission, thanks to Kent Nagano, and in its very different, but equally nonconformist way it is also a double concerto, for the word 'concerto' in this context is clearly meant in the Italian sense of mutual agreement, not in the Latin sense of conflict. So the *concertini* are two identical quintets formed from the first and second flutes, clarinets, horns and percussion. These sub-groups are placed high up, respectively to the left and right of the main orchestra. The work's title aptly describes the sense of space this creates, as indeed does the music itself, and one might again say that the work's Value is Seven, Treated as Structural, since without waxing too arithmetical it's possible to detect multiples of that value conditioning proportions and durations throughout the 14-minute, 252-bar work, which has seven main sections, and whose main climax occurs, time-wise, five sevenths of the way through at bar 98.

Much of the music up to the climax-point is slow and spacious, the *concertini* engaging in dialogue between themselves and commenting upon the orchestral 'vistas' presented in each contrasted section. Colour is all-important: indeed at the very outset, in the 'trademark' brief introduction, the ear is focused on timbre through the presence of multiphonic passages for the concertino flutes, wherein each flute independently plays two simultaneous parts in parallel motion. The faster sections are mercurial, with heightened, sometimes dramatic, tension. The powerful climax itself occurs at the end of the longest slow and increasingly expansive vista, before the music tips over into a lightly tripping triple-speed journey taking us almost without interruption through sometimes lush, sometimes brittle, landscapes in which the *concertini* become increasingly jostled until agreeing to join forces with the main orchestra for a celebratory ending.

Completing and complementing our triptych of works for soloists and orchestra we have the Flutes Concerto of 2000, written at the invitation of Kent Nagano for Vincent Lucas and the Berkeley Symphony Orchestra of San Francisco, who gave its first performances in early 2001. The orchestral forces match those of the Double Concerto, with the addition of harp, but instead of two soloists each playing one instrument we now have one, playing three. There are three movements, not quite in the normal quick-slow-quick relationship, since each movement alternates internally-related tempi, the faster speed generally having three beats to the slower one's two. Threes and their multiples abound in the textures, rhythms and lines, too. For instance, before the soloist slowly enters, he or she is heard playing, off-stage, two six-note phrases, one a rising bluesy scale in A and the other a chant-like melody in E flat. These lines, on concert flute, energise in their contrasted way not only the string harmonies but also, separately and intermingling, most of the melodic material in this mercurial, capricious movement.

More intermingled and not always in sixes, they reappear in the alternating slow, then faster, five-section central movement. Now the alto flute is solo, and the music is correspondingly calmer, more lyrical but only a little more stable due to the morphings of the orchestral textures from warm tutti harmonies to stark soli to muted *tremolandi* for the rest to echoes of the same on vibraphone to, finally, a peaceful closure for muted strings and soloist.

Strange, otherworldly sounds from a rattling rainstick and slapped harp usher in the once-more mercurial third movement, with the soloist now on piccolo, playing virtuoso, decorated lines – those initiated in the first movement – leading to a cadenza. Piccolo is then temporarily set aside for concert flute which, after a brief canonic passage on strings, enters at the slower tempo with gracious arabesques. Drama builds up somewhat breathlessly, in the characteristic Manduell time-signature of 11/8, to the work's main climax. All relaxes, the alto flute lazily returning with lyrical lines before being forced by the solo violin to mutate into piccolo for some delicate dancing. Now a whip interrupts, initiating hard vibraphone gesture and pizzicato strings. The concert flute intervenes, calling everyone to order for the calm ending before making a graceful exit, still performing – playing versions, in fact, of the same six-note phrases with which entry was made – as though nothing had happened in between. The work's recording is paired on CD with the Double Concerto above.

All three of these works have an extrovert, almost theatrical, quality and prompt one to hope for a John Manduell opera in which this characteristic could have fuller play. Sir John has in fact expressed the desire, perhaps in the face of possibility, to write such a work. Hearing Gustave Charpentier's *Louise* live at the Paris *Opéra* in 1947, in the presence of the composer indeed, may have initiated his life-long passion for the genre. For the time being, however, we have in a sense the complete opposite, but equally characteristic, works with words, the songs. The first surviving set, *Trois Chansons de la Renaissance*, were written in 1956 while still a student, and were given their first performance at the Royal Academy of Music. The poems are obviously French, and their setting among the best and most idiomatic of any by a British composer: vibrant, clear, highly expressive and in one case almost voluptuous. Yet there is a balance and restraint typical of Fauré or Ravel, and their wonderfully characteristic piano accompaniments clearly show the influence of these composers.

We had to wait fifty years, however, for a sequel to this elegant trilogy. The poet in this case, Carmen Bernos de Gasztold, was also French, from Arcachon. Her troubled early life and experiences under wartime German occupation caused her to withdraw to the Abbaye de Saint-Louis-du-Temple, where her sequence of poems *Prières dans l'Arche* came into being. These were translated in 1963 by Rumer Godden of *Black Narcissus* fame, and it is this version that Manduell has set. *Into the Ark*, for high voice, recorder and guitar, was not, however, his first foray into this territory, for as mentioned, in 1972 he had written *Prayers from the Ark* for clarinet, echoes of which are faintly heard in this song cycle. In both cases we have eloquence, concision and sharply-defined character and ,as with *Trois Chansons*, the melodic material is not just memorable, but haunting. The accompanying recorder and guitar add humour, but overall there is a kind of sad, ironic spirituality. 'The Goldfish' nervously laments her imprisonment in crystal, whence she sees terrifying things; 'The Ox' gently prays, with bass recorder, for men's understanding of slow creatures; 'The Glow-Worm' quietly prays for darkness, 'The Monkey', strutting with guitar, for respect and 'The Cock', dramatically, for recognition of his power to create sunrise. 'The Giraffe', in graceful arching curves, offers up an assertion of her own exalted nature. Both of these groups of songs are now available on the ASC CD *Gradi*, on which other works featured in these pages can also be heard. They leave one longing for a Manduell work for the stage.

Much of Sir John's recent work is brief, written for special occasions. Much, too, in its multi-faceted, sharp and expressive manifestations, involves recorder, for which we must offer thanks to Britain's mighty, multi-tasking recorderist, John Turner, who has been responsible for putting on innumerable concerts to celebrate the wealth of creative Mancunian talent, and whose work on behalf of all of us puts our local Arts Council-funded bodies to shame. Typical of such pieces are *Verses from Calvary*, an expressive setting of poems from a playlet by W. B. Yeats for a Basil Deane memorial concert (perhaps the closest so far that Manduell has come to writing for the operatic stage), and *Two Celebrations* for treble recorder, with and without piano, wittily gracious tributes to fellow Manchester-based composers. The final composition I have space to focus on is another such Turner-engendered work, one which does not feature the recorder in fact, but was commissioned by the Ida Carroll Trust for the centenary of Miss Carroll herself, daughter of composer Walter Carroll, double bass player and for many years Principal of the Northern School of Music before occupying a senior post at the RNCM. Its original title was *Nonet for Strings (a Rondo for Ida)*; however, when it appeared on the recently-released *Antiphon* CD by Dutton, its title had become *Rondo for Nine*. In its simple, straightforward way it encapsulates much of the characteristic vitality, warmth, depth yet structural simplicity of the music described above. Its rondo form allows focus on strong motifs, its changing and mostly irregular time-signatures maintain rhythmic vitality, its episodic cadenzas for double bass give it an electric charge and a close Carroll connection, and the overall celebratory tone is yet tinged with sadness.

Anthony Gilbert

Reprinted with permission from *Manchester Sounds*, Volume 8, 2009-10, published by The Manchester Musical Heritage Trust (Registered Charity no 1076473) in association with Forsyth Brothers Ltd.

Appendix 2

Discography

The following recordings of music by John Manduell are currently available:

Diversions, for chamber orchestra (1969)
    Northern Chamber Orchestra conducted by Nicholas Ward
    Manchester Accents, ASC CS CD45

Double Concerto, for oboe, cor anglais, strings and percussion (1985 / 2012)
    Richard Simpson *oboe*, Alison Teale *cor anglais*, Manchester Sinfonia conducted by Timothy Reynish
    "Mixed Doubles", MSV 77201

Flute Concerto, for flautist, harp, strings and percussion (2000)
    Michael Cox *flutes*, Manchester Sinfonia conducted by Timothy Reynish
    "Mixed Doubles", MSV 77201

Gradi, for oboe, clarinet, horn, violin and viola (1956)
    Julie Payne *oboe*, Simon Underhill *clarinet*, Angharad Jones *horn*, Tristan Gurney *violin*, Fiona Petersen *viola*
    Gradi – the music of John Manduell, PFCD027

Into the Ark, for voice, recorder and guitar (1997)
    Claire Bradshaw *mezzo soprano*, John Turner *recorder*, Craig Ogden *guitar*
    Gradi – the music of John Manduell, PFCD027

Prayers from the Ark, for clarinet, bass clarinet and narrator (1978)
    Sauro Berti *clarinet* & *bass clarinet*, Peter Rose *narrator*
    Solo non solo, RR7894

Rondo for Nine, for string nonet (2005)
    Manchester Chamber Ensemble conducted by Richard Howarth
    Antiphon: A tribute to John Manduell, CDLX 7207

String Trio (1956)
    Nossek String Trio
    Gradi – the music of John Manduell, PFCD027

String Quartet (1970)
    Nossek String Quartet
    Gradi – the music of John Manduell, PFCD027

Trois Chansons de la Renaissance, for baritone and piano (1956)
    Henry Herford *baritone*, Renna Kellaway *piano*
    Gradi – the music of John Manduell, PFCD027

Variations on a Trio Tune, for solo recorder (1985)
    John Turner *recorder*
    Gradi – the music of John Manduell, PFCD027

Verses from Calvary, for soprano, recorder, oboe, violin and viola (2007)
    Lesley-Jane Rogers *soprano*, John Turner *recorder*, Richard Simpson *oboe*, Richard Howarth *violin*, Richard Tunnicliffe *viola da gamba*
    The Rose Tree, PFCD005

APPENDIX 3

Cheltenham Firsts

First Performances 1962-67
1962

Lennox Berkeley	Song Cycle: *Autumn's Legacy*, op. 58 (Festival commission)
Gordon Crosse	*Villanelles*, op. 2
Peter Maxwell Davies	Sinfonia (first performance outside London)
Benjamin Frankel	Symphony No. 2, op. 38
Anthony Gilbert	Piano Sonata
Alexander Goehr	Violin Concerto, op. 13
David Harries	Clarinet Quintet, op. 15 (commissioned for the occasion by the Guild for the Promotion of Welsh Music)
Christopher Headington	Piano Sonata (first public performance)
Alun Hoddinott	Symphony No. 2, op. 29 (commissioned for the occasion)
Elisabeth Lutyens	*Quincunx* for orchestra, op. 44
William Mathias	Sonata for violin & piano, op. 15
Bo Nilsson	*Zwanzig Gruppen* (first performance outside London)
Ian Parrott	Septet for flute, clarinet, string quartet & piano (commissioned for the occasion by the Guild for the Promotion of Welsh Music)
Egon Wellesz	5 Piano Pieces, op. 83 (first public performance)
John White	Piano Scherzo (first public performance) Piano Sonata No. 10
Hugh Wood	String Quartet No. 1, op. 4 (commissioned for the occasion by the BBC)

1963

Richard Rodney Bennett	*Nocturnes* for chamber orchestra (British premiere, Festival commission)
David Blake	Variations for piano (first public performance)

Arthur Bliss	*A Knot of Riddles* for baritone & chamber orchestra (commissioned for the occasion by the BBC)
Reginald Smith Brindle	*Homage to H. G. Wells* for orchestra (first public performance)
Stephen Dodgson	Partita No. 1 for guitar
John Exton	*Fantasy* for violin & piano (first public performance)
Iain Hamilton	*Arias* for small orchestra
Harry Hancock	*Nocturne* for flute, violin & bassoon
John Joubert	*In Memoriam, 1820*, op. 39 (British premiere)
John Joubert	*Sonata à cinque*, op. 43 (commissioned by the players for this performance)
William Mathias	Wind Quintet, op. 22 (commissioned for the occasion by the BBC)
Thea Musgrave	Sinfonia (commissioned by the Festival committee)
Alan Ridout	Anthem: 'O Give Thanks unto the Lord'
Leopold Spinner	Variations for violin & piano
Hugh Wood	Three Piano Pieces, op. 5

1964

Lennox Berkeley	*Diversions*, four pieces for 8 instruments, op. 63 (commissioned for the occasion by Delphos Ensemble)
Harrison Birtwistle	*Entr'actes & Sappho Fragments*
David Cox	Four Pieces for piano
Peter Maxwell Davies	*Veni Sancte Spiritus*
Tony Hewitt-Jones	Canticles & Amen
Alun Hoddinott	Harp Sonata, op. 36 (commissioned for the occasion)
Robert Sherlaw Johnson	Piano Sonata (1963)
Elisabeth Lutyens	Music for Orchestra III, op. 56 (commissioned for the occasion by the BBC)
John McCabe	Three pieces for clarinet & piano
Wilfred Mellers	*Rose of May*, threnody for speaker, soprano, flute, clarinet & string quartet (commissioned for the occasion)
Alan Rawsthorne	Symphony No. 3 (Festival commission)
Edmund Rubbra	String Quartet No. 3, op. 112

William Schuman	Violin Concerto (first public performance in Britain)
Humphrey Searle	*Song of the Sun* for unaccompanied chorus, op. 42 (commissioned for the occasion by the BBC)
Robert Starer	Duo for violin & viola (British premiere)
John Wilks	*Beata l'Alma* for soprano & orchestra
William Wordsworth	Sonatina for viola & piano, op. 71 (first public performance)

1965

Don Banks	*Division for Orchestra* (commissioned for the occasion by the Feeney Trust)
David Bedford	*Music for Albion Moonlight* (British premiere)
Arthur Bliss	*Hymn to Apollo*, revised version
Frank Bridge	*Rhapsody Trio* for 2 violins & viola (first broadcast performance)
Alan Bush	*Variations, Nocturne & Finale on an English Sea-Song* for piano & orchestra, op. 60
David Carhart	Fantasy in Three Movements for piano
Gordon Crosse	Sinfonia Concertante, op. 13 (commissioned for the occasion by the Feeney Trust)
Benjamin Frankel	String Quartet No. 5. op. 43 (BBC commission)
John Gardner	Magnificat, Nunc Dimittis, Versicles & Responses, op. 72 (specially composed for the occasion)
Roberto Gerhard	Concerto for Orchestra (first public performance in Britain, commissioned for the occasion)
Cristobal Halffter	*Introducción fuga y final* for piano (British premiere)
Wilfred Josephs	Symphony No. 2, op. 42
Geoffrey Kimpton	Serenade for clarinet & piano
William Mathias	Piano Trio, op. 30
Alan Rawsthorne	*Tankas of the Four Seasons* for tenor, oboe, clarinet, bassoon, violin & cello (commissioned for the occasion by Macnaghten Concerts)

1966

Christopher Brown	Anthem: 'Laudate Dominum'
Christopher Brown	Sonata for violin & piano
Arnold Cooke	Piano Sonata No. 2 in B flat (1965)
Gordon Crosse	*Purgatory*, op. 18 – one-act opera (joint Festival & BBC2 television commission)
Petr Eben	Piano Concerto (first performance outside Czechoslovakia)
Jindrich Feld	Suite for string chamber orchestra (British premiere)
Tony Hewitt-Jones	Introit: 'O clap your Hands'
Alun Hoddinott	Piano Concerto No. 3, op. 44 (commissioned for the occasion)
Robert Sherlaw Johnson	Improvisations I & II for violin & piano
Norman Kay	Passacaglia for orchestra
David Lord	Divertimento for flute, violin & piano duet
Anthony Leach	Versicles & Responses
Anna Lockwood	*A Abelard, Héloise from the first letter*
John McCabe	Symphony No. 1 (*Elegy*) (commissioned by the Hallé)
Jan Novák	*Balletti à nove*
John Ogdon	Theme & Variations for piano
Tim Souster	*Poem in Depression at Wei Village*
Richard Stoker	Sextet for clarinet, horn, bassoon & string trio, op. 16
Richard Stoker	Sonatina in three movements for flute & violin
Clive Strutt	Piano Sonata (first public performance)
Phyllis Tate	*The What D'Ye Call It* – opera
Egon Wellesz	Symphony No. 6, op. 95 (British premiere)
Malcolm Williamson	Five Preludes for piano
Anna Wynne	*Improvisation*

1967

Grażyna Bacewicz	*Pensieri Notturni* (British premiere)
David Bedford	*Trona* for string quartet, flute, oboe, clarinet, bassoon, 2 trumpets & 2 trombones (British premiere)

Harrison Birtwistle	*Three Lessons in a Frame* for piano & five instruments (commissioned by Macnaghten Concerts)
Paul Broom	*Structures III* for flute, clarinet & bassoon
Brian Chapple	Quartet for clarinet, horn, violin & piano
Martin Dalby	*Eight Songs from the Chinese* (first public performance)
Peter Maxwell Davies	*Hymnos* for clarinet & piano
Brian Dennis	Piano Study No. 2 (first public performance)
Benjamin Frankel	Viola Concerto, op. 45 (BBC Third Programme & Festival joint commission)
Henryck Górecki	Refrain for orchestra, op. 21 (British premiere)
Michael Hurd	*Shore Leave: Poems by Charles Causley*
Wilfred Josephs	Fourteen Studies for piano, op. 53
Jeffrey Lewis	*Epitaphium – Children of the Sun*
Witold Lutosławski	*Three Postludes* (British premiere)
John McCabe	Fantasy on a theme of Liszt for piano (first public performance)
Sergei Prokofiev	Symphony No. 4, op. 47 / 112 (first performance in the West of revised version)
Priaulx Rainier	*Aequora Lunae* (commissioned by the BBC)
Thomas Rajna	Movements for strings (first public performance)
Howard Rees	*Sounds for Four* for flute, percussion & piano
Edmund Rubbra	Eight Preludes for piano, op. 131
Kazimierz Serocki	*Segmenti* (British premiere)
Robert Simpson	Piano Concerto (1967) (Festival commission)
Anton Webern	*Im Sommerwind – Idyll for large orchestra* (British premiere)
Dennis Wickens	Song Cycle: *The Everlasting Voices*
Malcolm Williamson	Sonata for 2 pianos (Festival commission)
Peter Wishart	Anthem: 'The Hevenly Kery' (specially commission for the occasion)

Hugh Wood	Quintet for clarinet, horn, violin, cello & piano, op. 9 (commissioned by the Music Group of London)

FIRST PERFORMANCES 1969-1994
1969

Lennox Berkeley	Three Pieces for organ, op. 72 no. 1 (first complete performance)
Lennox Berkeley	Symphony No. 3 in one movement, op. 74 (Festival commission)
André Boucourechliev	*Archipel 2*, for string quartet (British premiere)
Brian Brockless	Fantasia, Adagio & Fugue for organ (commissioned by Sir Arthur Bliss)
Alan Bush	*Time Remembered*, op. 67
Tristram Cary	*Continuum* (Festival commission)
David Cox	*Out of Doors* for a cappella choir
Peter Maxwell Davies	*St. Thomas Wake* – Foxtrot for orchestra (British premiere)
Jonathan Harvey	*Laus Deo* for organ
Alun Hoddinott	Sinfonietta 2, op. 67 (Festival commission)
Heinz Holliger	*Mobile* for oboe & harp (British premiere)
Gordon Jacob	Suite for bassoon & string quartet
André Jolivet	*Controversia* for oboe & harp (British premiere)
Daniel Jones	*The Ballad of the Standard Bearer* for tenor and piano
John Metcalf	Chorales & Variants (Festival commission)
Jiri Smutny	Two Pieces for oboe & harp
Christopher Steel	Anthem: 'O Praise the Lord of Heaven' (specially commissioned for the occasion)
Karlheinz Stockhausen	*Spiral* for oboe & radio (British premiere)

1970

William Alwyn	Sinfonietta for strings (Festival commission with funds from ACGB)
Jeffrey Bishop	*Spells and Incantations* for horn trio

George Brown	*Prisms* (Festival commission with funds from ACGB)
Howard Davidson	*Omega Centauri* (Festival commission with funds from ACGB)
Peter Dickinson	*Transformations* (commissioned by the Feeney Trust)
Patrick Gowers	Toccata for organ (Festival commission with funds from ACGB)
Robin Holloway	*Scenes from Schumann*, op. 13
Ian Kellam	*Festival Jubilate* (Festival commission with funds from ACGB)
Thea Musgrave	*Night Music* (British premiere)
Elizabeth Poston	Anthem: 'Benediction for the Arts' (Festival commission with funds from ACGB)
Howard Riley	*Textures* for string quartet
Humphrey Searle	*Zodiac Variations*, op. 53 (Festival commission with funds from ACGB)
Patric Standford	*Metamorphosis* for organ
Richard Stoker	*Nocturnal* for horn, violin & piano, op. 37 (commissioned by London Horn Trio)
John Tavener	*Coplas* for voices & tape (Festival commission with funds from ACGB)
Michael Tippett	*The Shires Suite* for orchestra & chorus (first complete performance)
Henry Weinberg	String Quartet No. 2 (British premiere)

1971

Sven-Erik Bäck	*In Principio* (British premiere)
Don Banks	Three Short Songs (Festival commission with funds from ACGB)
Reginald Smith Brindle	*Apocalypse*
Tristram Cary	Trios
Martin Dalby	*Concerto Martin Pescatore* (Festival commission with funds from ACGB)
Peter Racine Fricker	*Nocturne* for chamber orchestra, op. 63 (Festival commission with funds from ACGB)
Trevor Hold	Four Songs for baritone & ensemble
David Jenkins	*The Devil's Dream* (Festival commission with funds from ACGB)
Peter Lawson	*Valentia Extramaterial*

Nicola LeFanu	*Christ Calls Man Home* (Festival commission with funds from ACGB)
Bent Lorentzen	*Medea Suite* (British premiere)
Thea Musgrave	*From One to Another* for viola & tape (British premiere)
Bo Nilsson	*Exit* (British premiere)
Per Nørgård	*Luna* (British premiere)

1972

Arthur Bliss	*Two Contrasts* (British premiere)
Tristram Cary	*Peccata Mundi*
Charles Camilleri	Piano Trio (Festival commission with funds from ACGB)
Jean Coulthard	String Quartet No. 2, *Threnody* (British premiere)
Gordon Crosse	*Ariadne*, concertante for solo oboe & 12 players, op. 31
Chris Hazell	*Holy Moses!*
David Lumsdaine	*Caliban Impromptu* for piano trio (Festival commission with funds from ACGB)
Elizabeth Maconchy	String Quartet No. 10 (Festival commission with funds from ACGB)
Richard Meale	*Clouds Now and Then* (British premiere)
Wilma Paterson	*Five Poems of Charles d'Orléans* (commissioned by Neill Sanders)
Geoffrey Poole	*Lamentations & Prayer* (Festival commission with funds from ACGB)
Peter Sculthorpe	*Ketjak* for 6 male voices with feedback (Festival commission with funds from ACGB)
James Stevens	*Etheria* for organ
John Weeks	*Six Facets* for organ
Malcolm Williamson	*The Musicians of Bremen* (British premiere)
Malcolm Williamson	*The Icy Mirror*, Symphony No. 3 (Festival commission)

1973

Lennox Berkeley	Antiphon for string orchestra, op. 85 (Festival commission with funds from ACGB)

Anthony Gilbert	Symphony (Festival commission with funds from ACGB)
Nicholas Maw	*Lifestudies* for 15 solo strings (Festival commission with funds from ACGB)
Elis Pekhonen	*The Nightmare* for flute & strings
Raymond Premru	*Music from Harter Fell* (Festival commission with funds from ACGB)
Bernard Rands	*Wildtrack 2* (Festival commission with funds from ACGB)
Thomas Wilson	Refrains & Cadenzas for brass band (Festival commission with funds from ACGB)

1974

Richard Rodney Bennett	*Commedia II* for flute, cello & piano (first public performance)
Michael Blake-Watkins	*Presage of Storme*
Geoffrey Burgon	*Noche Oscura del alma*
Henri Lazarof	*Cadence 5* for flutes & tape (British premiere)
Elisabeth Lutyens	*Roads*, op. 95 (specially commissioned for occasion by Purcell Consort of Voices)
Nicholas Maw	*Lifestudies* for 15 solo strings (first complete performance of 7 studies)
John Mayer	Violin Concerto

The Seven Deadly Sins – group of works, all Festival commissions with funds from ACGB:

Anthony Gilbert	'Anger'
Carl Davis	'Covetousness – a Detective Opera'
Frank Cordell	'Envy'
Joseph Horovitz	'Gluttony'
Peter Dickinson	'Lust'
Humphry Searle	'Pride – Rhyme Rude to my Pride', op. 62
Elisabeth Lutyens	'Sloth'

1975

Kenneth Leighton	*Fantasy on an American Hymn Tune* for clarinet, cello & piano, op. 70 (commissioned by artists with ACGB funds)
Elizabeth Maconchy	*Epyllion* for solo cello & strings

Stephen Oliver	*Luv: a Study in Convention and Tonality* (Festival commission with funds from ACGB)
Richard Shephard	Preces & Responses (specially written for occasion)

1976

Anthony Payne	*The World's Winter* (Festival commission with funds from ACGB)
Malcolm Williamson	Piano Trio (British premiere: Festival joint commission)

1977

Gordon Crosse	Variations for oboe & cello, op. 39a *A Little Epiphany*
Jonathan Harvey	*Inner Light (2)* (commissioned for the Festival with Macfarlane Walker Trust funds)
Alun Hoddinott	*Passaggio* for orchestra, op. 94 (Festival commission with funds from ACGB)
Richard Orton	*Chansons perdues* (Festival commission with funds from ACGB)
Wilma Paterson	*Et in Arcadia Ego* (Festival commission with funds from ACGB)

1978

Richard Rodney Bennett	Music for strings (joint commission by Festival & Academy of St. Martin-in-the-Fields, with funds from ACGB)
Peter Racine Fricker	*Anniversary* for piano, op. 77
Iain Hamilton	*Cleopatra – a dramatic scene* for soprano & orchestra (Festival commission with funds from ACGB)
Grayston Ives	Anthem: 'O sing joyfully' (written for Tewkesbury Abbey School Choir)
Nicholas Maw	*Lifestudies* for 15 solo strings (first performance of all 8 studies)
Phyllis Tate	*Scenes from Kipling*, for baritone & piano

1979

Malcolm Arnold	Symphony for brass, op. 123
Geoffrey Burgon	*Dos Coros* (first concert performance)
Gordon Crosse	Cello Concerto, op. 44 (Festival commission with funds from ACGB)

Alun Hoddinott	*Ritornello No. 2* for brass quintet (Festival commission)
1980	
Edward Cowie	*Colombine* for soprano & chamber orchestra (Festival commission with funds from ACGB)
Anthony Hymas	Music for the ballet *Preludes & Song* (Festival commission with funds from ACGB)
Malcolm Lipkin	*Clifford's Tower*
Anthony Payne	*Song of the Clouds* (commissioned by Sarah Francis)
1981	
Erika Fox	*Litany* for strings (commissioned by Yehudi Menuhin School)
Robin Holloway	*Idyll*, op. 42 (commissioned by Northern Sinfonia)
George Lloyd	Symphony No. 4 in B (first public performance)
Elisabeth Lutyens	Concert Aria *Dialogo* for soprano & orchestra, op. 142 (commissioned by Richard Hickox & the CLS)
Elizabeth Maconchy	*Piccola Musica* for string trio (Festival commission with funds from Festival & SWA)
Paul Patterson	*Deception Pass* for brass ensemble, op. 43 (commissioned by Philip Jones Brass Ensemble)
1982	
George Benjamin	*Meditation on Haydn's name* for piano (first concert performance)
George Benjamin	*Sortilèges* for piano (commissioned by Paul Crossley)
Charles Camilleri	*Fantasia Concertante* for organ (Festival commission with funds from SWA)
Stephen Dodgson	*Essay No. 1* for orchestra
Peter Racine Fricker	Rondeaux for horn & orchestra, op. 87 (Festival commission with funds from SWA)

John Mayer	*Sangitara* (joint commission by Festival & Academy of St. Martin-in-the-Fields, with funds from ACGB)
Bruno Maderna	*Aulodia per Lothar* for oboe d'amore & guitar (British premiere)
Elis Pekhonen	Four Russian Folk Songs
André Tchaikovsky	*Trio Notturno* for piano trio

1983

Bouquet for Lennox – 16 original works commissioned by the Festival

John Manduell	Introduction & Theme – *Allegro molto*
Brian Chapple	*Energico*
Roy Teed	*Allegretto*
Sally Beamish	*Allegro*
Michael Berkeley	*Adagio calmo – Daybreak & a Candle End:* Prelude for orchestra
Christopher Headington	*Scherzando*
Christopher Brown	*Allegro molte e vivace*
Richard Stoker	*Sempre accelerando*
David Bedford	*Moderato*
Rory Boyle	*Fast*
John McLeod	*Allegro energico*
William Mathias	'A Birthday Roulade' – *Animé, avec joie*
Richard Rodney Bennett	'Freda's Fandango' – *con eleganza*
Jonathan Rutherford	*Allegro vivace – Andantino – Presto*
John Tavener	'Tropheia' – *molto legato sempre*
Nicholas Maw	*Allegro giocoso*
Lennox Berkeley	Cello Concerto
Arthur Butterworth	Piano Trio, op. 73 (Festival commission)
Gordon Crosse	*Chime* for brass quintet (Festival commission with funds from SWA)

1984

Michael Berkeley	Horn Concerto (Festival commission with funds from ACGB)
Martin Butler	String Quartet (Festival commission with funds from SWA)
Frederick Delius	*Paa Vidderne* (first professional public performance)
Peter Dickinson	Four Duos for oboe & cello
Peter Dickinson	Piano Concerto (Festival commission with funds from SWA)

Peter Racine Fricker	String Quartet No. 3, op. 73
Peter Racine Fricker	Madrigals for brass quintet, op. 89
Gustav Holst ed. Reynish	Three Folk Tunes, arr. wind band
Herbert Howells	Sonata for oboe & piano
John Tavener	*Ikon of Light*
John Tavener	*Towards the Son*
Jan van Vlijmen	*Faithful* for solo viola
James Wood	*Drama*

1985

Richard Rodney Bennett	Guitar Sonata
Edison Denisov	Sextet for flute, oboe, clarinet, violin, viola & cello (Capricorn commission with Festival funds)
Stephen Dodgson	Piano Sonata No. 3 (*Variations on a Rhythm*)
Zsolt Durkó	Sinfonietta for brass dectet
Peter Racine Fricker	Serenade No. 5 for violin & cello, op. 81 (British premiere)
Robin Holloway	Ballad for harp & orchestra, op. 61 (Festival commission with funds from ACGB & UK Harp Association)
Alain Louvier	*Etudes pour 14 Agresseurs,* XV & XVIII for harpsichord (British premiere)
Maurice Ravel	*Alcyone* (British premiere)
Dimitri Shostakovich	Six Poems of Marina Tsvetayeva for mezzo-soprano & chamber orchestra, op. 143a (British premiere)
Graham Whettam	Symphonic Prelude (Festival commission with funds from SWA)

1986

Kaiko Abe	*Frogs* for marimba (British premiere)
Edward Applebaum	*And with… and to* (British premiere)
Richard Rodney Bennett	Duo Concertante for clarinet & piano (Festival commission with funds from SWA & Royal Over-Seas League)
Michael Berkeley	*Songs of Awakening Love* (commissioned by City of London Sinfonia with funds from ACGB)
Christopher Brown	*A-courting we will go*
Conrad Cummings	*I wish they all could be…*

Ingolf Dahl	Piano Quartet (British premiere)
Claude Debussy	Piano Trio in G major (British premiere)
Peter Racine Fricker	*A Wish for a Party* (British premiere)
Peter Racine Fricker	Concerto for orchestra, op. 93 (Festival commission with funds from ACGB)
Mel Graves	String Quartet *Pangaea* (British première)
John Guinjoan	*Tension Relax* (British premiere)
Lou Harrison	Double Concerto for violin & cello with Javanese gamelan (British premiere)
Alun Hoddinott	Concerto for violin, cello, piano & orchestra, op. 124 (commissioned for Festival by Gloucestershire County Council)
Gustav Holst	*Dirge & Hymeneal, H124*
Gustav Holst	Five Part-songs, op. 12 (first complete performance)
Andrew Imbrie	*Pilgrimage* (European premiere)
William Kraft	*Gallery 4-5* (European premiere)
William Kraft	*Interplay* (British premiere)
William Kraft	*Mélange* (European premiere)
William Kraft	*Weavings* for string quartet & percussion (British premiere)
John Metcalf	Auden Songs (British premiere)
Robert Saxton	Viola Concerto (Festival commission with funds from ACGB)
Gerard Schumann	Piano Quartet
Neill Sorrell	*Mas in 1 minor* for gamelan
Virgil Thomson	*Party Pieces* (British premiere)
Henry Cowell	*Party Pieces* (British premiere)
John Cage	*Party Pieces* (British premiere)
Lou Harrison	*Party Pieces* (British premiere)
Tanaka Toshimitsu	Two Movements for marimba (British premiere)
Clive Wilkinson	*From the Flowering Currant* for gamelan

1987

Michael Ball	*Kabuki* for piano (commissioned by William Howard with funds from SWA)
David Bedford	*For Tess* for brass quintet
Richard Rodney Bennett	*After Ariadne* for viola & piano

Richard Rodney Bennett	*Ophelia* for counter-tenor, ondes martenot, harp & strings
Stephen Dodgson	String Quartet No. 1
Jean Françaix	Piano Trio
Frans Geysen	*Installaties* for recorder quartet (British premiere)
Anthony Gilbert	String Quartet No. 2 (BBC commission)
Marcel Landowski	*Blanc et feu* for brass quintet (British premiere)
Kenneth Leighton	*Earth, Sweet Earth... (Laudes Terrae)*, op. 94, for tenor & piano
Alain Louvier	*Cinq Pieces* for brass quintet (British premiere)
Alain Louvier	*Envois d'ecailles* for flute, viola & harp (British premiere)
Alain Louvier	*Etudes pour agresseurs, Livre 1* (nos. 1-7) (British premiere)
Alain Louvier	*Etudes pour agresseurs, Livre 6* (British premiere)
Alain Louvier	*Pentagone* for wind quintet (British premiere)
Alain Louvier	*Raga* for ondes martenot (British premiere)
Albert Roussel	*Andante* for oboe, clarinet & bassoon (British premiere)
Karel van Steenhoven	*Wolken* for recorder quartet (British premiere)
John Tavener	*Eis Thanaton*
Judith Weir	*A Night at the Chinese Opera* (BBC commission for Kent Opera)

1988

Malcolm Arnold	Brass Quintet No. 2, op. 132
Edison Denisov	String Quartet No. 2 (British premiere)
Keith Humble	*Ways – Byways* (European premiere)
Gordon Kerry	*Siderius Nuncius* for organ (European premiere)
Philip Lane	*Pageant Music* (Festival commission)
Paul Lansky	*Stroll* (European premiere)
Tigran Mansuryan	String Quartet No. 2 (British premiere)

Nigel Osborne	*Esquisses I & II* for 11 solo strings (British premiere)
Jeff Pressing	*If Nineteen were Twelve* (European premiere)
Peter Sculthorpe	*Songs of Sea & Sky* for clarinet & piano (British premiere of revised version)
Carl Vine	*Elegy* (European premiere)
Judith Weir	*A Spanish Liederbooklet*
Martin Wesley-Smith	For marimba & tape (European premiere)

1989

Mark Edgley-Smith	*Go-Round* for brass quintet (first public performance)
Anthony Gilbert	*Certain Lights Reflecting*
Alun Hoddinott	Piano Sonata No. 9, op. 134
Robin Holloway	*The Noon's Repose*, op. 39 (first public performance)
Gustav Holst	Quintet in A minor for piano & woodwind, op. 3 (first public performance)
Gustav Holst	*The Mystic Trumpeter*, op. 18 (first professional performance)
Leif Kayser	Trio No. 2 for flute, oboe & cello (British premiere)
John Marson	Fantasia for harp
John Mayer	*Ragamalika* for violin & tanpura (commissioned by Erich Gruenberg)
Harmut Pascher	String Quartet No. 1, op. 27 (British premiere)
Anthony Powers	Brass Quintet
Hans Stadlmair	String Quartet
John Woolrich	*The Kingdom of Dreams* for oboe & piano

1990

Simon Bainbridge	Double Concerto for oboe & clarinet (Festival commission with funds from ACGB)
Lennox Berkeley	Flute Sonatina, op. 13, orch. Newton (first public performance)
Stephen Dodgson	Partita No. 4 for guitar
David Gow	*Plaeiades Music* for saxophone quartet
Edward Harper	*Homage to Thomas Hardy* (Festival commission with funds from ACGB)

Ian McQueen	Triptych for piano
Paul Patterson	Symphony, op. 69
Robert Simpson	Brass Quintet
Roger Steptoe	Organ Concerto
Michael Tippett	*New Year Suite* (European premiere)
John Woolrich	*Favola in musica* for oboe, clarinet & piano

1991

Richard Rodney Bennett	*The Four Seasons* (Festival commission with funds from ACGB & RNCM)
Charles Camilleri	Clarinet Quintet
Peter Maxwell Davies	*Caroline Mathilde* – concert suite from Act I of the ballet
Peter Maxwell Davies	*Dangerous Errand* (English premiere)
Peter Maxwell Davies	*Jimmack the Postie* (English premiere)
Peter Maxwell Davies	*Mishkenot* (first public performance)
Peter Maxwell Davies	*Ojai Festival Overture* (British premiere)
Michael Finnissy	*O quam glorifica luce*
Elena Firsova	*Rakovjina* (Sea Shell), op. 49
Michael Nyman	*Where the Bee Dances* for saxophone & orchestra
Dmitri Smirnov	*Silent, silent night*
Graham Whettam	Violin Sonata No. 3

1992

Richard Arnell	String Quartet No. 6, op. 170
George Barcos	*Homenaje a la Selva* (British premiere)
Luciano Berio	*Call* for brass quintet (British premiere)
Stephen Dodgson	*Spice of Life (Essence & Variety)* for brass quintet
Philip Flood	*Movements & Repose* for brass quintet
Willy Hess	Divertimento in B flat, op. 51 (British premiere)
Klaus Huber	*Alveare Vernat* for flute & 12 solo strings (British premiere)
Rudolf Kelterborn	Chamber Music for 5 winds (British premiere)
Rudolf Kelterborn	*Musica luminosa* for chamber orchestra (British premiere)
Rudolf Kelterborn	7 Bagatelles for wind quintet (British premiere)

Rudolf Kelterborn	*Tableaux encadrés* for 13 solo strings (British premiere)
Malcolm Lipkin	Piano Sonata No. 3 (European premiere of revised version)
Michael Nyman	*Goodbye Frankie, Goodbye Benny* (later retitled *Time will pronounce*)
Paul Patterson	Violin Concerto, op. 72
Poul Ruders	Violin Concerto No. 2 (British premiere)
Othmar Schoeck	*Summer Night*, op. 58 (first professional public performance in Britain)
John Tavener	*The Last Sleep of the Virgin* – String Quartet No. 2
Richard Taylor	*Eternal Enigma* (Festival commission)
Judith Weir	*I broke off a golden branch* for piano quintet
Jacques Wildberger	*Retrospective II* for solo flute (British premiere)

1993

Simon Bainbridge	Clarinet Quintet (Festival commission with funds from SWA)
Sally Beamish	*Into the Furnace* for octet (Festival commission with funds from SWA)
Michael Berkeley	*Baa Baa Black Sheep* (Festival commission with funds from ACGB & BBC TV)
Michael Berkeley	*Elegy* for flute & strings
David Blake	Cello Concerto (BBC commission)
John Casken	*Darting the Skiff* for string orchestra
Cimarosa	*The Secret Marriage* (first performance of new production)
Robert Crawford	Variations on a Ground for treble recorder & piano
Jean Françaix	Quintet No. 2 for flute, harp & string trio (British premiere)
Edward Gregson	Processional (first concert performance)
Dave Heath	*Gorbachev* for piano trio
David Matthews	Oboe Concerto, op. 57 (first performance with a professional orchestra)
Alan Rawsthorne	Suite for recorder & piano

1994

Thomas Armstrong	*Broken Vows* (first professional performance)
Richard Rodney Bennett	Saxophone Quartet (commissioned by the Apollo Saxophone Quartet with funds from NWA)
Michael Berkeley	*Amen dico vobis* (first concert performance)
Michael Berkeley	*Laetentur coeli* (first concert performance)
Timothy Coker	*Odi profanum vulgus et arceo* (first public performance)
Dave Heath	*Free the Spirit*
Colin Matthews	Three Interludes
Thea Musgrave	Autumn Sonata (commissioned by Victoria Soames with funds from ACE & SWA)
Thea Musgrave	*Journey through a Japanese Landscape* (Festival co-commission)
Thea Musgrave	*On the Underground* (set no. 1) (commissioned by Canzonetta with funds from Sainsbury's)
Joseph Phibbs	String Quartet
Anthony Powers	*The Swing of the Sea*
Judith Weir	*Heroic Strokes of the Bow* (British premiere)

FEATURED COMPOSER CELEBRATIONS

Arnell	1992	(75th birthday)
Berkeley, Lennox	1973	(70th birthday)
	1983	(80th birthday)
	1993	(90th anniversary of birthday)
Berkeley, Michael	1993	
Birtwistle	1994	(60th birthday)
Bliss	1971	(80th birthday)
	1976	
	1991	(centenary)
Bridge	1979	(centenary)
Britten	1963	(50th birthday)

	1989	
Maxwell Davies	1991	
	1994	(60th birthday)
Delius	1984	(50th anniversary of death)
	1994	(60th anniversary of death)
Dodgson	1994	(70th birthday)
Elgar	1984	(50th anniversary of death)
	1994	(60th anniversary of death)
Fricker	1986	
	1990	
Goehr	1992	(60th birthday)
Handel	1985	(tercentenary)
Hoddinott	1989	(60th birthday)
	1994	(65th birthday)
Holst	1965	
	1974	(centenary)
	1984	(50th anniversary of death)
	1994	(60th anniversary of death)
Howells	1972	(80th birthday)
	1992	(centenary)
Ireland	1979	(centenary)
Lipkin	1992	(60th birthday)
Lutyens	1966	(60th birthday)
Maconchy	1987	(80th birthday)
Mathias	1994	(60th anniversary of birth)
McCabe	1989	(50th birthday)
	1994	(55th birthday)
Moeran	1994	(centenary)
Musgrave	1988	(60th birthday)
Rawsthorne	1965	(50th birthday)
	1972	(memorial)
Simpson, Robert	1991	(70th birthday)
Tate	1981	(70th birthday)
Tavener	1994	(50th birthday)
Tippett	1975	(70th birthday)
	1990	(85th birthday)
Vaughan Williams	1972	(centenary)
Warlock	1994	(centenary)
Weir	1987	

	1994	(40th birthday)
Wood, Hugh	1992	(60th birthday)
Woolrich	1994	(40th birthday)

Index

4-MALITY Percussion Quartet 180

A

Abe, Kaiko 255
Abraham, Gerald 115
Abramson, Elda 169
Abreu, José Antonio 196, 198
Academy of St Martin-in-the-Fields 179
Aeolian Quartet 76
Aldeburgh Music Festival 90, 161, 188, 217, 219
Alexandersson, Thomas 207
Allan, Richard van 124
Allegri String Quartet 170
All-India Radio 70
Allsop, Annie Amelia 53, 54
Allsop, Constance Ellen 54, 55
Allsop, Emily 54
Allsop, Tom 54, 55
Alsace 8, 28, 29, 30, 33, 34, 35 [Plate 3]
Alwyn, William 43, 44, 45, 48, 49, 68, 230, 248
Amadeus Quartet 125
Amanzimtoti 42
Ames, Les 35
Amy, Gilbert 182
Anders, Peter 38
Angadi, Ayana Deva 71
Angeles, Victoria de los 122
Angel, Martin 166
Applebaum, Edward 255
Arányi, Jelly d' 23
ARD International Music Competition, Munich 136, 137, 138, 139, 151
Argles, Michael 115, 118
Arkell, John 89
Armitage, Arthur 172
Armstrong-Jones, Anthony 37
Armstrong, Robert (Lord Armstrong of Ilminster) 51, 224
Armstrong. Sir Thomas 45, 51, 94
Arnell, Richard 259
Arnold, Malcolm 252, 257
Aronowitz, Cecil 9, 160, 179 [Plate 24] 9
Aronowitz, Nicola 160
Arts Council of Great Britain (ACGB) 7, 117, 121, 124, 127, 203, 204, 205, 206, 207, 212, 213, 214, 217, 229, 231, 240, 248, 249, 250, 251, 252, 253, 254, 255, 256, 258, 259, 260
  Housing the Arts Committee 205
  Music Department 204
  Music Panel 204
  'Spheres of Influence' 212
  The Glory of the Garden 206
  Touring Committee 204
Arts Council of N. Ireland 78, 120
Asian Music Circle 71
Associated Board 18
Atkins, Merton 59, 114

Attenborough, David 98
Attenborough, Richard 70
Attlee, Clement 26

B

Babbitt, Milton 118
Bacewicz, Grażyna 246
Bach, Johann Sebastian 34, 100, 117, 148, 163, 206
   Chaconne for Solo Violin 117
   Concerto for Two Violins 148
Bäck, Sven-Erik 249
Badings, Henk 68
Baer, Raymond 32
Bailey, Clive 188
Bainbridge, Simon 258, 260
Bain, Dean 150
Baird, Kenneth 5, 217
Baker, Janet 76, 94, 219
Bali 16
Ballet Rambert 170
Ball, Michael 256
Banks, Barry 187
Banks, Don 245, 249
Barber, Graham 178
Barber Institute, Birmingham University 94
Barbirolli, Sir John 45, 165, 221
Barcos, George 259
Bardsley, Bishop Cuthbert 95
Barrow, John 126
Bartók, Bela 39, 61, 101, 120, 121, 122, 123, 125, 150, 152, 153, 186
   Duke Bluebeard's Castle 152, 186
   Fifth Quartet 121
   Sonata (1926) 125
   Sonata for Two Pianos & Percussion 122

Audland, Christopher 5, 216, 217
Australasia 15, 16

   The Miraculous Mandarin 152
   The Wooden Prince 152
   Viola Concerto 150
Bartók Piano Competition 117
Basel 33
Baster, Miles 48
Bateman, Robert 126
Bath Festival 185, 218
Bayerischer Rundfunk 136
Beamish, Sally 254, 260
Beard, Paul 79
Beatles, The 70
Bedford, David 245, 246, 254, 256
Beecham, Sir Thomas 39, 75, 86, 87, 139
Beers, Adrian 160
Beeson, Colin 163
Beethoven, Ludwig van 14, 67, 68, 85, 103, 120, 122, 123, 124, 143, 163, 191, 198, 201
   A major Sonata op. 101 191
   C minor Piano Concerto 120
   E major Piano Sonata, op. 109 123
   E minor Sonata, op. 90 67
   'Emperor' Concerto 68
   Fidelio 123, 124
   Hymn of Joy 198
   Missa Solemnis 85
   Piano trios 123, 124
   Septet 122
   Violin sonatas 123
Belgrade 94, 107, 139
   British Embassy 139

Belgrade Theatre 94
Benjamin, George 253
Bennett, Richard Rodney 48, 121, 243, 251, 252, 254, 255, 256, 257, 259, 261
Benson, Clifford 103
Berg, Alban 120, 163
Berio, Luciano 120, 259
Berkeley, Freda 49, 51
Berkeley, Lennox 8, 48, 49, 50, 51, 61, 222, 223, 230, 234, 243, 244, 248, 250, 254, 258, 261
   [Plate 4]
   Quintet 79
   Ruth 37, 222
   Sextet for clarinet, horn & string quartet 49
   Sonatina 79
Berkeley, Michael 8, 11, 222, 254, 255, 260, 261
   Baa Baa Black Sheep 222, 260
   [Plate 4]
Berkeley Symphony Orchestra, San Francisco 237
Berlin Hochschule 151
Berlin Philharmonic Orchestra 94, 95
Berlin Symphony Orchestra 220
Berlioz, Hector 63, 87, 126
   Carnaval Romain 126
   Symphonie Fantastique 87
Besch, Anthony 183
Betjeman, Sir John 95, 96
Bevis, Elaine 5
Bezdüz, Bülent 218
Bickerdike, Allen & Rich (Architects) 146
   Allen, Bill 146
   Bickerdike, John 8, 146, 147, 167
      [Plate 16]

Biriucov, Lada 218
Birkelund, Paul 184
Birmingham 78, 80, 83, 88, 89, 90, 91, 93, 94, 95, 96, 97, 98, 100, 106, 126, 157, 159, 199, 221, 222
Birtwistle, Harrison 168, 180, 244, 247, 261
Bishop, Jeffrey 248
Bizet, Georges
   Carmen 17
Blacher, Boris 233
   Orkester Ornament 233
Black, Kitty 73
Blackstone, Tessa (Baroness) 224
Blaine, Diana 148
Blake, David 243, 260
Blake-Watkins, Michael 251
Bletchley 38
Bliss, Sir Arthur 121, 223, 244, 245, 248, 250, 261
   Angels of the Mind 121
   Clarinet Quintet 121
Bloomington, Indiana University 150
Boddington, Ewart 193
Bodenham, Peter 10
   [Plate 41]
Boettcher, Wilfried 187
Bogianckino, Massimo 206, 211
'Bomb' 105, 106
Bonington, Christopher 174
Borodin, Alexander
   Polovtsian Dances, Prince Igor 19
Bosch, Leon 179
Bosnia 139
Boucourechliev, André 248
Boulanger, Nadia 97, 103, 122, 140, 163, 230
Boulez, Pierre 48, 163

Le marteau sans maître 48
Boult, Adrian 80, 97, 200
Bourgue, Maurice 97
Bourne, David 37
Bourne, Paul 37, 50
Bourne, Percy 50
Bournemouth Symphony Orchestra 76, 82
Bowen, Miriam 183
Bowen, York 48
Bower, John 9, 166, 197 [Plate 31]
Boxall, Dorothy 15
Boyle, Edward (Lord) 176
Boyle, Rory 254
Bradbury, Colin 79
Bradbury, John 79
Bradman, Sir Donald 58
Bragg, Melvyn 223
Brahms, Johannes 46, 81, 123
  Vier ernste Gesänge (Four Serious Songs) 81
Brain, Dennis 169
Brandt, Michel 163, 182
Bream, Julian 76, 122, 125, 149
Brendel, Alfred 123, 191
Brezhnev, Leonid 140
Bridge, Frank 245, 261
Brighton Festival 218
British Broadcasting Corporation (BBC) 11, 23, 45, 46, 51, 61, 62, 66, 67, 69, 72, 76, 77, 81, 86, 88, 89, 91, 94, 113, 119, 121, 122, 123, 131, 133, 134, 143, 213, 214, 220, 221, 222
  BBC Beethoven Competition 103
  BBC Board of Governors 133
  BBC Composers Competition 122
  BBC Farringdon Studio 76
  BBC Home Service 23, 61, 63, 76, 84, 93, 102
    Musicale 93
    Music in Miniature 76
    *Music to Remembe*r 76
  BBC Midland Light Orchestra (MLO) 90, 92, 93, 96
  BBC Midland Region 6, 88, 89, 90, 91, 92, 93, 221
    Carpenter Road HQ & studios 91, 92
    The Archers 90, 91
  BBC Mozart Piano Concerto Competition 102
  BBC Music Division 61, 62, 64, 65, 88, 98, 101
  BBC Northern Region 90
  BBC Northern Singers 123
  BBC Northern Symphony Orchestra 122, 162, 170
  BBC Pebble Mill studios 91
  BBC Philharmonic Orchestra 122, 170
  BBC Singers 84, 85
  BBC Southern Region 90
  BBC Studios, Maida Vale 62, 63, 75, 84, 87, 88
  BBC Symphony Orchestra 6, 46, 78, 79, 80, 83, 87, 88, 89, 96
  BBC television 97, 98
  BBC Third Programme 48, 51, 63, 64, 65, 68, 69, 71, 73, 77, 84, 98, 101, 203, 229, 247
    Study on Three 98
  BBC Training Orchestra 99, 100
  BBC Welsh Orchestra 96, 102

BBC West Region 90
   Natural History Unit,
     Bristol 89
BBC World Service 72, 199,
   230
BBC Young Musician of the
   Year 6, 132, 133, 178,
   180
   Concerto Finals 133
Broadcasting House 71, 73, 77
Bush House 72
Dr. Who 92
General Overseas Service
   (GOS) 72, 73
gramophone records 99, 102
Green Book, The 62
music on television 132, 133
Music Programme, The 6,
   97, 100, 101, 102, 103,
   229, 230
   Music In Our Time 101
   Music Magazine 102
   University weekends 103
   Your Midweek Choice 101
Proms, The 67, 82, 84, 178,
   179, 198
Quadrophonic broadcasting
   77
Radio Times 62
Stereophonic broadcasting 77
Yalding House 61, 62, 63, 65,
   66, 67, 69, 88
British Council 7, 105, 113, 139,
   152, 196, 198, 199, 200, 201,
   204, 208, 231
   Music Advisory Committee
     198, 201
   Music Department 113, 199
Brittan, Leon 217
Britten, Benjamin 10, 39, 49, 94,
   170, 183, 184, 188, 190, 192,
   219, 231, 261
   A Midsummer Night's Dream
     10, 183
   Billy Budd 188
   Gloriana 188
   Les Illuminations 192
   Rape of Lucretia, The 188,
     190, 219
   Turn of the Screw, The 190
   War Requiem 94
Britten Quartet 170
Brockless, Brian 248
Brodsky, Adolf 181
Brodsky Quartet 181
Broom, Paul 247
Brossmann, Jean-Pierre 216
Brown, Christopher 246, 254, 255
Brown, George 249
Bruckner, Anton 84, 94, 181
   Sixth Symphony 84
   Te Deum 84, 85
Brussels 107, 201, 206, 209, 210,
   216, 217
Brymer, Jack 75, 235
Bucharest 6, 139, 140
   Academy of Music 140
Buckland, Rob 180
Buckley, Squadron Leader 164
Budapest Chamber Ensemble
   121
Budapest Franz Liszt Academy
   152
Budden, Julian 64
Budge, George 223
Buning, Robert 185
Burgon, Geoffrey 251, 252
Burnett, Jimmy 86
Burton, Humphrey 133
Bush, Alan 48, 245, 248

Busoni Piano Competition, Bolzano 142
Butler, Martin 161, 180, 254

C

Cage, John 256
Cahill, Teresa 124
Cairns, Peter 93
Callas, Maria 149
Cambridge 29, 36, 37, 38, 90, 103, 113
    Jesus College 13, 27, 28, 38, 113, 229
Camden Theatre 69, 70
Cameron, John 9
    [Plate 23] 9
Camilleri, Charles 250, 253, 259
Canada 6, 22, 73, 108, 134, 135, 136, 177
    British Columbia 135
    Prairies 135, 136
    Royal Canadian Ballet 136
Canadian Music Competition (CMC) 134, 135
Cantelli, Guido 56
Canterbury 17, 19, 21, 22, 23, 35, 58, 218
Caproni, Bruno 188
Caracas 196, 197, 198
Cardew, Cornelius 48
Cardiff 89, 102, 103, 123, 235
Cardiff University 123
    Cardiff University String Quartet 123
Carhart, David 245
Carl Rosa Opera 17
Carlton Green, Sir Hugh 98
Carroll, Ida 8, 9, 15, 145, 159, 171, 193, 240
    [Plate 16]

Butterworth, Arthur 254
Buxton, Nicholas 187
Buxton Opera House 205, 218

    [Plate 21]
Carroll, Walter 15, 159, 240
    Scenes at a Farm 15
Carter, Elliott 103
Carter, Sir Charles 8, 114, 115, 116, 145
    [Plate 13]
Cary, Tristram 118, 248, 249, 250
Casals, Pablo 66
Casken, John 260
Casson, Lewis 77
Cawdrey, Les 90
Cawood, Harry 117
Ceaușescu, President 140
Cecil Sharp House 120
Channel 4 224
Chapple, Brian 247, 254
Charpentier 35, 239
    Louise 35, 239
Cheltenham Festival 7, 11, 49, 90, 109, 205, 221, 222, 231, 232, 243
    Freedom of Cheltenham, 1994 10
    [Plate 47]
    Seven Deadly Sins, The (Festival Commission) 251
    Three Musical Knights 10
    [Plate 46]
Cherkassky, Shura 107, 108
Chetham's School 7, 170, 193, 194, 195
Chilingirian, Levon 103
Chinese Embassy, Portland Place 71

Chinese music 71, 72
Chopin, Frédéric 125, 174, 175
   B flat minor Sonata 125
Cimarosa, Domenico 260
cimbalom 153, 162
City of Birmingham Symphony
    Orchestra (CBSO) 80, 83,
    90, 96, 126, 127
   International competition
   for wind players 96
Clara Haskil Competition 178
Clayton, Shuttleworth & Allsop
   53
Clegg, John 113, 114, 115, 120
Clegg, Marcelle 115
Cleverdon, Douglas 77
Coates, Eric 96
Cohan, Robert 201
   Waterless Method of
   Swimming Instruction 201
Coker, Timothy 261
Coles, Jack 96
Collins, Michael 133
Cologne Hochschule 151, 152
Colston Hall, Bristol 100
commercial radio 98
   Classic FM 98
   Radio Caroline 98
   Radio Luxembourg 98
commercial television 98
   Committee for the Encourage-
   ment of Music & the Arts
   (CEMA) 78
Concours de Musique de
   Canada (CMC) 135
Concours Pan-Africain,
   Pretoria 142
Connell, John 188
Constantine, Leary 58
Cooke, Arnold 246

Copenhagen 10, 134, 184, 216,
   218, 219
Cordell, Frank 251
Cortot, Alfred 17
Couch, Thelma 92
Coulston, Sydney 162
Coulthard, Jean 250
Coventry Cathedral 68, 88, 91,
   94, 95
   Joseph Poole, Cathedral
   Precentor 95
Coventry Cathedral Festival
   68, 88, 94
Cowell, Henry 256
Cowie, Edward 253
Cox, Alison 186, 231
Cox, David 73, 230, 244, 248
Cox, Frederic 8, 145, 154
   [Plate 16] 8
Craft, Robert 73, 74
Cranston, Professor 223
Crawford, Robert 260
Craxton, Janet 79
cricket 13, 15, 18, 25, 35, 56, 57,
   58, 59, 60, 64, 90, 96, 115,
   173, 178, 208
   Edgbaston test ground 90
   Kent County Cricket Club 208
   Warwickshire County Cricket
   Club 90
Croatia 202, 203
Crosse, Gordon 10, 183, 184,
   231, 243, 245, 246, 250,
   252, 254
   Purgatory 10, 183, 184, 246
   [Plate 41]
Crossley-Holland, Peter 8, 63
   [Plate 6]
Crowe, Tom 65
Cruft, Adrian 69

Cruft, John 199, 204
Cummings, Conrad 255
Cundell, Edric 47
Curtis Institute, Philadelphia 180
Curzon, Clifford 76

D

Dahl, Ingolf 256
Dalby, Martin 247, 249
Dale, Caroline 132
Dali, Salvador 235
Dallapiccola, Luigi 103
Daniel, Nicholas 133
Danish Ministry of Culture 184
Danish Radio 134
Danks, Harry 80
Dankworth, John 123
d'Arcy, Michael 179
Dartford Grammar School 13
Dartington 103
Davidson, Howard 249
Davies, John 46
Davies, Noel 187
Davis, Carl 251
Davis, Colin 200
Davis, Noel 192
Dawson, Anne 186, 187
Dayan, Moshe 129
Day-Lewis, Cecil 123
Deakin, Richard 197
Deane, Basil 204, 235, 240
Dean, Robert 185
Debussy, Claude 25, 69, 256
de Gasztold, Carmen Bernos 239
    Prières dans l'Arche 239
de Lancie, John 180, 181
Delhi 70, 131
Delius, Frederick 254, 262

Czech Composers' Union 109, 110
Czech life 108
Czech Nonet 122, 123
Czechoslovakia 105, 107, 110, 140, 197, 246

Del Mar, Norman 169
Delphos Ensemble 93, 244
Denisov, Edison 255, 257
Dennis, Brian 247
Detmold Hochschule 152
Dickinson, Peter 249, 251, 254
Dobiáš, Václav 110, 111
Dodd, Geraint 188
Dodgson, Stephen 125, 244, 253, 255, 257, 258, 259, 262
    Fantasy-Divisions 125
Doig, Rodger 25
Donat, Misha 229
Donaueschingen Festival 87
Donizetti, Gaetano 220
    Emilia di Liverpool 220
Donohoe, Peter 178
Dorian Singers 69
Dougherty, Eric 77
Dowd, Ronald 124
Downes, Edward 187, 192
Drew, David 229
Drucker, Gerald 80
Drummond, Sir John 176
Dubček 140
Duchess of Kent 9, 171, 173, 191
Dudamel, Gustavo 198
Duffield, Vivienne 224
Duke of Edinburgh 171, 175, 196
Duke of Kent 207, 211
Dunbar, Geoff 220
Dunkerley, John 91, 92

Dunn, Edward 40, 41, 61
Dunn, Napier 40
Durban 6, 29, 38, 39, 40, 41, 42, 43, 55, 61, 229
Durkó, Zsolt 152, 255
Dutch East Indies 15
Dvořák, Antonin 83, 107, 123, 186

The Jacobin 186
Dyneley Studios 46
Dynevor Castle, Llandeilo, 126
   arts centre 126
   arts programme 125
Dynevor, Hugo 126
Dynevor, Richard, Earl of 125, 126
Dyson, James 214

E

Eaglen, Jane 187
East Anglia 45, 94, 96, 230
Eben, Petr 8, 109, 110, 180, 189, 246 [Plate 12]
Ebert, Peter 187
École Supérieur, Lyon 182
Edgley-Smith, Mark 258
Edinburgh University 133
Edrich, Bill 35, 56
Education Reform Act, 1989 176
Edwards, Philip 167
Edwards, Sian 180, 183
Egan, John 166
Elgar, Edward 53, 132, 181, 183, 262
   Cello Concerto 132
   Cockaigne Overture 181
Elliot, Sir Gerald 205
Ellis, David 189
El Sistema 7, 196, 198
Enescu Competition, Bucharest 140, 141
English folksongs 120
English, Matt 167
English National Ballet 212, 213
English National Opera 187, 217

English Touring Opera 204
Epstein, Gaby 116, 119
Eshowe, Zululand 38, 58, 63
European Broadcasting Union (EBU) 102, 134
European Young Musician of the Year 134
European Commission 216
European Music Year (EMY) 7, 200, 206, 207, 208, 210, 211
   Executive Committee 206, 208, 211
   Fêtes de la Musique 208
European Opera Centre (EOC) 7, 210, 215, 216, 217, 218, 220, 221
European Parliament 29, 209, 216
European Union 210, 217, 218, 219, 221
European Union Baroque Orchestra (EUBO) 210, 221
European Youth Orchestra 210
Europe, Council of 206
Everyman Theatre, Cheltenham 205
Exton, John 244

F

Fachiri, Adila 23
Fagiolini 133

Falklands War 177, 205
Falla, Manuel de 184

Master Peter's Puppet Show 184
Fassbaender, Brigitte 218
Fauré, Gabriel 239
Feld, Jindrich 246
Fell, Sidney 162
Ferguson, Howard 48
Ferrand, Emma 197
Finnissy, Michael 259
Firsova, Elena 259
Fischer, Ailine 126
Fischer Dieskau, Dietrich 85
Fisher, Archbishop 23
Fisher, Charles 223
Fisk, Eliot 131
fives 25
Flanders, Michael 73
Fleishman, Veniamin 220
Flood, Philip 259
Foggin, Myers 43, 48
Foreign Office 105, 107, 114, 198, 201
Forman, Sir Denis 169, 224
Forster, Michael 115
Forsyth Brothers, Manchester 240
Foster, Susan 169, 175
Fountain, Ian 178
Fox, Bryan 5, 8, 148
   [Plate 17]
Fox, Erika 253
Françaix, Jean 257, 260
France 28, 33, 167, 182, 208, 209
France, Canon William 21
France, Malcolm 21
Franck, César 63
Frankel, Benjamin 243, 245, 247
Frankfurt Hochschule für Musik 152, 181
Frémaux, Louis 96, 126
Fricker, Peter Racine 150, 223, 249, 252, 253, 255, 256, 262
Frommelt, Josef 207
Fry, Jeremy 214, 215
Fulgoni, Sara 189, 190
Fürst, János 120
Furtwängler, Zitla 82

G

Gable, Christopher 214
Gadd, Stephen 187
Galbraith, Paul 134
Gál, Hans 83
Gallois-Montbrun, Raymond 151
Galway, James 97
Gambold, Geoffrey 79
gamelan 69, 256
Gandhi, Mahatma 70, 130, 131
Gardner, John 245
Gascoigne, Bamber 224
Gaskell, Elizabeth 187
Gautier, Théophile 35
Georges Enescu Festival, Bucharest 139
Georgiadis, John 48
Gerhard, Roberto 103, 121, 245
   Leo 121
   Libra 103
German Music Council 216
   German national radio & television consortium (ARD) 136
Germany 30, 32, 82, 136, 151, 179, 206, 218
Geysen, Frans 257
Gibson, Lord 205
Gielgud, Val 23
Giggleswick School 157, 159
Gilbert, Anthony 3, 7, 9, 109, 117, 161, 180, 229, 240, 243, 251, 257, 258
   [Plate 25]

Gilbert & Sullivan
   Mikado, The 41
Gilchrist, Anne 120
Gilchrist, Roy 59
Gilels, Emil 67, 68
Giles, Allan 64
Gillard, Frank 8, 72, 99, 101, 104
   [Plate 9]
Gimpel, Bronislav 197
Glasgow 89
Glentworth, Mark 162
   Blues for Gilbert 162
Glock, William 8, 66, 88, 98, 99, 102, 104, 115, 143, 185, 221, 229
   [Plate 8]
Goble, Robert 127
Godden, Rumer 235, 239
Goehr, Alexander 121, 124, 168, 229, 243, 262
   Monteverdi Paraphrase 121
   Trio 124
Goethe Institute 152
Goldberg, Szymon 121
Goldsbrough Orchestra 69
Goodman, Arnold 203
Goodman, Roy 210
Goossens, Eugene 80
Goossens, Leon 79, 80
Goossens, Marie 80
Goossens, Sidonie 80

Górecki, Henryck 247
Gould, Glenn 73
Gould, Peter 63
Gow, David 258
Gowers, Patrick 249
Graeme, Peter 161
Granada Foundation 117
Granada Television 169
Grandjany, Marcel 72
Graves, Mel 256
Greaves, Terence 9, 157, 159
   [Plate 20]
Gregson, Edward 260
Grenfell, Joyce 174
Grenoble Maison de La Culture 185
Gretton, David 93
Griffiths, Paul Arden 183
Griffiths, Richard 167
Gromek 109
Groot, Cor de 68
Groves, Sir Charles 8, 10, 124, 143, 177, 183
   [Plate 14]
   [Plate 39]
Grummer, Elisabeth 38
Guinjoan, John 256
Gulbenkian Foundation 156
   Training Musicians report 156
Gustav Mahler Orchestra 221

H

Habsburg, Otto von 207
Hacker, Alan 121
Haileybury 6, 18, 19, 21, 25, 26, 27, 29, 34, 57, 58, 70, 159, 199
   Bartle Frere 27
   New Governors 27
Haines, Redvers 40

Haitink, Bernard 223
Halffter, Cristobal 245
Hallé Orchestra 45, 170, 181, 216, 217, 237, 246
Hall, Gillian 5, 15
Hall, Henry 25
Hall, John 5

Hall, Michael 25, 26
Hall, Richard 168
Hamilton, Iain 48, 244, 252
Hammond, Wally 58
Hancock, Harry 244
Handel, George Frideric 94, 95, 185, 189, 206, 262
    Alcina 189, 190
    Messiah 95
    Orlando 150, 185
Hanns Eisler Hochschule 151
Hanover Hochschule 151
Hardy, Maurice 76
Harewood, Earl of 198
Hargreaves, Glenville 10, 183
    [Plate 41]
Harper, Edward 258
Harper, Gerald 25, 26
harp music 72
Harries, David 243
Harrild, Patrick 127
Harrison, George 70
Harrison, Lou 256
Harrison, Sally 188
Harrow 26
Hartley Hall 9, 171, 172, 173
    [Plate 36]
Harvey, Jonathan 248, 252
Hassall, Christopher 73, 74
Hassett, Lindsay 58
Haydn, Franz Joseph 76, 163, 198, 253
    Toy Symphony 198
Hazell, Chris 250
Headington, Christopher 127, 243, 254
Headley, Christine 208
Heath, Dave 260, 261
Heath, Edward 124, 139, 175, 181, 211

three-day week 124
Hedges, Anthony 125
    String Quartet 125
Helliwell, Clifton 8, 65, 160
    [Plate 7]
Helliwell, Jessica 160
Hemsley, Thomas 170
Henderson, Gavin 5
Henson, Ronald 223
Henze, Hans Werner 182
Herbage, Julian 102
Herincx, Raimund 124
Herrera, President Luis 198
Herrmann, Bernard 66
    Wuthering Heights 66
Heslop, Jennifer 183
Hess, Willy 259
Hewitt-Jones, Tony 244, 246
Hext, Michael 132, 133
Hickox, Richard 183, 253
Hindemith, Paul 72
    Sonata for harp 72
Hirsch, Leonard 100
Hirsch Quartet 63
Hockley, Raymond 48
Hoddinott, Alun 102, 122, 123, 186, 231, 235, 243, 244, 246, 248, 252, 253, 256, 258, 262
    Octet 122
Hodges, Anthony 9, 165
    [Plate 30]
Holding, Michael 59
Hold, Trevor 249
Holland, Mildred 62
Holliger, Heinz 248
Holloway, Robin 249, 253, 255, 258
Holmes, Ralph 48
Holmstrom, John 70
Holst, Gustav 23, 200, 222, 255, 256, 258, 262

275

Planets 200
Savitri 222
The Wandering Scholar 222
Holt, Simon 9, 161, 180
   [Plate 26]
Hong Kong Academy of
   Performing Arts 235
Horenstein, Jascha 165
Horovitz, Joseph 251
Horsch, Gregor 179
Hotter, Hans 38
Hough, Stephen 178, 192
Howard, Yvonne 187
Howells, Herbert 255, 262
Howes, Frank 221, 223
Howgill, Pauline 65
Howgill, Richard 65, 66
Hsin-Ting, Tchen 71
Huber, Klaus 259
Hughes, Brian 184, 186
   Stars and Shadows 184, 186
Hull University 125
Humble, Keith 257
Humphreys, Karen 163
Hungarian National Opera 152
Hunter, Sir Ian 212
Hurd, Michael 247
Hurník, Ilja 110
Hutchinson, Jeremy (Lord) 203
Hylton, Jack 116
Hymas, Anthony 253

I

Ibert, Jacques 137
   Flute Concerto 137
Iliffe, Barrie 199
Iliffe, Caroline 199
Imai, Nobuko 179
Imbrie, Andrew 256
Incorporated Society of
   Musicians 79
Indian classical music 69, 71
Indonesia 15
Inoue, Yuko 179
Instone, Anna 102
IRA bombing of Manchester 191
Ireland, John 19, 262
   These things shall be 19
Irwin, Jane 190
Irwin, Robert 76
Isaacs, Jeremy 61, 63, 216, 224
Isaacs, Leonard 8, 61, 63
   [Plate 5]
Isserlis, Julius 63
Ives, Grayston 252

J

Jackson, Geoffrey 163
Jackson, Harry Croft 62, 63
Jacob, Gordon 132, 248
   Trombone Concerto 132
Janáček, Leoš 85, 189, 190, 220, 231
   House of the Dead 189
   Sinfonietta 85
   The Cunning Little Vixen 220
Janski, Stefan 188, 190
Japanese music 71
Jarman, Douglas 163
Java 16
Jeffreys, Stephen 114
Jenkins, David 249
Jeppe High School 13, 15
Joachim, Joseph 23

Jochum, Eugen 94
Johannesburg 13, 14, 15, 17, 54, 55, 229
John F. Kennedy Centre 148
Johnstone, Maurice 61, 62, 65, 66
Jolivet, André 248
Joll, Philip 185
Jones, Daniel 248
Jones, Geraint 155
Jones, Philip 9, 121, 161, 179, 253
   [Plate 27]
Jones, Richard 188
Jordan, David 185
Joseph, Keith 177
Josephs, Wilfred 245, 247
Joubert, John 42, 69, 230, 244
Joyce, Eileen 57
Juilliard School of Music, New York 141, 149

K

Kabeláč, Miloslav 110
Kaine, Carmel 48
Kalabis, Victor 110
Kallaway, Bill 129, 130, 131
Karasek, Franz 206
Karmel, Mohammed Ibrahim 129
Kárpáti, János 152
Kathleen Ferrier Award 187
Kay, Norman 246
Kayser, Leif 258
Keeffe, Bernard 62
Keenlyside, Simon 188
Keetch, David 167
Keith, Ian 200, 207
Kellam, Ian 249
Kellaway, Harold 55
Kellaway, Renna 5, 8, 9, 41, 42, 43, 47, 50, 51, 55, 62, 68, 74, 88, 89, 93, 97, 105, 106, 119, 123, 142, 153, 159, 178, 182, 202, 211, 229, 230, 242
   [Plate 11]
   [Plate 37]
   [Plate 38]
   [Plate 45]
Keller, Hans 104, 229
Kelterborn, Rudolf 259, 260
Kempe, Rudolf 79, 87
Kengyoin, Yatsuhashi 71
Kennedy, Joyce 5, 9
   [Plate 35]
Kennedy, Michael 9, 154, 176
   [Plate 35]
Kern, Jerome 41
   Sunny 41
Kerry, Gordon 257
Kettel, Gary 127
Khachaturian, Aram 44
   Sabre Dance 44
Khan, Ali Akbar 70
Khan, Ustad Vilayat 71
Kimpton, Geoffrey 245
King Peter of Yugoslavia 107
King's Lynn Music Festival 90
Kingston, Kent 19
Kinnock, Neil 217
Kirshbaum, Ralph 179, 192
Kitchen, Linda 187
Klemperer, Otto 84, 85, 86
Kłosiewicz, Władysław 138
Kodály, Zoltán 87, 88
   Háry János 88
Kok, Alexander 80
Kok, Felix 80
Kolberg Percussion Factory 138
Kolisch, Rudolf 149

Koopman, Ton 210
Kraft, William 256
Krapp, Edgar 182

Kurtág, György 121, 152
Kusche, Benno 39

L

Lade, John 102
Laine, Cleo 123
Lake Bala, N. Wales 14
Lake District Summer Music (LDSM) 211
Lal, Chatur 70
Lambert, Constant 19
Lancaster Ensemble 117, 122, 123, 125
Lancaster University 6, 59, 113, 114, 115, 116, 118, 119, 121, 123, 125, 126, 127, 143, 144, 145, 148, 193, 235
  Bowland College 116
  Cartmel College 116
  County College 116
  Furness College 116
  Fylde College 116
  Granada Fellow in Composition 117
  Great Hall 119, 121, 122, 126
  Lancaster University Chorus 124
  Lonsdale College 116
  Music Department 116, 119, 127
    Bartók, Beethoven and British subscription concerts 120
    Electronics studio 118
    Music of our time 117
    Redlich Collection 118, 119
    Skills in performance 117
    Turning Year concert 123
    Weekly concerts 119
  Nuffield Centre 125, 126
Landowski, Marcel 257
Lane, Philip 257
Lansky, Paul 257
Lanz, Igor 196, 198
La Scala 55
Latham, Angela 47
Latham, Peter 46, 47
Lawrenson, Tom 114
Lawson, Peter 249
Lazarof, Henri 251
Leach, Anthony 246
Ledbetter, David 163
Ledger, Philip 5
Leeds Castle 129, 130, 132
Leeds International Piano Competition 142
LeFanu, Nicola 250
Lehár, Franz 96
Leighton, Kenneth 251, 257
Lewis, Anthony 94
Lewis, Jeffrey 247
Lewis, Richard 68, 94, 200
Liebermann, Rolf 206, 211
Liechtenstein 207
light music 96
Lindwall, Ray 58
Lipkin, Malcolm 253, 260, 262
Liszt, Franz 125, 220, 247
  B minor Sonata 125
Liverpool University 124
Ljubljana 202, 203
Ljubljana Philharmonic 202

Lloyd, Emlyn 114
Lloyd, George 253
Lloyd Jones, David 188
Lloyd, Robert 124
Lloyds Arms pub, Manchester 144, 173
Lockley, W. P. 171
Lockwood, Anna 246
Lockwood, Graham 221
London Contemporary Dance Theatre 201
London Sinfonietta 121, 168, 231

London Symphony Orchestra (LSO) 44, 127
Lord, David 246
Lorentzen, Bent 250
Louvier, Alain 255, 257
Lowe, John 88, 89, 94
Lowry, L. S. 213, 214
Lucas, Vincent 237
Lumsdaine, David 250
Lutosławski, Witold 247
Lutyens, Elisabeth 243, 244, 251, 253, 262

M

Maazel, Lorin 87
Machado, Dr. 196, 197
Mackenzie, Graham 115, 118
Maconchy, Elizabeth 250, 251, 253, 262
Maderna, Bruno 87, 254
  Serenata no. 2 87
Mahler, Gustav 182
  Das Lied von der Erde 182
Malcolm, George 127
Manchester 89, 118, 127, 133, 168
  Free Trade Hall 133
Manchester Camerata 170
Manchester Cathedral 193
Manchester Musical Heritage Trust 240
  Manchester Sounds 240
Manchester School, the 168, 231
Manchester University 118, 172, 204, 235
Manduell, Anne 15
Manduell, David 8, 88, 100
  [Plate 11] 8
  [Plate 38] 10
Manduell, Helen 8, 88, 92, 100

  [Plate 11]
Manduell, John 8, 9, 229, 230, 231, 232, 238, 241, 242, 254
  at Buckingham Palace 10
  [Plate 38]
  BBC Music Producer 230
  BBC's Head of Music for the Midlands and East Anglia 230
  Belloc Variations 42
  Chief Planner, BBC Music Programme 230
  compositional idiom 233
  Director of Music, Lancaster University 18, 70, 208, 231
  Diversions 241, 244
  Double Concerto 234, 235, 237, 238, 241
    di-zi 235, 236
    er-hu 236
    ti-tzu 236
  first recipient of RPS / PRS Leslie Boosey Award, 1980 10
  [Plate 44]

Flutes Concerto 237, 238, 241
Founding Principal of
    RNCM 231
Freedom of Cheltenham,
    1994 10
    [Plate 47]
Gradi 230, 232, 233, 234, 239,
    241, 242
heart surgery 223
impact on Manchester's
    musical life 231
in Red Square, Moscow 10
    [Plate 45]
Into the Ark 239, 241
    'The Cock' 239
    'The Giraffe' 239
    'The Glow-Worm' 239
    'The Goldfish' 239
    'The Monkey' 239
    'The Ox' 239
John, the left-hander 9
    [Plate 19]
musical studies 39
    composition 39, 41, 42,
        43, 44, 46, 47, 229,
        230
    orchestration 39
Overture to Activity 42, 230
[Plate 11]
[Plate 15, receiving RCM
    Fellowship]
[Plate 35]
[Plate 37]
[Plate 46, at Cheltenham
    Festival]
Prayers from the Ark 235, 239,
    241
Programme Director,
    Cheltenham Festival
    231
retirement celebration 191
Rondo for Nine 240, 241
Scena for orchestra 230
String Quartet 11, 234, 242
String Trio 51, 230, 242
Sunderland Point overture
    120
time for composing 232
*Trois Chansons de la
    Renaissance* 230, 239,
    242
Two Celebrations 240
Variations on a Trio Tune 45,
    242
Verses from Calvary 240, 242
Vistas 234, 237
Manduell, Jonathan 8, 97, 100
    [Plate 11]
Manduell, Julius 8, 100
    [Plate 11]
    [Plate 38]
Manduell, Matthewman
    Donald 8, 13, 14, 15, 17,
    19, 27, 29, 55, 56
    [Plate 1]
Manduell, Theodora 13, 14, 15,
    29, 38, 57, 68
Manning, Peter 170, 179
Mansuryan, Tigran 257
Markland, Anna 133
Marriner, Neville 183, 184
Marriott, Richard 99, 101
Marson, John 258
Martinů, Bohuslav 122
    Nonet 122
Marychurch, Peter 223
Massenet, Jules 187, 190
    Cendrillion 190
    Manon 53, 187, 188
Mathias, William 243, 244, 245,

254, 262
Matthews, Colin 261
Matthews, David 260
Matthews, Denis 201
Matthews, Michael Gough 10
    [Plate 45] 10
Maw, Nicholas 251, 252, 254
Maxwell Davies, Peter 47, 79,
    120, 168, 180, 223, 243,
    244, 247, 248, 259, 262
    [Plate 46, at Cheltenham
        Festival] 10
    Trumpet Sonata 47
Mayer, John 251, 254, 258
McCabe, John 122, 244, 246,
    247, 262
    Nocturnal for piano quintet
        122
McCallum, David 87
McCurrach, Hector 8, 18, 19
McCurrach, Kathleen 8, 18, 19
    [Plate 2]
McGrath, Paul 190
McGuigan, Patrick 9
    [Plate 23]
McLeod, John 254
McQueen, Ian 259
Meale, Richard 250
Mechanical Copyright Protection
    Society (CPS) 99
Mellers, Wilfrid 116, 244
Melos Ensemble 93, 123, 160
Mendelssohn, Felix 220
Menotti, Gian Carlo 41
    The Consul 41, 183
Menuhin School 194, 253
Menuhin, Yehudi 70, 193, 253
Messiaen, Olivier 87, 235
    Chronochromie 87
Metcalf, John 248, 256

Methodist General Conference
    171
Metz 32
Mexico, Chamber Orchestra of
    148
Michelow, Sybil 81, 82
Middlemiss, Hugh 64
Mihály, András 121
Miles, Maurice 46, 51, 61, 230
Milhaud, Darius 150
Miller, Keith 58
Mills College, Orlando 150
Milner, Anthony 69
Milton, Ernest 73
Mitchell, Ena 157
MM Club 66
Moeran, E. J. 262
Montepulciano, Tuscany 182
Monteux, Pierre 74, 75, 76
Moore, Douglas 79
Moore, Gerald 23
Moreland, Claire 195
Morris, Gareth 66
Morris, John 64
Moss, Stirling 26
Mozart, Wolfgang Amadeus
    77, 85, 97, 102, 178, 186,
    187, 190, 218
    A minor Rondo 102
    Così fan tutte 190
    Die Zauberflöte 187
    Eine kleine Nachtmusik 85
    Idomeneo 187
    Lucio Silla 218
    Notturno in D K286 77
    Piano concertos 102
    The Magic Flute 186
MRP Party 31
Mukle, May 66
Mulhouse 33

Müller-Heuser, Franz 216
Munch, Charles 34
Munich Hochschule 151
Munich Philharmonic
    Orchestra 137
Murgatroyd, Keith 170
Musgrave, Thea 244, 249, 250,
    261, 262
Musicians Union (MU) 99, 100,
    127
Music Theatre Project 232
Mussorgsky, Modest 125
    Pictures from an Exhibition 125

N

Nagano, Kent 216, 218, 220, 237
Nag's Head pub, Manchester
    144, 173
Nakao, Tozan 71
Natal Daily News 40
Natal Technical College 40
National Orchestra of Wales
    102
National Trust 126, 203
National Youth Orchestra of
    Great Britain 196
Navotny, President 108
Netherlands Chamber
    Orchestra 121
Newby, Sir Howard 203
New England Conservatoire,
    Boston 149
Newman. Ernest 34
New Music Club, Duke's Hall
    47
Nicholas, Jane 204
Nicholson, Evelyn 187
Nicolet, Aurèle 137
Nilsson, Bo 243, 250
Nitschowa, Lidwika 174

Nono, Luigi 80
    Intolleranza 80
Nørgård, Per 250
Norris, Geoffrey 163
Northern Ballet (Theatre) 7,
    145, 170, 212, 213, 214, 215
    A Simple Man 214
    Coppélia 213
    Don Quixote 214
Northern College of Music
    (NCM) 6, 11, 15, 65, 147,
    148, 154, 231
Northern Ireland 78, 209
Northern School of Music
    (NSM) 8, 15, 144, 145, 147,
    154, 155, 156, 157, 158, 159,
    165, 193, 240
North Wales 14, 17
North West Arts Association
    (NWAA) 117
Novák, Jan 246
Nureyev, Rudolf 213
Nutland, Keith 223
Nyman, Michael 259, 260

O

Oberlé family 28
Oberlé, Joseph 28, 29, 31
Oberlé, Lucien 28, 29, 31
Offenbach, Jacques 220

Ogden, Craig 179, 241
Ogdon, John 10, 109, 202, 203, 246
    [Plate 39]
O'Hora, Ronan 192

Oliver, Robin Martin 186
Oliver, Stephen 252
Ollerenshaw, Dame Kathleen
    8, 9, 145, 146, 167, 168, 177
    Ollerenshaw Roof Garden 9
    [Plates 32 & 33]
    [Plate 16]
    [Plate 37]
Opéra de Lyon 216
Opéra du Rhin 35
Opera Europe 218, 219
Opera North 170, 187
Oram, Daphne 77
Oribi 13, 15, 159
Orion Trio 124
Ormandy, Eugene 181
Orton, Richard 252
Osborne, Steven 178, 258
Owens, Matthew 178
Oxford University
    Christ Church 51
    Green College 210

P

Padmore, Elaine 216
Paisiello, Giovanni 186
    The Barber of Seville 186
Paisley, Ian 209
Palmer, Wing Commander 164
Panenka, Jan 107
Papua New Guinea 16
Paris Conservatoire 135, 151, 163
Paris 'Rostrum' 232
Parkin, Simon 163
Parrot, Kenneth 126
Parrott, Cecil 106, 107, 113, 114
Parrott, Ellen 107
Parrott, Ian 107, 114, 243
Pascher, Harmut 258
Paterson, Wilma 250, 252
Patterson, Paul 200, 253, 259, 260
Payne, Anthony 241, 252, 253
Pearce, Leonard 40
Pearce, Michael 40
Pekhonen, Elis 251, 254
Penn, David 188
Performing Right Society (PRS)
    42, 125, 229, 230
Perlemuter, Vlado 135
Petrenko, Vasily 220
Petrof piano 67, 108
Phibbs, Joseph 261
Philadelphia Orchestra 180
Philharmonia Orchestra 66, 85
Philip Jones Brass Ensemble 121
Phipps, Jack 204
Pickup, Anne 102
Pierrot Players 120
Pijper, Willem 68
Pillot, Laurent 217
Pinches, Jack 80
Pinner Parish Church 50
Piper, John 95, 186
Piper, Myfanwy 186
Pittsburgh Symphony
    Orchestra 181
Plaistow, Stephen 229
Platt, Ian 187
Polonska, Elena 72
Poole, Geoffrey 250
Porter, David 92, 93
Poston, Elizabeth 249
Poulenc, Francis 49, 185
    Carmelites 185
Powers, Anthony 258, 261
Pragokonzert 107
Prague 6, 67, 105, 106, 107, 108,
    109, 111, 113, 125, 197, 220

British Embassy 107
Prague Academy 181
Prague Spring Festival 105
Premru, Raymond 251
Pressing, Jeff 258
Price, Janet 122
Prichard, Mathew 205
Primrose, William 150
Prince Edward 215
Prince Klaus 211, 212

Princess Margaret 37, 215
Pritchard, Edith 189
Pritchard, Eric 46
Prokofiev, Sergei 39, 67, 247
   Visions Fugitives 67
Puccini, Giacomo 101, 184
   La Bohème 101, 183, 184
   Madame Butterfly 190
Purcell, Henry
   King Arthur 37

Q

Quatuor Ebèn 138
Queen Beatrix of the
   Netherlands 211
Queen Elizabeth, Her Majesty
   19, 154, 171, 195
Queen Mother, Her Majesty
   The 8
   [Plate 15]

R

Rachmaninov, Sergei 127, 133,
   134, 163
   Paganini Variations 127
   Third Piano Concerto 133
Raikes, Raymond 77
Rainier, Priaulx 247
Rajna, Thomas 247
Rameau, Jean-Phillippe 220
Rands, Bernard 251
Ranger, Brigid 51, 119, 123, 153
Rankl, Karl 39
Rattle, Simon 83, 96
Ravel, Maurice 23, 66, 184, 239, 255
   L'heure espagnole 184
   Tzigane 23
Rawnsley, John 183
Rawsthorne, Alan 68, 102, 103,
   119, 165, 183, 244, 245, 260,
   262
   Ballade 102
Rawsthorne Bequest 165

Rawsthorne Society 165
Redlich, Hans 118
Rees, Howard 247
Rees-Mogg, Sir William 205
Remedios, Alberto 200
Resch, Beate 182
Resch, Hans Dieter 181
Reynish, Hilary 5
Reynish, Timothy 5, 161, 179,
   190, 241
Reynolds, Philip 114
Rice, Christine 190
Richards, Jack 25
Richardson, Stephen 186, 187
Richards, Sir Gordon 25
Ridout, Alan 244
Rignold, Hugo 96
Riley, Howard 249
Roberts, Bill 92
Roberts, Hannah 179
Robinson, Sir Kenneth 205

Robson, Nigel 183
Roche, Suzanne 135
Rodgers, Joan 187, 191
Rodrigo, Joaquín 134, 189
    Guitar Concerto 134
Rogé, Pascal 140
Romania 139, 140, 200
Ronnefeld, Renate 137
Roocroft, Amanda 189
Rosbaud, Hans 87
Rossini, Gioachino 186, 219
    La Scala di Seta 219
    The Barber of Seville 186
Roussel, Albert 63, 257
Rovinj Music Competition 202
Rowe, Miss 17
Rowland, Christopher 235
Royal Academy of Music (RAM) 42, 43, 45, 46, 47, 48, 49, 50, 51, 61, 94, 177, 230, 239
Royal Albert Hall 57, 84, 198
Royal Ballet 212, 224
Royal College of Music (RCM) 79, 118, 193
Royal Danish Academy, Copenhagen 184
Royal Danish Opera 216, 219
Royal Festival Hall 84, 85, 86
Royal Liverpool Philharmonic Orchestra 124, 143, 220
Royal Manchester College of Music (RMCM) 8, 144, 145, 147, 154, 155, 156, 157, 158, 159, 160, 163, 165, 168, 172, 178, 181
Royal Northern College of Music (RNCM) 6, 8, 9, 10, 11, 15, 51, 65, 81, 104, 109, 133, 143, 145, 148, 152, 153, 157, 162, 163, 171, 179, 182, 183, 186, 187, 188, 189, 190, 192, 215, 231, 235, 237, 240, 259
    Board of Governors 176
    catering provision 166
    coat of arms 153
    College library 165
    College motto 153
    College opera theatre 167
    commissions 186
    concert hall 167, 168, 170
        acoustics 169
        tapestry 169
    Constituent Authorities 143, 144, 145, 168
        Joint Committee 143, 144, 145, 146, 154, 155, 166
    Degree Congregation Day welcome line-up 9
    [Plate 37]
    Duchess of Kent, RNCM President 171
    [Plate 35]
    [Plate 37]
    first auditions 169, 170
    Foundation Stone 8
    [Plate 16]
    Hradetzky organ 155, 156, 175
    inaugural concert 168
    individual tuition 158
    John Manduell's retirement celebrations 191, 192
    motto 154
    Ollerenshaw Roof Garden 167
    [Plates 32 & 33]
    opera theatre 182, 183, 231

pianos, purchase of 155
RNCM Junior Department 163
RSA Design Centre award 170
Schools of Study 159, 177
   School of Strings 179
staff conferences 156, 157
staffing 157, 158
statue of Chopin 174
Student Travel Scholarship 160
under construction 9
   [Plate 18] 9
undergraduate courses 156
view at time of formal opening 9
   [Plate 34]
Royal Opera, Copenhagen 184
Royal Opera House, Covent Garden 7, 38, 39, 170, 180, 188, 203, 216, 217, 223, 224, 231
Royal Philharmonic Orchestra (RPO) 40, 75, 86, 87
Royal Shakespeare Company 170, 185
Royal Society of Musicians 204
RTF 131
   France Musique 131
   Monsieur Plug-in 132
Ruane, Peter 189
Rubbra, Edward 244, 247
Rubinstein Piano Competition 178
Ruders, Poul 260
Russell, Oswald 103
Rutherford, Jonathan 254
Růžičková, Zuzana 110

S

Sabata, Victor de 56
Sadler's Wells 184, 185
Sainsbury, Lord (John) 224, 261
Salt, Chrys 123
Salter, Lionel 140, 141
Santa Barbara, University of Calafornia 150
Sargeant, Kim 223
Sargent, Sir Malcolm 57, 81, 84, 86
Sartori Quartet 235
Saxton, Robert 256
Sayers, Dorothy 23
   The Man Born to be King 23
Scarlatti, Domenico 67, 68, 206
Scheel, Walter 206, 208, 211
Schmidt, Ole 189
Schoeck, Othmar 260
Schoenberg, Arnold 120, 149, 190, 231
   Erwartung 190
   Fourth String Quartet 149
Schouvaloff, Alexander 117
Schubert, Franz 14, 19, 61, 123, 125, 161, 170
   Die schöne Müllerin 125
   String Quintet 123
   The Trout 123
   Winterreise 125
Schumann, Gerard 256
Schumann Piano Competition, Zwickau 142
Schumann, Robert 19, 41
   Faschingsschwank aus Wien 41
   Kinderscenen 19
Schuman, William 245
Schütz, Heinrich 206

Schwarz, Rudolf 8, 82, 83
 [Plate 10]
Schweitzer, Albert 34, 64
Scotland, Tony 51
 Lennox and Freda 51
Scottish Opera 170
Scott, Percy 173
Scriabin, Alexander 67, 68
 Fourth Sonata op. 30 68
Sculthorpe, Peter 250, 258
Searle, Humphrey 245, 249, 251
Segovia, Andrés 6, 129, 130, 131, 132
Segovia Competition 129
Seiber, Mátyás 69, 230, 233
 Permutazioni a Cinque for wind 233
Serbian nationalism 139
Serkin, Rudolf 180
Serocki, Kazimierz 247
Shankar, Ravi 69, 70, 71
 Raga Bhimpalasi 70
 Raga Charukeshi 70
Shephard, Richard 252
Shepheard, Peter 116
Sherlaw Johnson, Robert 244, 246
Sherry Shippers, Jerez 129
Shirley-Quirk, John 125, 170
Shore, Bernard 204
Shostakovich, Dmitri 126, 220, 255
 Tenth Symphony 126
Sillito, Ken 48
Simpson, Bob 73
 Canzona for Brass 73
Simpson, John 153
Simpson, Robert 63, 64, 247, 259
 The Symphony (1975) 63
Sims, Jim 58
Slater, Andrew 189

Slatford, Rodney 160, 179
Slovenia 202
Smetana Quartet 125
Smirnov, Dmitri 259
Smith Brindle, Reginald 244, 249
Smith, Daphne 88
Smith, Euan 185
Smutny, Jiri 248
Snowdon, Bill 25
Society for the Promotion of New Music (SPNM) 229
Sorrell, Neill 256
Souster, Tim 201, 229, 246
South Africa 11, 13, 14, 15, 28, 38, 39, 40, 41, 44, 48, 56, 58, 59, 63, 81, 89, 160, 229, 230
South African Broadcasting Corporation (SABC) 40, 41
Southampton University 124
Spence, Basil 94
Spillett, Adrian 180
Spinner, Leopold 244
Spooner, Sir James 224
Stadlmair, Hans 258
Staicu, Paul 97
Standford, Patric 249
St. Andrew's Hall, Glasgow 77
Stanley, John 211
Starer, Robert 245
Steel, Christopher 248
Steenhoven, Karel van 257
Steinway piano 67, 108, 155
Stevens, Denis 64, 65
Stevens, James 250
Stirling, Angus 203, 224
St. Martin's College, Lancaster 124
St. Michael's Tenbury Wells 95, 96
Stockhausen, Karlheinz 122, 248

Zyklus 122
Stojanović, Josip 202
Stoker, Richard 246, 249, 254
Stone, David 64
St. Petersburg 219
Strasbourg 6, 28, 29, 30, 31, 32, 34, 36, 55, 207, 208, 209, 211, 229
Strauss, Johann 195
    Hunting Polka 195
Strauss, Richard 170, 181, 182
    Der Rosenkavalier 192
    Ein Heldenleben 170, 182
    Oboe Concerto 181
Stravinsky, Igor 40, 73, 74, 96, 121, 161, 183
    Rite of Spring 40, 75, 96, 169
The Rake's Progress 161, 183
The Soldier's Tale 73, 74
Strutt, Clive 246
Stuart-Roberts, Deborah 188
Suffield, Raymond 77
Suk, Josef 107
Sumatra 16
Surrans, Alain 208
Sutherland, Graham 95
Sutherland, Joan 73
Swann, Lord (Michael) 133
Switzerland 33, 73, 178
Sydney, Australia 16, 17
Syrus, Peter 163
Székely, Zoltán 121
Szeryng, Henryk 148, 149

T

Tansman, Alexandre 130, 131
Tate, Phyllis 246, 252, 262
Tavener, John 249, 254, 255, 257, 260, 262
Taylor, Richard 260
Tchaikovsky, André 254
Tchaikovsky, Pyotr Ilych 19, 178, 190, 192
    Maid of Orleans 190
    Rococo Variations 192
Teed, Roy 254
Thatcher, Margaret 51, 177
Thatcher, Reginald 43, 45
Theatre Museum, Covent Garden 117
Theatre Royal, Bath 205, 214, 215
Thionville 32
Thomas, Dylan 77
    Under Milk Wood 77
Thompson, Jane 5
Thomson, Bryden ('Jack') 122
Thomson, Virgil 256
Thorndike, Sybil 77
Three Choirs Festival 90
Tillett, Emmie 107, 108, 202
Tinkler, Mark 188
Tinsley, Pauline 124
Tippett, Michael 68, 69, 94, 102, 125, 180, 200, 202, 223, 249, 259, 262
    Boyhood's End 69
    Fourth Symphony 180
    King Priam 68, 94
    Knot Garden, The 180
    Midsummer Marriage, The 200
    Piano Concerto 202
    [Plate 46, at the Cheltenham Festival]
    Second Quartet 125
    The Heart's Assurance 69
Tipping, Roy 133
Todds, Walter 132

Tomlinson, Ellis 153
Toshimitsu, Tanaka 256
Towneley, Simon 145, 154, 155, 212
Trethowan, Ian 104
Trinity College of Music 43, 162
Troughton, Charles 199
Trowell, Brian 94, 185
Tunnell, John 48
Turner, Dame Eva 165
Turner, John 5, 45, 240, 241, 242
Twin Towers 138
Tyndall, Jeremy 223
Tyrrel, Timothy 185

U

UFAM (Union Feminim des Artistes Musicales) Competition, Paris 142
Ulster Orchestra 120

V

Vaduz School of Music 207
van Vlijmen, Jan 255
Vardigans, Richard 185, 189
Vaughan, Mansel 9, 164, 168, 177
    [Plate 29] 9
Vaughan Williams, Ralph 23, 38, 66, 86, 87, 184, 190, 231, 262
    Pastoral Symphony 87
    Pilgrim's Progress, The 190
    Riders to the Sea 184
    Sinfonia Antartica 38
    Six Studies in English Folk Song 66
    Sixth Symphony 87
Vegh Quartet 121
Venezuela 196, 197
    National Youth Orchestra 196, 197
Venice Biennale 80, 84
Verdi, Giuseppe 49, 56, 64, 187, 188
    Aida 35, 183
    Don Carlo 188, 189, 190
    Ernani 187
    Il Trovatore 41
    La Traviata 53
    Otello 49
    Requiem 56
    Rigoletto 188
Verwoerd, Henryk 89
Vickers, Harry 194
Vick, Graham 183
Vienna State Opera 82
Vine, Carl 258
Vinter, Gilbert 96
Vyner, Michael 168
Vyrnwy 14, 17
Vyvyan, Jennifer 126

W

Wade, Frank 65
Wagner, Richard 34, 42, 50, 75, 82, 185
    Das Rheingold 185
    Die Meistersinger 38, 192
    Ring of the Nibelungen 42
    Siegfried Idyll 75
    Tannhäuser 50
Walsworth, Ivor 77
Walton, Sir William 121, 183,

184, 231
Bear, The 183, 184
Façade 121
Ward, Joseph 10, 183, 185, 187, 188, 190
    [Plate 40]
Warlock, Peter 262
Warren, Eleanor 160, 179
Warren, Robert de 213, 214
Warr, Eric 61
Watendlath 50
Waterhouse, William 161
Waterson, Juanita 10, 183
    costume design for Oberon & Puck 10
    [Plates 42 & 43]
Webern, Anton 121, 223, 247
Webster, Gilbert 81, 162
Weeks, John 250
Weill, Kurt 231
Weil, Terence 160
Weinberg, Henry 249
Weir, Judith 222, 257, 258, 260, 261, 262
    A Night at the Chinese Opera 222, 257
Wellard, Arthur 58
Wellesz, Egon 243, 246
Welsh National Opera 186, 187
Welton, Percy 162
Wesley-Smith, Martin 258
Wessels, Cecilia 44, 50
Whettam, Graham 255, 259
Whewell, Michael 78, 120
Whitefield, Caleb Gordon 27, 28
Whitehouse, Richard 190
White, John 243
Whittaker, Doug 78
Wickens, Dennis 247
Wildberger, Jacques 260
Wilde, David 117, 120, 122, 124, 126
Wilkinson, Clive 256
Wilkinson, George 222
Wilkinson, Stephen 123
Wilks, John 245
Willcocks, David 193
Williams, John 125
Williamson, David 217
Williamson, Malcolm 125, 126, 246, 247, 250, 252
    The Growing Castle 125, 126
Williamson, Vanessa 185
Willoughby, George 81, 82
Wilson, Hazel 200
Wilson, John 9
    [Plate 23]
Wilson, Rodney 220
Wilson, Thomas 251
Wimbledon Theatre 215
Wishart, Peter 247
Wolf-Ferrari, Ermanno 220
Woodage, Wesley 80
Wood, Avril 200
Wood, Hugh 243, 244, 248
Wood, James 255
Woods, Wesley 108
Woolrich, John 258, 259, 263
Woolrych, Austin 114
Wootton Court Prep School 17
Wordsworth, William 245
World music 69
World War, First 27, 73
World War, Second 15, 221
Wray, John 9, 159, 162
    [Plate 22]
Wright, Anna 5
Wright, Doug 58
Wright, Ian 162
Wynne, Anna 246

Y

Yamamoto, Hozan 71
Yates, Christopher 5
Yates, Mr. 17, 18
Yeats W. B. 240
Yorkshire Symphony Orchestra 46
York University 114, 116
Young, Alexander (Basil) 9, 125, 161 [Pate 28]
Young Concert Artists Trust 205
Young, David 163
Young, Jane 161
Yugoslavia 107, 202
Yuize, Shinichi 71

Z

Zabaleta, Nicanor 72
Zagreb Biennale 202
Zanetti, Miguel 122

www.ingramcontent.com/pod-product-compliance
Lightning Source LLC
Chambersburg PA
CBHW040314170426
43195CB00021B/2964